AF845074

UNDERSTANDING CRIME TRENDS

WORKSHOP REPORT

Committee on Understanding Crime Trends
Committee on Law and Justice
Division of Behavioral and Social Sciences and Education

NATIONAL RESEARCH COUNCIL
OF THE NATIONAL ACADEMIES

THE NATIONAL ACADEMIES PRESS
Washington, D.C.
www.nap.edu

THE NATIONAL ACADEMIES PRESS 500 Fifth Street, N.W. Washington, DC 20001

NOTICE: The project that is the subject of this report was approved by the Governing Board of the National Research Council, whose members are drawn from the councils of the National Academy of Sciences, the National Academy of Engineering, and the Institute of Medicine. The members of the committee responsible for the report were chosen for their special competences and with regard for appropriate balance.

This project was supported by Contract Grant No. 2001-MU-MU-0007 between the National Academy of Sciences and the National Institute of Justice, Office of Justice Programs, U.S. Department of Justice. Any opinions, findings, conclusions, or recommendations expressed in this publication are those of the author(s) and do not necessarily reflect the views of the sponsors.

International Standard Book Number-13: 978-0-309-12586-4
International Standard Book Number-10: 0-309-12586-3

Additional copies of this report are available from the National Academies Press, 500 Fifth Street, N.W., Lockbox 285, Washington, DC 20055; (800) 624-6242 or (202) 334-3313 (in the Washington metropolitan area); Internet http://www.nap.edu.

Copyright 2008 by the National Academy of Sciences. All rights reserved.

Printed in the United States of America

Suggested citation: National Research Council. (2008). *Understanding Crime Trends: Workshop Report*. Committee on Understanding Crime Trends, Committee on Law and Justice, Division of Behavioral and Social Sciences and Education. Washington, DC: The National Academies Press.

THE NATIONAL ACADEMIES

Advisers to the Nation on Science, Engineering, and Medicine

The **National Academy of Sciences** is a private, nonprofit, self-perpetuating society of distinguished scholars engaged in scientific and engineering research, dedicated to the furtherance of science and technology and to their use for the general welfare. Upon the authority of the charter granted to it by the Congress in 1863, the Academy has a mandate that requires it to advise the federal government on scientific and technical matters. Dr. Ralph J. Cicerone is president of the National Academy of Sciences.

The **National Academy of Engineering** was established in 1964, under the charter of the National Academy of Sciences, as a parallel organization of outstanding engineers. It is autonomous in its administration and in the selection of its members, sharing with the National Academy of Sciences the responsibility for advising the federal government. The National Academy of Engineering also sponsors engineering programs aimed at meeting national needs, encourages education and research, and recognizes the superior achievements of engineers. Dr. Charles M. Vest is president of the National Academy of Engineering.

The **Institute of Medicine** was established in 1970 by the National Academy of Sciences to secure the services of eminent members of appropriate professions in the examination of policy matters pertaining to the health of the public. The Institute acts under the responsibility given to the National Academy of Sciences by its congressional charter to be an adviser to the federal government and, upon its own initiative, to identify issues of medical care, research, and education. Dr. Harvey V. Fineberg is president of the Institute of Medicine.

The **National Research Council** was organized by the National Academy of Sciences in 1916 to associate the broad community of science and technology with the Academy's purposes of furthering knowledge and advising the federal government. Functioning in accordance with general policies determined by the Academy, the Council has become the principal operating agency of both the National Academy of Sciences and the National Academy of Engineering in providing services to the government, the public, and the scientific and engineering communities. The Council is administered jointly by both Academies and the Institute of Medicine. Dr. Ralph J. Cicerone and Dr. Charles M. Vest are chair and vice chair, respectively, of the National Research Council.

www.national-academies.org

COMMITTEE ON UNDERSTANDING CRIME TRENDS

RICHARD ROSENFELD (*Cochair*), Department of Criminology and Criminal Justice, University of Missouri, St. Louis
ARTHUR S. GOLDBERGER (*Cochair*), Department of Economics, University of Wisconsin, Madison
ALFRED BLUMSTEIN, John Heinz III School of Public Policy and Management, Carnegie Mellon University
PHILLIP J. COOK, Stanford Institute of Public Policy, Duke University
STEVEN N. DURLAUF, Department of Economics, University of Wisconsin, Madison
KAREN HEIMER, Department of Sociology and Public Policy Center, University of Iowa
JANET L. LAURITSEN, Department of Criminology and Criminal Justice, University of Missouri, St. Louis
MICHAEL G. MAXFIELD, School of Criminal Justice, Rutgers University

CAROL PETRIE, *Study Director*
LINDA DePUGH, *Administrative Assistant*

COMMITTEE ON LAW AND JUSTICE

JAMES Q. WILSON (*Chair*), Department of Political Science, Pepperdine University
DAVID H. BAYLEY, School of Criminal Justice, State University of New York, Albany
RICHARD J. BONNIE, Institute of Law, Psychiatry and Public Policy, University of Virginia
PHILIP J. COOK, Stanford Institute of Public Policy, Duke University
MARTHA CRENSHAW, Department of Government, Wesleyan University
ROBERT D. CRUTCHFIELD, Department of Sociology, University of Washington, Seattle
JOHN DILULIO, JR., Department of Sociology, University of Washington, Seattle
STEVEN N. DURLAUF, Department of Economics, University of Wisconsin, Madison
JOHN A. FEREJOHN, Hoover Institution, Stanford University
ARTHUR S. GOLDBERGER, Department of Economics, University of Wisconsin, Madison
BRUCE HOFFMAN, RAND Corporation, Arlington, Virginia
ROBERT L. JOHNSON, Department of Pediatrics, New Jersey Medical School, University of Medicine and Dentistry of New Jersey
JOHN H. LAUB, Department of Criminology and Criminal Justice, University of Maryland
TRACEY L. MEARES, Center for Studies in Criminal Justice, School of Law, University of Chicago
TERRIE E. MOFFITT, SGDP Research Center, Institute of Psychiatry, University of London
MARK H. MOORE, Hauser Center for Nonprofit Organizations, Cambridge, Massachusetts
RUTH D. PETERSON, Department of Sociology, Criminal Justice Research Center, Ohio State University
RICHARD ROSENFELD, Department of Criminology and Criminal Justice, University of Missouri, St. Louis
ROBERT J. SAMPSON, Department of Sociology, Harvard University
JEREMY TRAVIS, John Jay College of Criminal Justice, City University of New York
CHRISTY A. VISHER, Justice Policy Center, Urban Institute, Washington, DC

CONTRIBUTORS

ERIC P. BAUMER, Department of Criminology and Criminal Justice, University of Missouri, St. Louis
ALFRED BLUMSTEIN, John Heinz III School of Public Policy and Management, Carnegie Mellon University
STEVEN N. DURLAUF, Department of Economics, University of Wisconsin, Madison
JEFFREY FAGAN, Mailman School of Public Health, Columbia University
ARTHUR S. GOLDBERGER, Department of Economics, University of Wisconsin, Madison
KAREN HEIMER, Department of Sociology and Public Policy Center, University of Iowa
JANET L. LAURITSEN, Department of Criminology and Criminal Justice, University of Missouri, St. Louis
SALVADOR NAVARRO, Department of Economics, University of Wisconsin, Madison
JOHN V. PEPPER, Department of Economics, University of Virginia
DAVID A. RIVERS, Department of Economics, University of Wisconsin, Madison
RICHARD ROSENFELD, Department of Criminology and Criminal Justice, University of Missouri, St. Louis

Acknowledgments

This report has been reviewed in draft form by individuals chosen for their diverse perspectives and technical expertise, in accordance with procedures approved by the Report Review Committee of the National Research Council. The purpose of this independent review is to provide candid and critical comments that assist the institution in making the published report as sound as possible and ensure that the report meets institutional standards for objectivity, evidence, and responsiveness to the study charge. The review comments and draft manuscript remain confidential to protect the integrity of the deliberative process.

We thank the following individuals for their participation in the review of the report: Julie Horney, School of Criminal Justice, University at Albany, State University of New York; Gary LaFree, National Center for the Study of Terrorism and Responses to Terrorism, Department of Criminology/Democracy Collaborative, University of Maryland; James P. Lynch, John Jay College of Criminal Justice, New York, NY; Steven Raphael, Richard and Rhonda Goldman School of Public Policy, University of California, Berkeley; Ronald B. (Ralph) Taylor, Department of Criminal Justice, Temple University; and Wesley G. Skogan, Political Science and the Institute for Policy Research, Northwestern University.

Although the reviewers listed above provided many constructive comments and suggestions, they were not asked to endorse the conclusions or recommendations nor did they see the final draft of the report before its release. The review of this report was overseen by Darnell F. Hawkins, African American Studies, Sociology, and Criminal Justice, University of Illinois. Appointed by the National Research Council, he was responsible for making certain that an independent examination of this report was carried out it in accordance with institutional procedures and that all review comments were carefully considered. Responsibility for the final content of this report rests entirely with the authoring panel and the institutions.

Contents

1

Introduction

Richard Rosenfeld and Arthur S. Goldberger

Changes over time in the levels and patterns of crime have significant consequences that affect not only the criminal justice system but also other critical policy sectors. Yet compared with such areas as health status, housing, and employment, the nation lacks timely information and comprehensive research on crime trends. Consider a recent example. After declining or remaining stable for over a decade, violent crime rates rose in many American cities in 2005 and 2006. What is known about these changes? What brought them about? Could they be anticipated? The honest answers are: very little, no one knows, and no.

Descriptive information and explanatory research on crime trends across the nation that are not only accurate but also timely are pressing needs in the nation's crime-control efforts. Without useful and reliable information, national and local policy makers fly blind when formulating and evaluating the effectiveness of policy interventions or, as a recent National Research Council (NRC) report on criminal justice evaluation research observes, they must generate ad hoc outcome indicators for each new policy assessment (National Research Council, 2005, pp. 59-60). In the absence of common and timely crime indicators, the U.S. Department of Justice sent teams of "auditors" to a select group of cities in 2007 to examine local records and consult with law enforcement officials concerning local crime trends. Although there may be good reasons for proceeding in this way, the contrast with using available employment indicators to evaluate local labor market conditions is illuminating. Faced with concerns about a rise in unemployment, the U.S. Department of Labor would not have to, at least in the first instance, send auditors across the country to examine local employment records. That information is routinely compiled, stored, and updated in centralized records systems that can be accessed by local, state, and national officials, researchers, the press, and the public. These information systems constitute the basis of a policy evaluation infrastructure that is indispensable for assessing economic policy in the United States. Comparable evaluation capabilities do not exist in the policy area of criminal justice (Rosenfeld, 2006).

MONITORING CRIME TRENDS

The nation lacks a comprehensive, coherent, and up-to-date infrastructure to monitor crime trends and relay the resulting information to law enforcement agencies, researchers, policy makers, and the public. The federal government sponsors two major crime data collection programs, the Uniform Crime Reports (UCR) of the Federal Bureau of Investigation (FBI) and the National Crime Victimization Survey of the Bureau of Justice Statistics. Although both programs provide essential information about crime levels, patterns, and trends, neither does so with the speed and level of detail necessary to inform local law enforcement planning or state and national policy responses to emerging crime problems. The paucity of high-quality information for criminal justice planning and research stands in sharp contrast to the rich assortment of monthly and quarterly data collections on specific topics that characterizes other policy areas. The rapid and continuous public dissemination of economic data and forecasts ("economists predict slowdown in next quarter," "monthly housing starts off by 2 percent") has no equivalent in criminal justice, even though timely information on changes in serious violent and property crime rates is just as vital to the nation's health and welfare as information on changing levels of industrial production or consumer prices.

The FBI's UCR do provide national and local crime indicators, but the UCR data are released several months after the relevant reporting period. The year-end 2005 data, for example, were not released until September 2006, and the preliminary data for the first six months of 2006 were not available until December of that year (http://www.fbi.gov/ucr/ucr.htm). Even though the time lags have been shortened in recent years, they often extend well beyond the planning and response horizons of local jurisdictions. Without timely crime indicators to draw on, Justice Department officials were caught short when police chiefs and mayors from around the country assembled in Washington, DC, in August 2006, to demand federal assistance in combating local crime increases (Files, 2006). The Police Executive Research Forum (PERF) later reported sharp crime increases on the basis of a survey of the cities represented at the August meeting (Johnson, 2006; the PERF report is available at http://www.policeforum.org). But the representativeness of the survey results is uncertain, and they offer only a snapshot of local crime patterns rather than the kind of continuous monitoring needed for rapid and ongoing policy assessment and intervention.

THE NRC WORKSHOP

In April 2007 the NRC held a two-day workshop to address in a preliminary way key substantive and methodological issues underlying the study of crime trends and to lay the groundwork for a proposed multiyear NRC panel study of these issues. Six papers were commissioned from leading researchers and discussed at the workshop by experts in sociology, criminology, law, economics, and statistics. The authors revised their papers based on the discussants' comments. In accordance with standard NRC procedures, the papers were sent out for external review and revised again. The six final workshop papers are the basis of the current volume.

The workshop committee was necessarily selective regarding the range of topics that could be covered in a two-day workshop. The committee asked Alfred Blumstein and Richard Rosenfeld to summarize changes in rates of serious crime in the United States over the past several decades and identify factors that may be driving those changes. Karen Heimer and Janet Lauritsen were asked to address trends in victimization and offending by sex. Jeffrey Fagan addresses the prospects and challenges of analyzing neighborhood-level crime trends. Two researchers, Eric Baumer and John Pepper, were asked to perform separate analyses, including forecasting crime rates, on a city-level dataset specially created for the committee by Robert Fornango of Arizona State University. Finally, the committee asked Steven Durlauf to discuss statistical and theoretical issues in drawing causal inferences from observational data on crime rates.

The workshop was intended to highlight outstanding issues in the analysis of crime trends rather than to develop a consensus agenda for research, let alone offer consensus recommendations for policy makers. Thus the chapters do not form an integrated whole but rather an exploration of the field. Although the six papers cover a diverse assortment of substantive and analytical issues, clearly they do not exhaust the range of relevant topics of interest to the scientific community or policy makers.

For example, no effort was made to draw on trends in other countries. None of the papers deals specifically with the problem of race, ethnicity, and crime. That issue, as well as the related question of the impact of immigration on crime trends, requires much more extensive evaluation than is possible in a workshop format and could be a major topic to be considered by an NRC panel study of crime trends (see Peterson, Krivo, and Hagan, 2006, for a recent treatment). Nor did the workshop address the research and policy implications of trends in so-called white-collar crime or in the multiple forms of cyber crime. Little systematic research exists on the use of the Internet as a conduit for stolen goods, child pornography, identity theft, or fraud. Building the science in this important area of public concern might also be on the agenda of any future panel study of crime trends to emerge from this workshop.

RESEARCH CONTEXT

Rates of serious violent crime in the United States have exhibited marked fluctuations over the past 30 years (see Blumstein and Rosenfeld, this volume). Homicide and robbery rates rose to peaks in 1980 and the early 1990s and fell by over 40 percent through the end of the century, during what one analyst has termed "the great American crime decline" (Zimring, 2006). Social scientists, policy makers, and law enforcement officials were caught off guard by these changes, in part because they did not become apparent in the available statistical indicators until well after they had begun. Little planning for spikes in resource demands or timely responses are possible under such circumstances. The local police department is perhaps the last remaining complex organization in American society without the capacity to anticipate and plan for changes in its environment, yet it is assigned virtually all of the responsibility for responding to crime increases and more than its share of the blame when the responses prove inadequate.

Although research on crime trends remains quite limited, the emerging assessments of the 1990s crime decline yield some useful insights on which more comprehensive and sustained efforts can build (Blumstein and Wallman, 2005; Rosenfeld, 2004; Zimring, 2006). The first lesson from that research is that disaggregating total crime rates by age, race, sex, city size, and other factors reveals important differences in the timing, magnitude, and duration of group-specific trends. The second lesson is that multiple causes underlie the crime drop and, by extension, longer term variations in crime rates. Some progress has been made in identifying candidate explanatory factors, which include the quadrupling of the nation's prison population since 1980; cyclical variations in unemployment, wages, and other economic conditions; and the changing dynamics of illegal drug markets (Blumstein and Wallman, 2005). But the relative contribution of these factors to the 1990s crime drop or more recent local-level crime trends remains uncertain (Levitt, 2004; Rosenfeld, Fornango, and Rengifo, 2007). Nor is it clear whether they are themselves sufficiently predictable to serve as the basis for useful crime forecasts.

Another lesson from recent research is the value of distinguishing short- from long-run changes in crime rates and in the factors hypothesized to explain those changes. Consider how changes in the economy may affect crime over the long and short run. A well-known account suggests that the move from a manufacturing-based to a service-based economy during the latter half of the 20th century contributed to an increase in crime among population groups, young minority men in particular, lacking the training and skills needed for the better paying jobs in the rising service sector (Wilson, 1987, 1996). Cities hit hardest by deindustrialization experienced large and sustained crime increases (Parker, 2004).

But deindustrialization and the social changes attributed to it, such as the growth of "oppositional cultures" among minority youth in distressed urban areas (Anderson, 1999) are, by themselves, unlikely to account for short-run swings in crime rates, such as those occurring in some cities in 2005 and 2006. Better candidate explanations include cyclical economic changes, prison admissions and releases, local enforcement initiatives, and other factors subject to year-to-year fluctuation, some of which may activate local grievances or more widespread and long-standing psychological or cultural conditions.

A final and related insight from the recent research on crime trends distinguishes sources of change in crime rates that apply across local areas from those that may be specific to particular jurisdictions. Some factors, such as economy-wide changes in unemployment or wage rates, potentially affect crime conditions across the nation, whereas others, such as gang conflicts or local changes in policing strategies, influence crime rates in some places but not others. A good example of the importance of this distinction is the dramatic fall in New York City's crime rates during the 1990s, at roughly double the rate of decline registered at the national level (Zimring, 2006). The difference suggests that New York's crime drop is related to distinctive local conditions as well as factors common to other cities. One candidate for explaining New York's crime reduction "bonus" is its CompStat initiative and accompanying order-maintenance enforcement strategies begun in the early 1990s. New York clearly differs from other cities in other respects that may have influenced its crime trends, and recent research has found either small or no effects of CompStat on the New York City crime drop (Fagan, this volume; Harcourt and Ludwig, 2006; Rosenfeld, Fornango, and Rengifo, 2007).

THE CURRENT VOLUME

Four lessons from the emerging research on the crime drop—(1) disaggregating crime rates, (2) identifying multiple sources of variation, (3) distinguishing long swings from year-to-year variation, and (4) differentiating general and specific changes—form the context for the contributions to this volume. None of the chapters addresses all four of the issues but taken as a whole the volume illustrates the importance of each of them. In Chapter 2, Alfred Blumstein and Richard Rosenfeld underscore the value of disaggregating recent crime trends by age, race, and ethnicity to disclose the multiple and differing factors associated with group-specific variation in trends. Their chapter identifies factors that had been established by prior research to be associated with changes in crime rates, such as demographic shifts, growth in incarceration, drug markets, and changing economic conditions. They identify other factors, such as policing innovations, firearm availability, street gangs, childhood socialization, and investments in social services that may influence crime trends but for which the existing evidence is fragmentary or inconsistent.

The authors conclude that developing sound empirical explanations of past crime trends is an important means of improving the capacity to make informative and reasonably accurate forecasts of future changes. They suggest that only with a large investment of resources can criminologists hope to make their forecasting models as worthwhile as those produced in other disciplines. To be most useful, it is also important to differentiate efforts at generating national, regional, and local (for a particular city or neighborhood) crime trend estimates.

Blumstein and Rosenfeld conclude that the influence of research on policy will be limited in the absence of a substantial upgrading in the nation's capacity to monitor crime trends. That will require additional resources devoted to compiling, disseminating, and updating the data. They suggest that the National Institute of Justice can play an important part in this process by establishing an ongoing research program devoted to analyzing crime trends.

In Chapter 3, Karen Heimer and Janet Lauritsen use data from the National Crime Victimization Survey to examine changes between 1980 and 2004 in female and male violent offending and victimization and victim-offender relationships in violent incidents. This work has not been done previously except for homicide, and so the chapter constitutes a unique contribution to the field. Among the authors' findings are a widening of the gender gap in intimate partner homicide victimization due to a greater decline in victimization among men, a narrowing of the gender gap in overall violent offending, an increase in the proportion of assaults involving female victims, and an increasing likelihood of female involvement in violent interactions, both as perpetrators and as victims.

The authors note that the modal category of violent crime in 2004 is not the same as it was in earlier decades. Recent declines in stranger violence have been such that, by 2004, male victimization by strangers was no longer greater than male or female victimization by nonstrangers. Why stranger violence has declined more rapidly than nonlethal acquaintance violence is a challenging question for future research. In addition, although female violent offending against strangers has always been low, the large percentage increase in such violence that occurred before violence rates peaked in the mid-1990s warrants further investigation. The authors conclude that nonstranger violence remains a critical part of violence in the United States, and women and men are now affected equally by violence by acquaintances. At the same time, they caution that violence prevention strategies may not work equally well for men and women and that gender differences in the effectiveness of interventions to reduce violence should be evaluated systematically.

In Chapter 4, Jeffrey Fagan reviews research on factors that influence changes in crime rates between and within neighborhoods in cities over time. He examines local area studies of neighborhood and crime, focusing on neighborhood structures and processes. The study of neighborhoods has stimulated a rich body of sociological theory to conceptualize space and its effects on individuals and populations. But studies of the impact of neighborhood change on crime have been rare and are usually limited to a few neighborhoods in single cities. Fagan identifies several challenges to theory, measurement, and analysis that affect estimates of why and how neighborhood crime rates change. He offers a causal account that frames changes in violence within and between neighborhoods as contagion and diffusion processes. The challenges are illustrated with data from a panel study of violent crime in New York City neighborhoods from 1985 to 2000.

Fagan notes the difficulties associated with compiling systematic data on these issues and calls for building an infrastructure in cities for neighborhood data to support research on neighborhoods and crime. To overcome some of the political challenges to achieving this goal, he calls for the shifting of social and professional norms toward more open and transparent data systems to monitor changes in local crime rates that mirror changes in each city's neighborhoods.

The chapters by Eric Baumer and John Pepper analyze crime trends in U.S. cities between 1980 and 2004. The units of analysis are 240 large U.S. cities with populations of 100,000 or more according to the 2000 census. The data consist of rates of homicide, robbery, burglary, and motor vehicle theft as measured by the FBI's Uniform Crime Reports. The data also include annual measures of drug arrests, state-level incarceration rates, the number of police per 100,000 population, and demographic, social, and economic indicators drawn from the 1980, 1990, and 2000 censuses. Each researcher was free to augment the common dataset with additional indicators. The committee asked them to use their analysis of 1980-2004 crime trends to forecast crime rates into 2005.

In Chapter 5, Baumer develops a comprehensive assessment that significantly expands the typical set of factors considered in crime trends research. He includes in his models most of the major factors identified in prior cross-sectional and longitudinal research on crime rates. Advocates for the role of particular factors, such as policing, incarceration, abortion, or immigration, have drawn relatively strong empirical conclusions, which ignore other factors that may be equally or more relevant. Baumer highlights five noteworthy findings from his analysis:

1. Changes in incarceration and crime are significantly related during the period under consideration. Increases in state prison committals per 100,000 residents tend to reduce crime the following year, whereas increases in the number of persons released from state prisons per 100,000 residents tend to increase crime the next year.
2. Policing variables yield inconsistent findings. A measure of public order and weapons offenses is unrelated to crime rates, but increases in police force size and the certainty of arrest are associated with crime reductions.
3. Overall results point to a relatively limited role for short-run changes in the economy.
4. Evidence for an association between guns or drugs and recent crime trends is mixed. Alcohol consumption trends do not appear to influence recent crime trends. Firearm prevalence is significantly associated with homicide but not other crimes. Indicators of change in crack cocaine use and market activity exert significant effects on recent crime trends, albeit in somewhat inconsistent ways across measures and crime types.
5. Some of the demographic variables—age, cohabitation rates (but not marriage), percentage of the youth cohort born to teenage mothers—exert significant effects on crime trends.

Regression results—coefficients, standard errors, etc.—are not themselves indicators of the influences of factors on past trends. Changes in the values of the corresponding explanatory variables need to be considered as well. Doing so to estimate the relative contributions of the explanatory variables to observed change in crime rates, Baumer's analysis supports the conclusion that the rise in youth firearm violence, robbery, and some forms of auto theft during the 1980s can be attributed to the emergence and proliferation of crack cocaine markets. In addition, consistent with other reports, the analysis indicates that lethal violence would have increased even more during the 1980s had it not been for a substantial increase in levels of incarceration and a considerable decline in the relative size of the youth population ages 15-24. Incarceration also emerged as a primary contributor to the decline in burglary and adult homicide during the 1990s, accounting for more than half of the observed declines in both of these crimes.

While Baumer's models fit the sample period reasonably well, his forecasts diverge substantially from the observed 2005 crime rates. He concludes that empirical literature on crime trends is in the early stages of development, and much more research is needed before confident conclusions can be provided.

In Chapter 6, Pepper takes a different approach using several time-series regression models to forecast crime rates. While Baumer included once-lagged crime rates along with a long list of covariates, Pepper focused on the lagged rates, supplemented in part by a very short list of covariates. He examines the possibility of predicting a crime rate series from its past history, thus treating forecasting as distinct from causal analysis. He first illustrates his approach using national data and then turns to the city-level database. He compares the performance of basic panel data models with and without covariates and with and without lags. He also compares two naïve models, one in which the forecast equals the city-level mean or fixed effect, and one in which the forecast equals the last observed rate (random walk forecast). He examines the basic plausibility of the models as well as their prediction accuracy and bias over 1-, 2-, 4-, and 10-year forecast horizons.

Pepper found that the forecast models are fragile, in that seemingly minor changes to a model can produce qualitatively different forecasts. Naïve models do relatively well for short-term forecasts, but forecasts are invariably error ridden around turning points, especially, he speculates, when these movements are largely the result of external events that are themselves unpredictable.

In Chapter 7, Steven Durlauf, Salvador Navarro, and David Rivers examine the use of aggregate regressions—of the sort run by Baumer and Pepper—as a basis for informing policy decisions. Starting with a formulation at the level of an individual, the authors indicate how the individual-level model can be aggregated to produce crime regressions of the type found in the literature. They demonstrate some of the limitations of these regressions, focusing particularly on how empirical findings may be over-interpreted when the link between aggregate data and individual behavior is treated casually. They then discuss the analysis of policy counterfactuals, consider issues of model uncertainty in crime regressions, and illustrate these arguments in the context of two prominent papers in the capital punishment and deterrence literatures.

The authors note that assumptions are embedded in any scientific approach, and they attempt to clarify various assumptions needed to interpret aggregate crime regressions in terms of individual behavior. They outline ways of using model-averaging methods and statistical decision theory to broaden the basis of forecasts. (Baumer also discusses the problem of model uncertainty.)

The NRC workshop committee asked several researchers to comment on the papers prepared for the workshop: Philip Cook, John Donohue,

Rosemary Gartner, Lauren Krivo, Kenneth Land, Daniel Nagin, Robert Sampson, Justin Wolfers, and Franklin Zimring. Although space limitations precludes publication of the comments in this volume, each of the chapters has benefited from the discussants' criticisms and suggestions, some of which stand as original contributions to the emerging body of research on crime trends. To take one example, Wolfers suggests that "prediction markets"[1] of the kind used to forecast economic changes and election outcomes may have a useful role in forecasting crime rates (Wolfers and Zitzewitz, 2004). Given the poor forecasting track record of criminologists (Land and McCall, 2001, 2006), some experimentation with differing forecasting methods seems warranted.

From this summary of the chapters, it is clear that the current volume does not offer an integrated whole, but rather explores the range of issues that will be addressed as progress is made. What is clear is that progress will require a substantial improvement in infrastructure in the form of current and comprehensive databases. Past empirical and theoretical analysis has focused on cross-sectional data, sometimes over a few periods. What emerges from this work are correlates of crime rates, which may not be the ones that are relevant for temporal analysis. For example, ethnic composition and income distributions may have strong associations with crime rates across localities at a point in time, yet vary so little over time that they cannot have contributed to the time paths seen.

The NRC workshop and this resulting volume represent some of the most serious thinking and research on crime trends currently available. But they also reveal how far there is to go in improving information and research in order to provide useful policy guidance. The hope is that the current volume will stimulate other social scientists to contribute fresh insights and innovative methods to the study of crime trends.

REFERENCES

Anderson, Elijah. (1999). *Code of the street: Decency, violence, and the moral life of the inner city*. New York: Norton.

Blumstein, Alfred, and Joel Wallman (Eds.). (2005). *The crime drop in America* (2nd ed.). New York: Cambridge University Press.

Files, John. (2006). Police chiefs want U.S. aid in crime fight. *New York Times,* August 31. Available: http://www.nytimes.com/2006/08/31/us/31crime.html?_r=1&adxnnl=1&oref=slogin&adxnnlx=1219237826-uj+VjluE1+WysknxZi+/hg [accessed August 2008].

Harcourt, Bernard E., and Jens Ludwig. (2006). Broken windows: New evidence from New York City and a five-city social experiment. *University of Chicago Law Review, 73*, 271-320.

[1]Wolfers and Zitzewitz also submitted an unpublished paper subsequent to a discussion at the 2007 workshop.

Johnson, Kevin. (2006). Dozens of cities see jump in murders, robberies. *USA Today,* October 12. Available: http://www.usatoday.com/news/nation/2006-10-12-violent-crime_x.htm [accessed August 2008].

Land, Kenneth C., and Patricia L. McCall. (2001). The indeterminacy of forecasts of crime rates and juvenile offenses. In National Research Council, *Juvenile crime, juvenile justice.* Panel on Juvenile Crime: Prevention, Treatment, and Control, Joan McCord, Cathy Spatz Widom, and Nancy A. Crowell (Eds.). Committee on Law and Justice, Division of Behavioral and Social Sciences and Education. Washington, DC: National Academy Press.

Land, Kenneth C., and Patricia L. McCall. (2006). *Uncertainty in crime forecasts: A reconsideration.* Paper presented at the meeting of the American Sociological Association, Montreal (August).

Levitt, Steven D. (2004). Understanding why crime fell in the 1990s: Four factors that explain the decline and six that do not. *Journal of Economic Perspectives, 18*, 163-190.

National Research Council. (2005). *Improving evaluation of anticrime programs.* Committee on Improving Evaluation of Anti-Crime Programs, Committee on Law and Justice, Division of Behavioral and Social Sciences and Education. Washington, DC: The National Academies Press.

Parker, Karen F. (2004). Polarized labor markets, industrial restructuring and urban violence: A dynamic model of the economic transformation and urban violence. *Criminology, 42*, 619-645.

Peterson, Ruth D., Lauren J. Krivo, and John Hagan. (2006). *The many colors of crime: Inequalities of race, ethnicity, and crime in America.* New York: New York University Press.

Rosenfeld, Richard. (2004). The case of the unsolved crime decline. *Scientific American,* February, 82-89.

Rosenfeld, Richard. (2006). Connecting the dots: Crime rates and criminal justice evaluation research. *Journal of Experimental Criminology, 2*, 309-319.

Rosenfeld, Richard, Robert Fornango, and Andres Rengifo. (2007). The impact of order-maintenance policing on New York City robbery and homicide rates: 1988-2001. *Criminology, 45*, 355-383.

Wilson, William Julius. (1987). *The truly disadvantaged: The inner city, the underclass and public policy.* Chicago: University of Chicago Press.

Wilson, William Julius. (1996). *When work disappears: The world of the new urban poor.* New York: Knopf.

Wolfers, Justin, and Eric Zitzewitz. (2004). Prediction markets. *Journal of Economic Perspectives, 18*, 107-126.

Zimring, Franklin E. (2007). *The great American crime decline.* New York: Oxford University Press.

2

Factors Contributing to U.S. Crime Trends

Alfred Blumstein and Richard Rosenfeld

Over the past 30 years, crime has become a major issue of public concern, of political discussion and action—often intemperate and not likely to reduce crime—and of major public expenditure. Despite its salience in the public arena, very little is known about the factors driving the crime trends, and the knowledge base is too limited to support intelligent forecasts of the direction in which crime rates are moving, especially when changing direction. Developing such a knowledge base is important for enhancing the rationality of public policies and public expenditures related to crime, particularly because many such commitments have to be made well in advance of their actual use. These include, for example, recruiting and training police forces, building prisons, and developing other interventions outside the criminal justice system.

In this chapter we summarize the crime trend history over the past 35 years, examine the factors that appear to have been particularly influential in driving those trends, consider whether change in those factors could have been known in advance, and use that information to indicate some of the potential directions for enhancing the knowledge needed for better explanations and forecasts.

One can expect that different crimes will be affected by different factors. In particular, one might anticipate that property crimes would be responsive to the state of economic opportunity, whereas violent crimes might be responsive to the availability of guns or to societal factors stimulating conflict. Many of these factors would be difficult to know in advance to warrant their serving as leading indicators to indicate future trends. The one factor that is often important in affecting crime is population composition: Different demographic groups, particularly different age and ethnic groups, display very different rates of involvement in crime.

Some of these factors could be addressed in the context of generating policies intended to reduce crime. For example, to the extent that unemployment among teenagers and young adults is a major contributing factor to the crimes they commit, then efforts at providing job assistance, job training, or extending unemployment support for those groups could well be stimulated by their anticipated crime trends.

ANALYSIS OF SOME RECENT CRIME TRENDS[1]

We begin by examining trends in violent crimes, which are the most serious crimes and attract the greatest public concern. We focus on robbery and murder, the two violent crimes that are best measured. We devote less attention to the other two violent crimes, forcible rape and aggravated assault, both of which exhibit important measurement problems. Aggravated assault is troubled by the room for discretion in classifying an assault as either "aggravated" or "simple"; only if it is aggravated is it recorded as a Part I crime in the Federal Bureau of Investigation's Uniform Crime Reports (UCR). Moreover, comparisons with the assault trends measured in the National Crime Victimization Survey (NCVS) suggest that the police have "upgraded" the recording and classification of assaults over time and classify many as aggravated that they would have treated as lesser offenses in the past (Rosenfeld, 2007a). The measurement of forcible rape is subject to important variations in whether the incident is reported to the police and counted as a Part I crime.

Trends in Robbery and Murder

In Figure 2-1 we compare the rates of homicide and robbery from 1972 to 2006. To provide a comparison of the two trends, we have divided the robbery rate by 25 to put robbery and murder on a comparable scale.

The first observation from comparing the murder and robbery trends is their striking similarity. Both reach their peaks and their troughs within a year of each other. This may suggest that similar factors are affecting both trends, but not necessarily. It also is possible that one is driving the other. Explaining the correspondence between trends in different types of crime is an important issue for future research (see LaFree, 1998).

[1]Except where indicated otherwise, we use the term "trends" in this chapter to refer to year-to-year variation in crime rates and associated conditions.

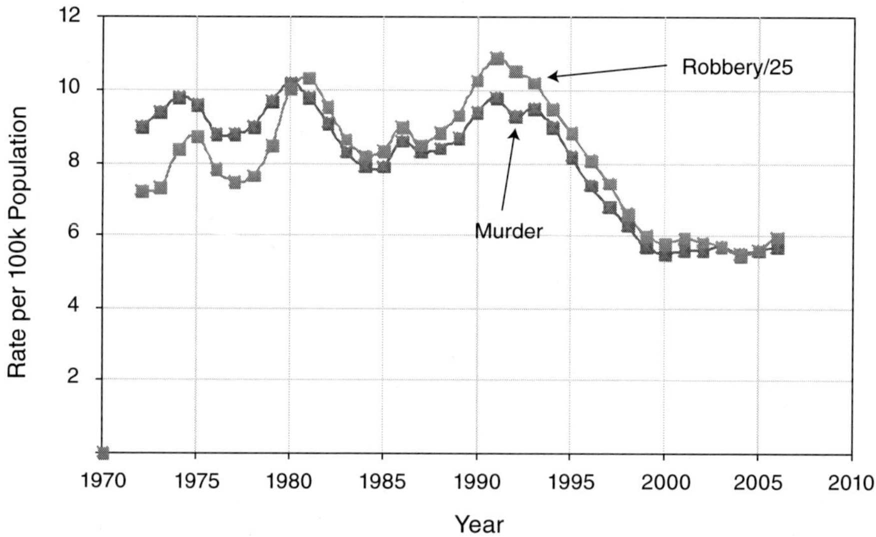

FIGURE 2-1 Trends in murder and robbery, 1972-2006.

Turning Points

It is useful to examine the peaks and the troughs of these two curves as a way of identifying knowledge about the factors contributing to crime trends. The turning points are of particular interest because, once a trend has been established, the value for the current year and the current trend often yield a good prediction of the value for the next year. But the turning points are usually not easy to predict without a strong model of the factors accounting for such changes in direction.

1980 and Age Composition

There was an important turning point in 1980. The rather steady rise in both rates until 1980 can be attributed to factors associated with the postwar baby boom that began with the 1947 birth cohort. As the baby boom cohorts moved into the high-crime ages of about 15 to 20, they were important contributors to the crime rise of the 1960s and 1970s. This was a consequence of there being more people in those high-crime ages and also perhaps a cohort-size effect, whereby a larger cohort in those ages stimulated more of its members to engage in crime (Easterlin, 1987; O'Brien, Stockard, and Isaacson, 1999). The peak cohort in the baby boom era is the 1960 cohort, which had about 4.5 million members. By 1980 that group and large fractions of the baby boom population were moving out of the high-crime ages. Indeed, a detailed analysis of demographic effects on crime rates published in 1980, and therefore based on data for the 1970s, forecast that crime rates would peak in 1980 (Blumstein, Cohen, and Miller, 1980). Of course, that forecast was relatively easy to make because demographic factors can be reliably traced well into the future, and indeed they are among the few factors that can easily be used as a leading indicator of crime rates.

1985 and the Recruitment of Young People into Crack Cocaine Markets

A second turning point in robbery and murder trends took place in 1985. Crime rates declined between 1980 and 1985, the decreases associated with the demographic trends already identified. There was no prior expectation that crime rates would turn up after 1985. Undoubtedly, some other factor emerged that overwhelmed the continuing demographic trend. A detailed account (Blumstein, 1995; Blumstein and Rosenfeld, 1998) highlighted the importance of the recruitment of young people into crack markets as replacements for the older sellers who were being sent to prison at a very high rate in the early 1980s. Because crack was typically sold in street markets, these young sellers had to carry guns to protect themselves against street robbers (Jacobs, 2000). They were far less restrained then their older predecessors in the use of guns, and that diminished restraint contributed to a major rise in firearm violence. The violence was augmented by the tight networking of these young people, resulting in other young people with no involvement in drug markets arming themselves for self-defense or for the status derived from carrying a gun (Fagan and Wilkinson, 1998; Sheley and Wright, 1995).

Popular accounts at the time directed attention to crack as an important factor in violent crime. The street markets were located in inner-city neighborhoods, where violence was a norm for dispute resolution (Anderson, 1999), and it arrived with widespread appeal, particularly for poor people who could not afford powder cocaine but could readily afford the low cost of crack, typically sold in small quantities. The "high" associated with crack is short-lived, 8-15 minutes, necessitating frequent purchases by regular users. The high-volume street trade facilitated violence by street robbers who preyed on sellers and buyers, conflicts among sellers, and robberies by users seeking funds to purchase the drug (Jacobs, 1999).

Although it was widely recognized that violence was associated with crack markets, it would have been difficult to know precisely when the turning point would occur. Crack markets began in Miami, New York, Los Angeles, and other larger coastal cities in the early 1980s, but the turning point did not occur until the major recruitment of the young replacements, rather than with the introduction of crack. This effect is not very likely to have been anticipated in advance.

1993 and the Decline in Demand for Crack by New Users

The third major turning point depicted in Figure 2-1 occurred about 1993, which was the start of the major downturn documented in *The Crime Drop in America* (Blumstein and Wallman, 2006; see also Zimring, 2006). That book discusses the shrinkage in crack markets that resulted from a major drop in demand for crack by new users and the consequent departure from the crack markets of the young recruits (Johnson, Golub, and Dunlap, 2006). A robust economy could absorb those young people; unemployment rates for African-American teenagers reached 20- to 30-year lows by the mid-1990s (Nasar, 1998; Nasar and Mitchell, 1999). Between 1992 and 2000, unemployment dropped by 30 percent among African Americans without a high school diploma and by over 50 percent among similarly situated Hispanics (U.S. Census Bureau, 2006). Aggressive policing focused on young people with guns probably also contributed to the violent crime drop, although the effects of such programs have been documented for only a few cities (e.g., Kennedy et al., 2001).

Another contributor was the continued drop in violent crime by people over 30, resulting in part from the growing prison population (Blumstein, 2006; Rosenfeld, 2006a). During the 1990s, the median age of state prisoners reached the early 30s, which criminal career research suggests is the age with the longest residual career following a criminal justice intervention. Thus, the departure of young people from the crack markets combined with the continuing decline of violence by the over-30 population were major factors contributing to the steady decline in violent crime from about 1993 until 2000. The role of aggressive policing of young people with guns or of other innovative policing strategies introduced during the decade is less easy to identify strongly (Eck and Maguire, 2006; Rosenfeld, Fornango, and Baumer, 2005).

2000 and the End of the Crime Drop

The year 2000 was not quite a turning point in the sense that it showed a trough in the crime rate, but it was certainly a turning point in converting the steady decline of the 1990s to a very flat trend that continued at least until 2005. It is not surprising that the strong downward trend of the 1990s finally flattened out, but at the time it was not at all clear when that flattening would occur. The fact that the crime drop continued until 2000, resulting in low crime rates that had not been seen since the 1960s, was fortunate but not readily predictable.

The Blip in 2005

That flat trend continued over the next few years, with no changes greater than 2.5 percent. The increases continued through 2006, but in 2007 homicide and robbery rates decreased by 1.3 percent and 1.2 percent respectively (http://www.fbi.gov/ucr/cius2007/data/table_01a.html). These small changes do little to encourage a belief that neither the two previous increases nor the following decrease in 2007 represent any more than fluctuations around a continuing flat trend (Police Executive Research Forum, 2006, 2007; Rosenfeld, 2007b).

It is easy to identify a number of factors that could be contributing to a new upward trend in violent crime, including:

- reduced job opportunities for young people with minimal education,
- reduced social services as a result of federal funding cuts,
- reductions in the size of police forces,
- diversion of police attention to terrorism issues,
- slower growth in the prison population, and
- diminished attention to gun control.

The problem is that one could have enumerated these same factors in at least several of the preceding years or in 2007. Why they should be particularly relevant in 2005 or 2006 is part of the dilemma of whether there is currently merely a blip or the start of a clear upward trend in violent crime.

Trends in Burglary and Motor Vehicle Theft

We have been examining just the trends in murder and robbery, the two most well-defined and well-measured violent crimes. Among property crimes, burglary and motor vehicle theft are of particular interest because of their seriousness, prevalence, and reliable measurement in the UCR. Well over half of burglaries documented in the NCVS are reported to the police, compared with only 32 percent of larcenies (http://www.albany.edu/sourcebook/tost_3.html#3_x). Victims are even more likely to report motor vehicle thefts, partly because they depend on the police to recover their car and partly because of insurance requirements. But an important and poorly understood source of heterogeneity in motor vehicle theft is the large fraction of vehicles stolen for "joyriding" as opposed to economic gain.

Figure 2-2 presents the time trends in burglary and motor vehicle theft rates (the latter scaled up by a factor of 2 to be comparable to burglary). We see a somewhat different pattern for burglary from that in Figure 2-1

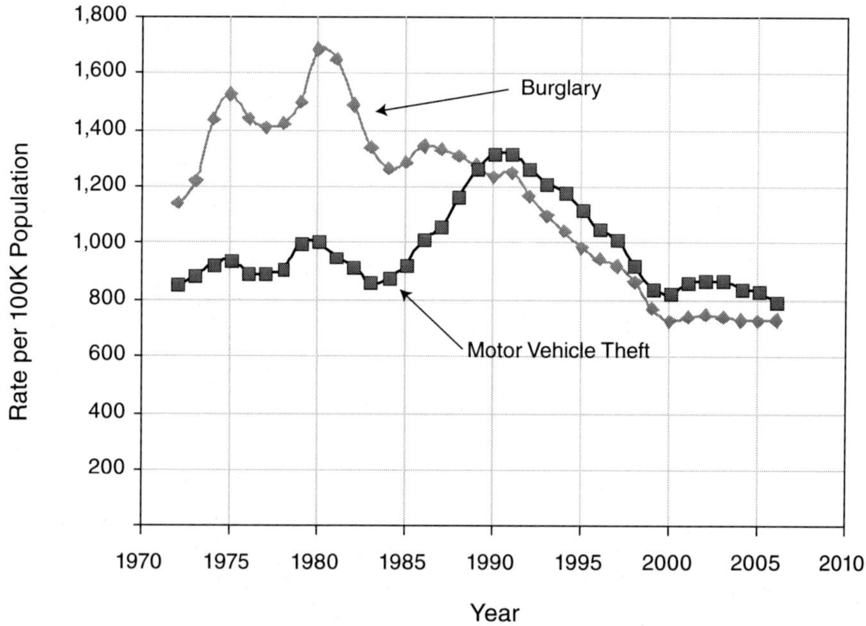

FIGURE 2-2 Burglary and motor vehicle theft, 1972-2006.

for murder and robbery. Burglary has been on an almost steady downward trend since 1980. It is not clear why burglary, which shares with robbery the motive of economic gain, should have such a different pattern. It is possible that many offenders began to substitute robbery, with its "one-stop shopping" characteristic, for burglary as the traditional fencing operations for stolen goods disappeared during the crack epidemic (Baumer et al., 1998). It is also possible that sanctions against burglary have increased faster than sanctions against robbery, thereby diminishing the difference between them and making robbery relatively more attractive as an illicit means of economic gain. The trend in motor vehicle theft, with a turning point in the early 1990s, is more similar to those for robbery and homicide than to the burglary trend, and it is consistent with qualitative accounts of stolen cars traded for drugs during the crack era (Jacobs, 1999) or for use by drug dealers to avoid having their own cars confiscated as forfeited assets. A clear need exists for research on the divergence between burglary and motor vehicle theft trends over the past 25 years.

LOOKING FOR GOOD LEADING INDICATORS

Although some candidate explanations are more compelling than others, the factors underlying the recent crime trends in the United States, and especially those that might help to explain the abrupt reversals in trend we have documented, remain poorly understood (Levitt, 2004; Rosenfeld, 2004; Zimring, 2006). Given the social science community's poor track record in explaining past crime trends, it is not surprising to find that efforts to forecast future changes are even less promising. Reliable forecasting requires either strong time-series predictors or knowledge of leading indicators that can be used to predict future changes in crime rates, such that knowledge of the indicator's value at t_0 yields an accurate prediction of the change in crime at t_1, some later time. We consider the forecasting possibilities of several of the factors already mentioned and a few additional ones that appear to hold some promise at both the national and local levels.

Demographic Trends

As noted previously, demography provides one of the best leading indicators. On one hand, it is well established, and it can be forecast well into the future. It invokes the information contained in the well-known age-crime curves and in racial and ethnic differences in victimization and offending patterns. When there are no other comparably strong influences, demographic changes may provide the best prediction of future crime trends. On the other hand, we also have mentioned in earlier sections other important factors that can dominate the demographic effects. This is particularly true when the demographic changes are relatively slow. Indeed, during the sharp crime drop of the 1990s, age composition changes were trending in the wrong direction: the number of 18-year-olds in the U.S. population was increasing while crime rates were declining for other reasons.

Age Composition

The role of age composition can be assessed from Figure 2-3, which shows the number of people of each age in 2005. The strong effect of the baby boom is seen in the right-hand portion of the curve. There was a 30 percent increase in cohort size between 1945 and 1947 (the two cohorts were 60 and 58 years old, respectively, in 2005). Subsequent cohorts were increasing in size until the peak 1960 cohort (which was 45 years old in 2005). Looking at the cohorts between ages 0 and 20 one does not see any important changes in cohort sizes, with most of those cohorts varying around 4 million persons per cohort. Thus, changing age composition is not likely to provide a substantial influence on crime rates for the next 20 years.

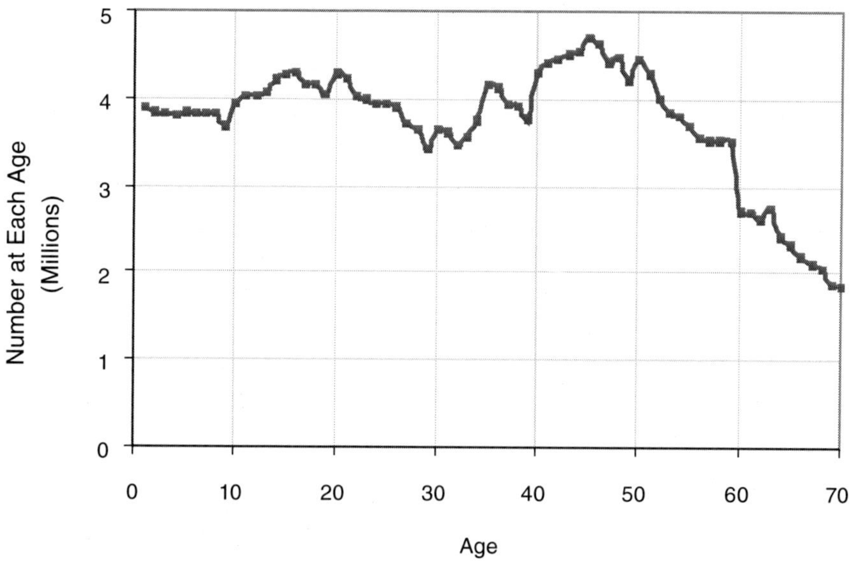

FIGURE 2-3 Demography: Age distribution of the U.S. population in 2005.

Race and Ethnicity

Because there are sizable differences in crime involvement among racial and ethnic groups, changes in their size might be important in affecting crime trends. We can assess the probable race-ethnic effects with the data in Table 2-1, which presents projected changes in the composition of the U.S. population by race and ethnicity in five-year intervals through age 25 (based on data in http://www.census.gov/ipc/www/usinterimproj/usproj2000-2050.xls). The table shows that the growth rate in the white and black populations is generally quite slow (less than 1 percent per year for almost all age-year combinations), while the growth in the Hispanic population is somewhat greater (typically on the order of 1-2 percent per year). These aggregate growth rates are generally quite small and so are not likely to have a major effect on crime rates during a period of major change, such as the 1990s, when the homicide and robbery rates fell by about 5 percent per year, or between 1985 and 1991, when they rose by 3 to 4 percent per year.

It is possible, of course, that during more limited periods or for particular ages the demographic shifts could become important. Table 2-2 presents the projected trends for 15-year-olds as an illustration of that effect. We note that during the 2000-2005 period, both blacks (2.9 percent) and His-

TABLE 2-1 Annual Percentage Change in U.S. White, Hispanic, and Black Populations by Age Over Five-Year Intervals, 2000-2020

Age	White	Hispanic	Black
5	0.1	1.9	0.64
10	–0.6	1.9	–0.02
15	–0.6	2.5	0.36
20	–0.6	1.6	0.09

TABLE 2-2 Annual Percentage Change in U.S. White, Hispanic, and Black 15-Year-Olds Over Five-Year Intervals, 2000-2020

Years	White	Hispanic	Black
2000-2005	0.5	4.5	2.9
2005-2010	–2.2	1.6	–2.1
2010-2015	–1.0	1.5	–1.2
2015-2020	0.5	2.4	1.7

panics (4.5 percent) had appreciably larger annual growth than over the entire 20-year period. This might well have introduced a demographic effect into the crime changes in recent years, as the 15-year-olds move toward the peak ages of the age-crime curve. But the rate of change for the later years is smaller for Hispanics and negative for blacks, so it is likely that any such demographic effect would be short and transient.

Incarceration

Another factor with some promise as a leading indicator for crime is the extent of incarceration. There is little question that incarceration at the levels used in the United States has a crime reduction effect, most specifically through incapacitation. But that effect varies with crime type, and it is quite dubious for offenders engaged in illicit markets, like drug dealers, in which replacements can be recruited when offenders are sent to prison (Blumstein, 1993, 1995). Also, the effect will differ with the offender's age (e.g., those in their 30s have the longest residual career length) and with the length of the sentence being served. Some policy analysts argue that incarceration is the dominant influence on crime, with the growth of incarceration during the 1990s crime drop given as a dramatic case in point. But incarceration was also increasing during the 1980s, when crime rates were going up. This highlights the fact that crime rates are affected by a multiplicity of factors—some pushing them up and others pushing them down—and at any time one or another could be dominating the rest. It is the net sum of these factors that results in a net positive or negative effect on crime rates.

Such considerations call for multivariate investigations of the impact of incarceration on crime rates. That research has, with exceptions, shown that crime rates decline with increases in incarceration, net of other influences (Levitt, 1996; Marvell and Moody, 1994; but see DeFina and Arvanites, 2002). Rosenfeld and Fornango (2007) estimate that rising incarceration rates accounted for about 19 percent of the decline in national robbery rates and 23 percent of the drop in burglary rates during the 1990s, controlling for the effects of economic conditions, growth in police per capita, changes in age and race composition, and lagged crime rates. These results are similar to those reported by Spelman (2006), Rosenfeld (2006a), and Levitt (2004).

This convergence in results does not guarantee a similar effect under any other circumstances, but it does highlight the ability to make reasonable estimates of the effects of incarceration on recent U.S. crime trends. Using the elasticity estimates that derive from these analyses and the time lag between observed increases in imprisonment and crime reductions (generally estimated as one year but sometimes longer), one should be able to anticipate future effects on crime as incarceration rates and related policies change. For example, given the recent decline in the net growth of incarceration, the large numbers of individuals being released from prison (about 700,000 per year), and potential difficulties in readjusting to civilian life, one might have expected some reduction of the incarceration effect on robbery and homicide over the past few years.

Future research, however, should consider two limits on the relationship between incarceration and crime. First, if the crime reduction effects of incarceration are assumed to operate mainly through incapacitation, they are likely to be strongly age-graded. The crime rates of younger people, who have a comparatively low risk of incarceration, should not be affected as much as those of adults by aggregate changes in the incarceration rate, which largely reflects the incapacitation of offenders in their late 20s and 30s (again, the median age of prisoners is early 30s).

A second condition limiting the crime reduction effects of imprisonment concerns the diminishing effect of incapacitation as imprisonment rates increase. Research indicates that the effect of imprisonment on crime varies with the scale of incarceration. The crime reduction effects of imprisonment grow larger as incarceration rates increase and then level off and could well diminish (Canela-Cacho, Blumstein, and Cohen, 1997). There is some indication that additional expansion in incarceration may actually be associated with crime increases (Clear et al., 2003; Liedka, Piehl, and Useem, 2006).

If replicated, these findings can help to reconcile rival theoretical claims about the impact of incarceration on crime. Some analysts point to the disruptive effects of high incarceration rates on family functioning and community organization, maintaining that under such conditions incarceration increases crime (Rose and Clear, 1998). Others argue that the incapacitation effects of incarceration must diminish with the incarceration of less serious offenders inherent in prison expansion (Spelman, 2006). And others cite the now substantial econometric literature on imprisonment as evidence for the deterrent and incapacitation effects of incarceration on crime (Levitt, 2002). All may be correct. There is a clear need for research on the impact of incarceration on age-specific crime rates as the scale of imprisonment changes.

The Economy

The idea that crime rates rise and fall with economic conditions has a long pedigree in criminology. Early studies sought to connect crime rates to the changing prices of staple commodities, such as wheat or rye (Cook and Zarkin, 1985, p. 118). More recent research has generally used the unemployment rate to measure economic performance. Employment opportunities represent an important means of diverting people from need-based criminal activity. This is especially the case with teenagers, for whom employment represents the natural role transition to adult status. Although many studies have attempted to link unemployment rates with crime, the results have been strikingly diffuse: some find a positive association, some find a negative association, and many find not much of an association at all (Kleck and Chiricos, 2002).

These disparate results can be attributed, in part, to the meaning of "unemployment rate." On one hand, for example, the unemployment rate may have been high in Silicon Valley following the "dot-com" bust, but the newly unemployed people were not likely to turn to crime—or, at any rate, the types of crime counted in the FBI's Part I crimes. On the other hand, employment opportunities for teenagers can have a powerful influence on whether they begin or continue to engage in crime (Freeman, 1996). Changes in the aggregate unemployment rate are likely to be a very blunt instrument for identifying the effects of economic conditions on crime trends. Changes in age-, race-, and sex-specific unemployment should yield better estimates of the criminal involvement of groups that have a disproportionate influence on crime trends at both the national and local levels.

Other economic indicators have shown some promise in explaining aggregate and age-specific crime trends, including wages (Grogger, 2006) and state-level gross domestic product (GDP) (Arvanites and DeFina, 2006). However, the forecasting potential of such indicators is limited because they are generally estimated as coincident and not leading indicators of crime changes, and they are themselves difficult to anticipate. It would be extremely desirable to find macroeconomic indicators that can serve as leading indicators of crime rates.

One possible candidate is consumer sentiment. Aggregate consumer expectations derived from monthly population surveys may outperform formal economic models and the forecasts of professional economists in predicting future unemployment and inflation trends (Curtin, 2002, 2003). They also have proven to be relatively accurate predictors of subsequent changes in real GDP (Golinelli and Parigi, 2004). The Index of Consumer Expectations, taken from the University of Michigan's monthly consumer surveys, is included in the Leading Indicator Composite Index published by the Bureau of Economic Analysis of the U.S. Department of Commerce.

Perhaps the most salient advantage of the consumer surveys over the standard measures of economic conditions is that they measure the subjective experience of economic hardship and change. Individuals may, of course, misjudge the timing or significance of various economic conditions, but they are likely to be more reliable guides to their own perceptions of economic conditions than researchers who must rely on more or less informed assumptions about those perceptions.

Recent research has revealed sizable and robust effects of a summary measure of consumer sentiment on trends in U.S. robbery and property crime rates (Rosenfeld and Fornango, 2007). Year-over-year increases since 1970 in consumer confidence and optimism are associated with year-over-year reductions in robbery, burglary, larceny, and motor vehicle theft rates. These effects withstand controls for age and race composition, imprisonment rates, police per capita, lagged crime rates, and the possible reciprocal influence of crime on public economic perceptions. They are largely independent of the effects of unemployment and real GDP per capita. Perhaps most importantly, consumer sentiment leads (by one year) and is not simply a contemporaneous indicator of robbery and property crime changes. If these results are replicated in future research, they hold some promise for perceptual measures of economic conditions as leading indicators of crime rate changes.

The findings to date on the impact of the public's economic perceptions on crime rates are limited to property crimes and the violent crime of robbery. In light of the similarity between the homicide and robbery trends shown in Figure 2-1, one might anticipate a similar relationship to homicide. An initial indication is the correspondence between homicide rates and the Index of Consumer Sentiment over the past 45 years, as shown in Figure 2-4. To better reveal the correspondence between the two series, the consumer sentiment measure has been inverted so that low values reveal consumer confidence and optimism. Both series have been regressed on a

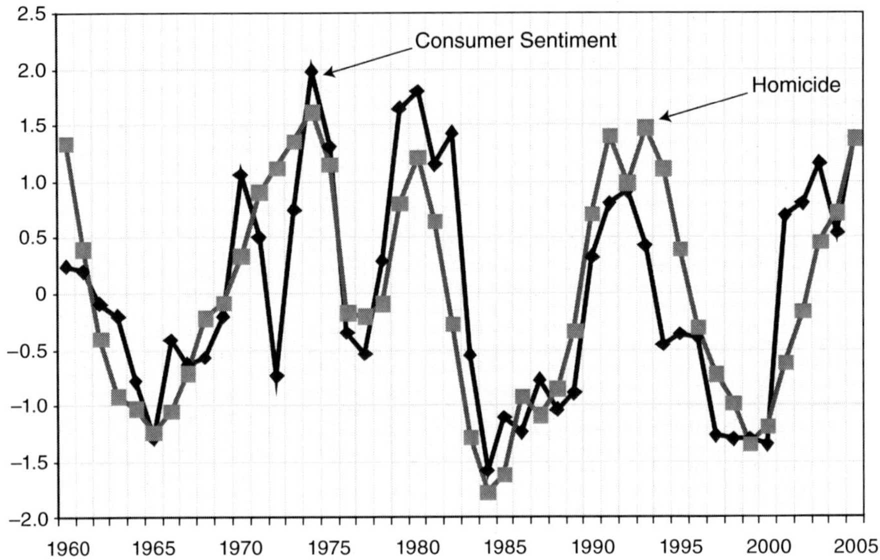

FIGURE 2-4 Detrended index of consumer sentiment (inverted) and U.S. homicide rate, 1960-2005.

linear counter to highlight year-to-year deviations from their respective time trends. The two series move in strikingly similar patterns, reaching peaks and troughs at about the same time, including the important turning points during the 1980s and 1990s discussed earlier. Public economic perceptions certainly warrant attention in future research on changes in both property and violent crime rates.

Other Proposed Factors

Aside from the previous enumeration, a number of other explanations have been proposed in the literature. The one that has probably received the most currency, perhaps because of the creativity of the suggestion and also because of its elaboration in the bestselling book, *Freakonomics* (Levitt and Dubner, 2005), is that of Donohue and Levitt (2001). This analysis appears to show that the legalization of abortion in 1973 as a result of the *Roe v. Wade* Supreme Court decision resulted in fewer unwanted births and hence reduced the criminality of subsequent birth cohorts. Their original analysis suggested that at least half of the crime drop of the 1990s was thus attributable to the legalization of abortion, although in a subsequent analysis they dropped that factor to one-quarter (Donohue and Levitt, 2004).

There has been considerable challenge to the Donohue-Levitt conclusion. Joyce (2004) challenged the salience of abortion by showing no significant drop in fertility, suggesting that the legalization could well have been matched by illegal abortions prior to 1973. Comparing crime rates of similar cohorts born before and after legalization, he found only period effects. His various analyses conclude with a strong and consistent finding of no appreciable effect of abortion on crime rates.

Zimring (2006) argues that if there were a profound effect of abortion legalization on unwanted births resulting in a major crime decline, one should see that effect replicated in school performance, labor force participation, and many other facets of the enhanced socialization of the post-*Roe* cohorts. He suggests that finding it only with respect to crime is an artifact of the shortcomings of the analysis rather than the hypothesized abortion effect. He also points out that the liberalization of abortion policy in other nations evidently has not produced corresponding reductions in crime.

These criticisms imply that the Donohue-Levitt analysis omits important factors other than abortion policy changes that have influenced crime trends. A critical omission is any consideration of the influence of the changes in the crack market and its participants in the late 1980s and early 1990s. A key part of the Donahue-Levitt argument hinges on the different effects in five states—importantly including New York and California—that legalized abortion before 1973. As demonstrated by Cork (1999), these two states' largest cities, New York and Los Angeles, were early initiators of the crack epidemic and that could have accounted for the early start of the crime drop in those two states.

Thus, it seems reasonable to conclude that, while among the many factors affecting crime rates there may well have been some limited effect of abortion and the consequent reduction in unwanted children, the important omitted variables in the initial analysis and the replications showing no significant effect suggest that any such effect is likely to be quite small.

Similarly, studies by Reyes (2007) and Nevin (2000) comment on children's exposure to lead and its effect on intelligence and on violence. This research builds on early work by Needleman (1995) on the effects of children's exposure to lead on their intelligence measured by IQ scores. Lead was introduced into gasoline in the early 1940s, reached a peak in the early 1970s as environmental controls were introduced, and declined thereafter. There is a clear similarity between time trends in environmental lead levels and violent crime rates lagged by 23 years. But demographic trends—the arrival and waning of the baby boom generation from the high-crime ages—coincided roughly with the arrival and departure of leaded gasoline, and so the apparent effect of exposure to lead on crime rates may be confounded with demographic change.

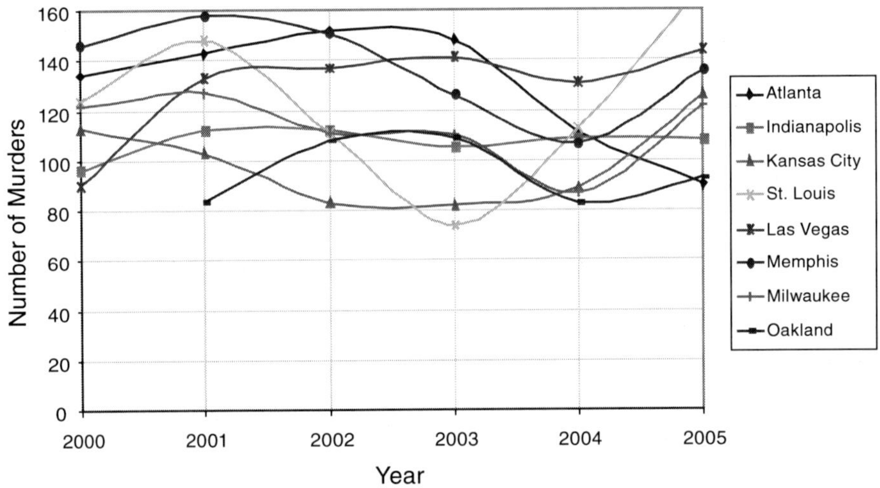

FIGURE 2-5 Number of murders in eight cities over six years.

LOCAL VARIATION IN CRIME TRENDS

The general consistency across cities of the large crime drop during the 1990s could leave the impression that crime trends are reasonably uniform across cities. In fact, crime trends are much more likely to vary across cities, and that has been very much the case since 2000, when the aggregate national trend has been flat. This is reflected in Figure 2-5, which depicts recent patterns across eight cities, each of which had about 100 homicides per year. This graph clearly highlights the diverse patterns of change across cities, although most of them turned up in 2005. This suggests that, at least until 2005, the recent crime trends have been driven more by local conditions than by any general national demographic, incarceration, or economic trend.

Nor were the crime increases recorded in 2005 and 2006 uniform across cities. Figure 2-6 displays changes in robberies in 28 cities between 2004 and 2006.[2] On average, robberies in the 28 cities increased 2.9 percent over the two years, and several cities registered declines. An average yearly robbery increase of 1.5 percent, as well as a decrease or an increase of less than 10 percent over two years for almost two-thirds of the cities, do not constitute the "gathering storm" of violence chronicled in a recent influential report based on a different sample of cities (Police Executive Research Forum, 2006, 2007).

[2]The full-year 2006 data were drawn from the police department websites of the 28 cities at about the time that the preliminary six-month results were reported by the UCR.

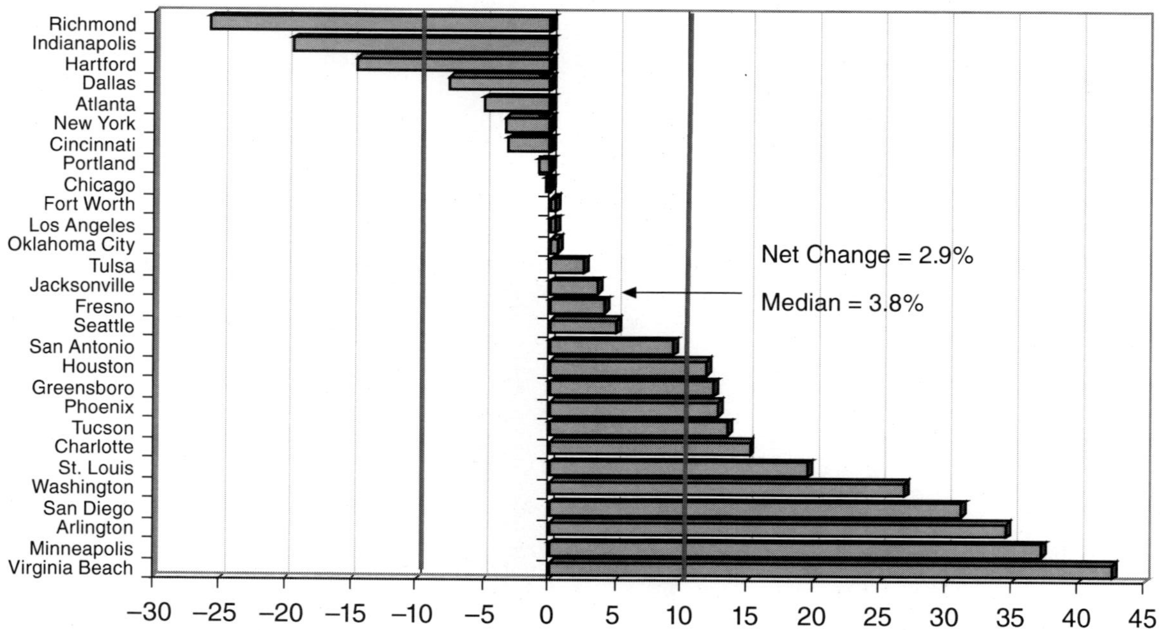

FIGURE 2-6 Percentage change in robberies in 28 cities, 2004-2006.

The natural place to turn for identifying local factors affecting crime rates is the rich body of criminological theory and research, including longitudinal investigations of factors affecting the development of criminality, and evaluation research on local crime-control initiatives. Some of these factors may be distinctively local, such as particular policing tactics; some may be regional, such as the progression of a particular drug market; and some may be national, such as the result of a change in federal public assistance policies. Of course, such factors may be as difficult to forecast as crime rates themselves. Furthermore, the existing research generally does not link specific factors affecting individual criminality (e.g., parenting styles or temperament) or specific local interventions (e.g., hot spots policing) to broader changes in crime rates, so one knows very little about the probable effects of such conditions and programs on crime trends were they brought to scale (Rosenfeld, 2006b; Wilson, 2002).

We now consider factors that are relevant at the local level: policing strategies, tactics, and management; firearm availability; drug markets; the presence of local gangs or other oppositional groups; and variation in socialization and the availability of social services.

Policing

A recent review concluded that the many and diverse changes in policing strategies and tactics in the United States during the 1990s probably contributed little to the national crime drop (Eck and Maguire, 2006). But that conclusion is as much a reflection of the sparseness and quality of the underlying research as of the effectiveness of the policing innovations (Rosenfeld, Fornango, and Baumer, 2005).

For example, we are aware of only four investigations of the effects on precinct-level violent crime trends of New York City's widely emulated program of increasing arrests for minor quality-of-life offenses. Two of these studies concluded that the quality-of-life initiative had statistically significant but small effects on New York's violent crime decline during the 1990s (Messner et al., 2007; Rosenfeld, Fornango, and Rengifo, 2007); one concluded it had no effect (Harcourt and Ludwig, 2006); and the other maintained that the initiative was responsible for all of New York's violent crime drop (Kelling and Sousa, 2001). Until the disparate results of these investigations are reconciled in future research, the effects of quality-of-life policing on rates of serious crime in New York—and the many other cities where similar strategies have been instituted—will remain an open question and a very contentious policy issue.

The innovation that has received the most consistent research support is so-called hot spots policing. This strategy concentrates police resources in areas of elevated criminal activity identified on the basis of continuous monitoring of crime reports. Hot spots policing has been shown to reduce localized crime without displacement to other areas (Braga, 2005). But it is not known what effect such programs have, net of other influences, on the crime trends in the cities where they have been implemented.

Firearms

Firearms are phenomenally ubiquitous in the United States. There are perhaps 75 million handguns in civilian hands. In the great majority of cases, these guns belong to generally law-abiding individuals who pose no threat of using their guns in criminal activity. But this ubiquity also ensures that many guns will find their way into the hands of people, especially young people, who acquire them illegally, who are much more likely to use them with much less restraint, and who are likely to use them in a criminal way, either for interpersonal violence or as a weapon for robbery.

Various policing efforts are targeted at suppressing illicit gun trafficking or at confiscating guns from inappropriate carriers. Reports of "shots fired" provide a key indicator of the presence of guns and their likely misuse, and so warrant police efforts to interdict such activities. Recent evidence suggests that shots-fired calls may serve as a reliable leading indicator for short-term forecasts of more serious offenses (Cohen, Gorr, and Olligschlaeger, 2007).

A relationship between firearm possession and firearm homicide rates in local areas has been documented (Cook and Ludwig, 2006; Hemenway, 2004; National Research Council, 2005). The causal direction of this relationship remains in dispute, however, with some researchers maintaining that firearm violence elevates rates of gun ownership, but not the reverse (Kleck, 1997). A recent study using instrumental-variable methods found a mutually reinforcing relationship between firearm ownership and firearm homicide rates for a nationally representative sample of metropolitan and nonmetropolitan counties (Rosenfeld, Baumer, and Messner, 2007; see also Cook and Ludwig, 2006). Firearm ownership increased rates of firearm homicide, and they, in turn, increased ownership. Additional research on the relationship between trends in firearm possession and firearm violence in the United States is clearly needed, especially research on the acquisition of firearms by persons at high risk for criminal violence (see National Research Council, 2005).

Drug Markets

As indicated earlier, drug markets can be an important source of violent crime. They generate violence because disputes between buyers and sellers or between competing sellers cannot be settled through recourse to the police, courts, or other formal means of conflict resolution. They also generate property crime and robbery resulting from many drug users being unable to maintain jobs, or, even if they do work, being unable to generate the income needed to support their addiction and turning to crime to provide the money to buy drugs. It is also the case that drug markets vary considerably in the degree to which they stimulate violent or property crimes. It is rare, for example, for marijuana markets to generate much violent crime. But crack street markets have been strongly involved in both violent and property crimes.

Typically, a new drug does not show itself in all places at the same time but rather takes hold in some places, often in the largest cities on the coasts, and spreads over time to other places. That pattern then provides an early warning of its diffusion. In some cases the diffusion will be very rapid, as was the case with crack and the firearm violence associated with it (Cork, 1999; Messner et al., 2005). The drug getting the most attention in recent years is methamphetamine, which started in the West several years ago and has been slowly working its way east, still not much further than the Midwest. Abundant anecdotal evidence, mainly from law enforcement agencies, suggests that methamphetamine stimulates violent crime in small towns and rural areas, but systematic research is lacking on the relationship between methamphetamine and criminal violence.

One important source of information on the local features of drug use is the program managed by the National Institute of Justice (NIJ) initially entitled Drug Use Forecasting (DUF) and later changed to Arrestee Drug Abuse Monitoring (ADAM). In this program, booked arrestees in cities across the country were interviewed and given urine tests quarterly to assess the prevalence of illicit drugs and to identify the drugs being used by this population. This program provided valuable information to local communities on the time trends of drug abuse and the nature of the drugs being used. Collectively, it also provided a corresponding national picture of the time trends in drug abuse. The program was canceled by NIJ because of a shortage of funds, even though those funds were minuscule compared with the national effort at drug control.

Gangs and Other Special Groups

There will always be certain population subgoups that are disaffected from or actively hostile to their social environment. In *Code of the Street*, Elijah Anderson (1999) describes a small segment of the inner-city poor as "street people" who live among much larger numbers of "decent people." The street people see little prospect for their future, have a very low threshold of insult, and are prepared to use even extreme violence to avenge perceived disrespect. The violence often involves groups, and sometimes more formal gangs, and exhibits processes of retaliation that can escalate into a sequence of assaults. Indeed, when they see a significant jump in criminal violence within a city, local officials and criminologists often link that jump to the actions of such groups. It is difficult to know in advance when such escalation will occur or the extent to which retaliatory violence spirals are themselves a consequence of changing economic conditions, incarceration levels, drug market conflicts, police actions, or other factors.

More formal street gangs engage in similar kinds of retaliatory activity with each other. American street gangs and the peer groupings Anderson (1999) describes probably differ more in degree than in kind. Los Angeles and Chicago are notorious for the long-term operation of gangs with formal names, hierarchical structures, and formal signs and colors, but most street gangs are loosely organized, fragmented groups with fleeting membership (Klein, 1995).

The number of street gangs and gang members increased during the 1980s and early 1990s, in tandem with the national rise in youth homicide, fell through the end of the decade, and has flattened in recent years—not unlike the pattern for youth violence generally (Egley and Ritz, 2006). This correspondence between the rise and decline of street gangs and street crime implies that gangs might have been an important cause of the broader crime trends. Although entirely plausible, it is just as likely that gangs formed in response to the rising tide of violence and diminished in number as the violence decreased.

The causal relationship between the trends in gangs and violent crime is probably reciprocal, a hypothesis supported by two well-established facts about why adolescents join gangs and the consequences of membership for individual offending and victimization. An important motive for joining is protection from violence in the local community (Decker and van Winkle, 1996; Klein, 1995). Once in the gang, however, adolescents' criminal offending and victimization increase, and when they leave the gang, their offending and victimization levels fall (Peterson, Taylor, and Esbensen, 2004; Thornberry et al., 2003). Gangs may therefore arise as youths seek protection from escalating violence, and as they proliferate their internal dynamics may generate further increases in violence. When the level of violence begins to drop, gangs stop forming or break up, which hastens the decline in violence. Testing these hypotheses with aggregate-level data on gang and violence trends is an important topic for future research.

Socialization and Social Services

The propensity for young people to be involved in crime is affected by the socialization processes they experience from birth through adolescence. Family disruption, family size, and parental supervision, conflict, and criminality are all important determinants of individual delinquency and criminality. Family-based crime prevention programs have been shown to reduce children's antisocial behavior and arrests during adolescence. The family factors affecting delinquency and crime may be modifiable by investments in a wide array of social services, but especially in pre- and postnatal home visits and parent training programs, which demonstration projects have shown to be especially effective (Farrington, 2002). The availability of such services, even when supported by local funding, is particularly sensitive to federal social welfare investments. As federal budget deficits have grown in recent years, such services have been cut back and become more dependent on local financing, which has been under considerable strain in many urban areas, where such support is most needed. The same is true of more narrowly focused violence prevention programs, including those of proven effectiveness, such as the Blueprints program evaluated by the Center for the Study and Prevention of Violence at the University of Colorado (http://www.colorado.edu/cspv/blueprints/index.html).

A challenging research need is to link individual-level data on childhood socialization to aggregate trends in social welfare investments, and both of these to crime trends. It should be possible in principle to integrate data from longitudinal studies of child and adolescent development with aggregate budgetary and crime data for those cities in which the longitudinal developmental studies have been conducted over an extended period (e.g., Pittsburgh, Rochester, Denver, Montreal). Until such multilevel studies are undertaken, one will not know to what extent the risk factors identified in developmental research can serve as leading indicators of changes in crime rates or to what degree public investments in social services can help to ameliorate childhood risks for delinquency and crime.

FUTURE RESEARCH NEEDS

We have identified several factors that prior research suggests have been associated with changes in crime rates in the United States over the past several decades. These include demographic shifts, growth in incarceration, drug markets, and changing economic conditions. We have discussed other factors, such as policing innovations, firearm availability, street gangs, childhood socialization, and investments in social services that may influence crime trends but for which the existing evidence is too fragmentary to develop accurate effect measures. Much remains to be learned about the factors affecting crime trends, including those we already know something about.

For example, the crack markets were implicated in the rise of youth firearm violence during the late 1980s, and an important reason was because young people replaced the adult drug sellers who were sent to prison

(Blumstein, 1995). That interpretation is consistent not only with the rising imprisonment rates for adult drug dealers during the 1980s but with the rising rates of drug arrests and gun violence among minority adolescents that occurred after 1985. The evidence for this explanation could be augmented by results from panel studies showing that the largest increases in youth firearm violence were concentrated in those cities with the largest increases in drug arrests of crack dealers. Those increases, in turn, should have happened in those cities displaying the largest increases in the incarceration of adult drug sellers. Such evidence would further support a leading explanation of the upturn in violent crime during the 1980s that has important policy implications: an unanticipated negative consequence of the intensive sentencing policies initiated as part of the war on drugs was its contribution to the rise in youth violence.

To take another example, we have argued that the strong economy of the 1990s contributed to the decline in violence. During the longest peacetime economic boom on record, tight labor markets were able to absorb minority youth who no longer could make money in the shrinking drug markets. The implication is that the economic expansion conditioned the effect on crime of the drop in demand for crack. In the absence of legitimate employment opportunities, more young people would have pursued other illegitimate opportunities for making money. Again, this story is compatible with several co-occurring trends at the national level in the 1990s, including falling unemployment rates among minority youth and declining demand for crack (Golub and Johnson, 1994). Stronger evidence, with direct relevance for employment policies, would come from studies showing that the impact of declining drug markets on crime reduction was strongest in those cities exhibiting the sharpest increases in minority youth employment and earnings.

The Future of Crime Forecasting

Developing sound empirical explanations of past crime trends is an important means of improving the capacity to make informative and reasonably accurate forecasts of future changes. As approaches are developed to estimating and forecasting the factors contributing to crime trends, it is useful to recognize that there are few significant social or even natural phenomena for which there are good forecasts. For example, a leading group of weather forecasters inaccurately predicted a "very active" 2007 hurricane season. The group's forecast for 2006 overpredicted hurricanes; the year before that, when Hurricane Katrina hit, they erred on the low side. Forecasts of when and where emerging tropical storms will land tend not to be very accurate (Merzer, 2007; see National Research Council, 2006, for a useful discussion of incorporating uncertainty into the dissemination of weather forecasts).

The field of macroeconomics offers another example of considerable effort to develop forecasting models and abundant forecasting failures (Gross, 2007). Despite the large industry devoted to economic forecasts, one week saw the current and former chairmen of the Federal Reserve come out at the same time with strongly differing forecasts, one suggesting the possibility of a recession within the year and the other commenting on the current strength of the economy. Given the resources available and the experience they both bring, and given that the forecast extended for only one year, it is humbling—but also encouraging—to enter the challenge of forecasting crime.

The encouragement comes not from the accuracy of weather or economic forecasts but from the seriousness of the efforts, stimulated no doubt by the strong economic interest in their forecasts. Criminologists are notorious for the inaccuracy of their crime forecasts; consider only the widely publicized prediction of a crime boom brought on by marauding "super predators" (Dilulio, 1995) issued just as crime rates began their historic plunge in the 1990s. The problem with such forecasts is not simply that they are wrong, but also that they are based on minimal systematic analysis. One therefore learns nothing from them. When meteorologists or economists fail to accurately predict the next tropical storm or recession, they can acquire new knowledge about the conditions affecting the weather or economy, which can be used to enhance the data and refine the models used in making the forecasts. Opportunities for such self-correction are absent when forecasts are created in the interest of advocacy, with no opportunities for challenge and replication. Only with a large investment of resources can criminologists hope for their forecasting models to become as meaningful as those from economists, let alone meteorologists.

National and Regional Estimates

It is useful to differentiate efforts at generating national estimates, regional estimates, and local estimates for a particular city or neighborhood. For the national estimates, it is difficult at this point to identify any reliable leading indicators other than demographic shifts. Nevertheless, efforts to identify such indicators are desirable, at least in part because such forecasts could influence the level of federal financial support for policing and other local criminal justice initiatives. A measure of collective economic perceptions from consumer surveys seems to be a strong contemporary correlate of changes in several crime types and may well be a leading indicator of some (Rosenfeld and Fornango, 2007). Similar considerations would apply in the search for multistate regional indicators. There are good reasons to believe that reliable regional indicators might be found because regions are generally more homogeneous than the nation as a whole. The consumer sentiment data are available for the four major census regions. For both the nation and regions, one would also look to drug activity, particularly drugs that are sold in street markets or that start a rapid escalation of demand, as primary indicators of rising crime rates ahead.

Local-Level Estimates

Both economic and drug market indicators should also be evaluated for their contributions to crime forecasts at the neighborhood or city level. Local efforts could be more effectively targeted than national resources or policies, and so developing better estimates for local application would be particularly desirable. The consumer sentiment data are not available for cities or metropolitan areas, but the crime-forecasting capabilities of other economic indicators of local conditions, such as youth unemployment and wage rates, should be investigated. A useful research task would be to use traditional regression-based clustering models to aggregate a large number of cities into subgroups that display similar patterns in crime trends. Alternatively, one might use trajectory analysis (Nagin, 2005) to aggregate into groups cities that have displayed similar crime trends. One could then look for leading indicators of the patterns for each of these trajectory groups. Because the different trajectory groups will have different patterns, there is a strong likelihood that different factors affect them. We anticipate that in the contemporary environment, drug markets, incarceration levels, and employment opportunities for unskilled young men are likely to be important factors affecting crime trends in the larger cities. Whether the same factors also help to explain the trends in smaller cities is a research question for which regression analysis, including interactions with city size, or trajectory analysis could well contribute.

At the neighborhood level, crime, especially violent crime, is concentrated in relatively few areas of the city, a pattern similar to the highly skewed distribution of serious offending across individuals (Chaiken and Chaiken, 1982). Researchers have begun to use trajectory methods at the neighborhood and even smaller levels of aggregation with some promising initial results (Griffiths and Chavez, 2004; Weisburd et al., 2004). Forecasting at this level poses special research challenges but also some distinctive opportunities for acquiring information from individuals familiar with the local environment. Police, youth workers, social service providers, and neighborhood residents are often sensitive to changes in mood and activity patterns and signs of disorder that can serve as early warnings of an upturn in crime. Short-term forecasts of crime patterns at the neighborhood level, such as those recently produced for the Pittsburgh Police Department (Cohen, Gorr, and Olligschlaeger, 2007), also are likely to be of more immediate interest to police managers than forecasts of crime rates for the entire city.

An exciting potential for forecasting at the local level lies in the rich individual and family data from long-standing longitudinal investigations of delinquent and antisocial behavior that are situated in several cities. The challenge is to evaluate the indicators that provide good predictions, sometimes years ahead, of individual criminal involvement for their potential as leading indicators of neighborhood or city crime trends. This will require multilevel analyses that go beyond the now common practice of assessing "neighborhood effects" on individual criminal behavior by estimating the effects of aggregated individual propensities on community crime rates. Such research will necessitate bringing together researchers with quite different interests and skills into collaborative projects. The science of crime forecasting could be advanced significantly by incorporating findings from longitudinal research on individual criminal behavior into analyses of changes in crime rates over time.

Building the Research Infrastructure

The relevance of these proposals for future research on crime trends to assessments of crime control policy will be limited in the absence of a substantial upgrading in the nation's capacity to monitor crime trends. We have already observed the divergent interpretations following reports of some recent crime increases, which stem in large part from the time delay between the availability of local crime data and the UCR's dissemination of aggregate crime statistics. Such delays can provide an opportunity for advocacy groups to leap into the information breach with data of uncertain reliability. There is no technical reason why the recording and dissemination of crime data cannot be as rapid as, say, the compilation and online dissemination of unemployment data by the Bureau of Labor Statistics (Rosenfeld, 2007b). As with many economic time series, the UCR crime data could be released on a quarterly and eventually a monthly basis, with dissemination of the annual data three months after the collection year a reasonable goal. More rapid dissemination, however, would lead to a need for more imputation to develop estimates for nonreporting agencies and require corresponding improvement in the methodology for developing those imputed estimates.

One attempt to significantly enhance the data from the UCR was the introduction of the National Incident-Based Reporting System (NIBRS). Rather than relying merely on aggregate counts of incidents or of arrestees, this approach involved compiling detailed information on individual crime incidents, the perpetrators and the victims, the multiple offenses that occurred in the incident, and aggregating those data as needed to generate population counts and rates. Participation in NIBRS by local police departments has still not exceeded 25 percent of the U.S. population, even though the system has been in operation for over 20 years. It would be most desirable to find ways to increase that participation in a major way to develop the rich data potentially available from the NIBRS approach. One method would be to tie federal funding of state and local crime control initiatives to participation in NIBRS, with some of that funding directed specifically to NIBRS implementation.

The FBI is currently developing an incident-based data system called N-DEX that involves much richer detail on each incident. It is possible that the more detailed data, especially if disseminated more rapidly, could generate much greater participation than has been the case with NIBRS. But the NIBRS experience suggests that participation is likely to be even less extensive without additional incentives.

Much more can be done to improve the current minimal efforts related to crime measurement and forecasting. The precision of crime estimates from the NCVS, which was conducted initially with a much larger sample and with more face-to-face interviewing, has eroded considerably because funding limitations have reduced the sample size and resulted in more telephone interviews, even as declining crime rates warranted larger samples to maintain statistical power. Also, the NCVS, which now regularly provides only national estimates of victimization experience, could well provide subnational estimates, at least for the larger metropolitan areas (see Lauritsen and Schaum, 2005). It might also be able to provide some limited number of characteristics of each respondent's census tract if those characteristics were modified with some random error to protect the respondents' privacy. Doing so would permit linking socioeconomic characteristics to crime prevalence.

Improving the nation's capacity to monitor crime trends will require additional resources devoted to compiling, disseminating, and updating the data. The National Institute of Justice can play an important part in this process by establishing an ongoing research program devoted to analyzing crime trends. Building the infrastructure for understanding changes in crime rates over time is an important criminal justice policy priority and a major focus of more extensive investigations of crime trends emerging from this workshop.

REFERENCES

Anderson, Elijah. (1999). *Code of the street: Decency, violence, and the moral life of the inner city*. New York: Norton.

Arvanites, Thomas M., and Robert H. DeFina. (2006). Business cycles and street crime. *Criminology, 44*, 139-164.

Baumer, Eric, Janet L. Lauritsen, Richard Rosenfeld, and Richard Wright. (1998). The influence of crack cocaine on robbery, burglary, and homicide rates: A cross-city, longitudinal analysis. *Journal of Research in Crime and Delinquency, 35*, 316-340.

Blumstein, Alfred. (1993). Making rationality relevant: The American Society of Criminology presidential address. *Criminology, 31*, 1-16.

Blumstein, Alfred. (1995). Youth violence, guns, and the illicit-drug industry. *Journal of Criminal Law and Criminology, 86*, 10-36.

Blumstein, Alfred. (2006). Disaggregating the violence trends. In Alfred Blumstein and Joel Wallman (Eds.), *The crime drop in America* (revised ed.). New York: Cambridge University Press.

Blumstein, Alfred, and Richard Rosenfeld. (1998). Explaining recent trends in U.S. homicide rates. *Journal of Criminal Law and Criminology, 88*, 1175-1216.

Blumstein, Alfred, and Joel Wallman. (2006). *The crime drop in America* (revised ed.). New York: Cambridge University Press.

Blumstein, Alfred, Jacqueline Cohen, and Harold Miller. (1980). Demographically disaggregated projections of prison populations. *Journal of Criminal Justice, 8*, 1-25.

Braga, Anthony A. (2005). Hot spots policing and crime prevention: A systematic review of randomized controlled trials. *Journal of Experimental Criminology, 1*, 317-342.

Canela-Cacho, Jose A., Alfred Blumstein, and Jacqueline Cohen. (1997). Relationship between the offending frequency (λ) of imprisoned and free offenders. *Criminology, 35*, 133-175.

Chaiken, Jan, and Marcia Chaiken. (1982). *Varieties of criminal behavior.* (RAND Report No. R-2814-NIJ.) Santa Monica, CA: RAND Corporation.

Clear, Todd R., Dina R. Rose, Elin Waring, and Kristen Scully. (2003). Coercive mobility and crime: A preliminary examination of concentrated incarceration and social disorganization. *Justice Quarterly, 20*, 33-64.

Cohen, Jacqueline, Wilpen L. Gorr, and Andreas M. Olligschlaeger. (2007). Leading indicators and spatial interactions: A crime-forecasting model for proactive police deployment. *Geographical Analysis, 39*, 105-127.

Cook, Philip J., and Jens Ludwig. (2006). The social costs of gun ownership. *Journal of Public Economics, 90*, 379-391.

Cook, Philip J., and Gary A. Zarkin. (1985). Crime and the business cycle. *Journal of Legal Studies, 14*, 115-128.

Cork, Daniel. (1999). Examining space-time interaction in city-level homicide data: Crack markets and the diffusion of guns among youth. *Journal of Quantitative Criminology, 15*, 379-406.

Curtin, Richard T. (2002). *Surveys of consumers: Theory, methods, and interpretation.* Paper presented at the September 30, 2002 meeting of the National Association for Business Economics, Washington, DC.

Curtin, Richard T. (2003). Unemployment expectations: The impact of private information on income uncertainty. *Review of Income and Wealth, 49*, 539-554.

Decker, Scott H., and Barrik van Winkle. (1996). *Life in the gang*. New York: Cambridge University Press.

DeFina, Robert H., and Thomas M. Arvanites. (2002). The weak effect of imprisonment on crime: 1971-1992. *Social Science Quarterly, 83*, 635-653.

DiIulio, John J. (1995, November 27). The coming of the super predators. *The Weekly Standard.*

Donohue, John J., and Steven D. Levitt. (2001). The impact of legalized abortion on crime. *Quarterly Journal of Economics, 116*, 379-420.

Donohue, John J., and Steven D. Levitt. (2004). Further evidence that legalized abortion lowered crime: A reply to Joyce. *Journal of Human Resources, 39*, 29-49.

Easterlin, Richard. (1987). *Birth and fortune: The impact of numbers on personal welfare* (2nd ed.). Chicago: University of Chicago Press.

Eck, John E., and Edward R. Maguire. (2006). Have changes in policing reduced violent crime? An assessment of the evidence. In Alfred Blumstein and Joel Wallman (Eds.), *The crime drop in America* (revised ed.). New York: Cambridge University Press.

Egley, Arlen, and Christina E. Ritz. (2006). *Highlights of the 2004 National Youth Gang Survey*. Fact Sheet 2006-01. Washington, DC: U.S. Department of Justice, Office of Juvenile Justice and Delinquency Prevention.

Fagan, Jeffrey, and Deanna L. Wilkinson. (1998). Guns, youth violence and social identity in inner cities. *Crime and Justice, 24*, 105-188.

Farrington, David P. (2002). Families and crime. In James Q. Wilson and Joan Petersilia (Eds.), *Crime: Public policies for crime control.* Oakland, CA: ICS Press.

Freeman, Richard B. (1996). Why do so many young American men commit crimes and what might we do about it? *Journal of Economic Perspectives, 10*, 25-42.

Golinelli, Roberto, and Giuseppi Parigi. (2004). Consumer sentiment and economic activity: A cross-country comparison. *Journal of Business Cycle Measurement and Analysis, 1,* 147-170.

Golub, Andrew, and Bruce D. Johnson. (1994). A recent decline in cocaine use among youthful arrestees in Manhattan (1987-1993). *American Journal of Public Health, 84,* 1250-1254.

Griffiths, Elizabeth, and Jorge M. Chavez. (2004). Communities, street guns, and homicide trajectories in Chicago, 1980-1995: Merging methods for examining homicide trends across space and time. *Criminology, 42,* 941-978.

Grogger, Jeffrey. (2006). An economic model of recent trends in violence. In Alfred Blumstein and Joel Wallman (Eds.), *The crime drop in America* (revised ed.). New York: Cambridge University Press.

Gross, Daniel. (2007, March 4). The forecast for the forecasters is dismal. *New York Times.*

Harcourt, Bernard E., and Jens Ludwig. (2006). Broken windows: New evidence from New York City and a five-city social experiment. *University of Chicago Law Review, 73,* 271-320.

Hemenway, David. (2004). *Private guns, public health.* Ann Arbor: University of Michigan Press.

Jacobs, Bruce A. (1999). *Dealing crack: The social world of streetcorner selling.* Boston: Northeastern University Press.

Jacobs, Bruce A. (2000). *Robbing drug dealers.* Hawthorne, NY: Aldine.

Johnson, Bruce D., Andrew Golub, and Eloise Dunlap. (2006). The rise and decline of hard drugs, drug markets, and violence in inner-city New York. In Alfred Blumstein and Joel Wallman (Eds.), *The crime drop in America* (revised ed.). New York: Cambridge University Press.

Joyce, Theodore J. (2004). Did legalized abortion lower crime? *Journal of Human Resources, 39*, 1-28.

Kelling, George, and William H. Sousa, Jr. (2001). Do police matter? An analysis of the impact of New York City's police reforms. *Manhattan Institute Civic Report,* 22(December). Available: http://www.manhattan-institute.org/pdf/cr_22.pdf [accessed August 2008].

Kennedy, David M., Anthony A. Braga, Anne M. Piehl, and Elin J. Waring. (2001). *Reducing gun violence: The Boston Gun Project's Operation Ceasefire.* (National Institute of Justice Research Report.) Washington, DC: U.S. Department of Justice.

Kleck, Gary. (1997). *Targeting guns: Firearms and their control.* New York: Aldine.

Kleck, Gary, and Ted Chiricos. (2002). Unemployment and property crime: A target-specific assessment of opportunity and motivation as mediating factors. *Criminology, 40,* 649-680.

Klein, Malcolm W. (1995). *The American street gang: Its nature, prevalence, and control.* New York: Oxford University Press.

LaFree, Gary. (1998). *Losing legitimacy: Street crime and the decline of institutions in America.* Boulder, CO: Westview.

Lauritsen, Janet L., and Robin J. Schaum. (2005). *Crime and victimization in the three largest metropolitan areas, 1980-1998*. Washington, DC: U.S. Department of Justice.

Levitt, Steven D. (1996). The effect of prison population size on crime rates: Evidence from prison overcrowding litigation. *Quarterly Journal of Economics, 111*, 319-352.

Levitt, Steven D. (2002). Deterrence. In James Q. Wilson and Joan Petersilia (Eds.), *Crime: Public policies for crime control.* Oakland, CA: ICS Press.

Levitt, Steven D. (2004). Understanding why crime fell in the 1990s: Four factors that explain the decline and six that do not. *Journal of Economic Perspectives, 18*, 163-190.

Levitt, Steven D., and Stephen J. Dubner. (2005). *Freakonomics: A rogue economist explores the hidden side of everything*. New York: William Morrow.

Liedka, Raymond V., Anne Morrison Piehl, and Bert Useem. (2006). The crime control effect of incarceration: Does scale matter? *Criminology and Public Policy, 5*, 245-276.

Marvell, Thomas B., and Carlisle E. Moody. (1994). Prison population and crime reduction. *Journal of Quantitative Criminology, 10*, 109-139.

Merzer, Martin. (2007, April 4). Strong hurricane season is forecast. *St. Louis Post-Dispatch*, A2.

Messner, Steven F., Glenn D. Deane, Luc Anselin, and Benjamin Pearson-Nelson. (2005). Locating the vanguard in rising and falling homicide rates across U.S. cities. *Criminology, 43*, 661-696.

Messner, Steven F., Sandro Galea, Kenneth J. Tardiff, Melissa Tracy, Angela Bucciarelli, Tinka Markham Piper, Victoria Frye, and David Vlahov. (2007). Policing, drugs, and the homicide decline in the 1990s. *Criminology, 45*(2), 385-414.

Nagin, Daniel. (2005). *Group-based modeling of development.* Cambridge, MA: Harvard University Press.

Nasar, Sylvia. (1998, May 9). U.S. jobless rate plunges to 4.3%, lowest since 1970. *New York Times*, A1, B3.

Nasar, Sylvia, and Kirsten B. Mitchell. (1999, May 23). Booming job market draws young black men into fold. *New York Times*, 1, 21.

National Research Council. (2005). *Firearms and violence: A critical review.* Committee to Improve Research Information and Data on Firearms, Charles F. Wellford, John V. Pepper, and Carol V. Petrie (Eds.). Committee on Law and Justice. Division of Behavioral and Social Sciences and Education. Washington, DC: The National Academies Press.

National Research Council. (2006). *Completing the forecast: Characterizing and communicating uncertainty for better decisions using weather and climate forecasts.* Committee on Estimating and Communicating Uncertainty in Weather and Climate Forecasts. Washington, DC: The National Academies Press.

Needleman, Herbert. (1995). Environmental lead and children's intelligence. *British Medical Journal, 310*, 6991.

Nevin, Rick. (2000). How lead exposure relates to temporal changes in IQ, violent crime, and unwed pregnancy. *Environmental Research, A.83,* 1-22.

O'Brien, Robert M., Jean Stockard, and Lynne Isaacson. (1999). The enduring effects of cohort characteristics on age-specific homicide rates: 1960-1995. *American Journal of Sociology, 104*, 1061-1095.

Peterson, Dana, Terrance J. Taylor, and Finn A. Esbensen. (2004). Gang membership and violent victimization. *Justice Quarterly, 21*, 794-815.

Police Executive Research Forum. (2006). *A gathering storm: Violent crime in America.* Washington, DC: Author. Available: http://www.policeforum.org/upload/Gathering-Storm-PRINT-Final_110473745_1027200610304.pdf [accessed August 2008].

Police Executive Research Forum. (2007). *Violent crime in America: 24 months of alarming trends*. Washington, DC: Author. Available: http://www.policeforum.org/upload/Violent%20Crime%20Report%203707_140194792_392007143035.pdf [accessed August 2008].

Reyes, Jessica Walpow. (2007). *Environmental policy as social policy? The impact of childhood lead exposure on crime*. (NBER Working Paper No. 13097.) Cambridge, MA: National Bureau of Economic Research. Available: http://www3.amherst.edu/~jwreyes/papers/LeadCrimeNBERWP13097.pdf [accessed August 2008].

Rose, Dina R., and Todd R. Clear. (1998). Incarceration, social capital and crime: Examining the unintended consequences of incarceration. *Criminology, 36*, 441-479.

Rosenfeld, Richard. (2004, February). The case of the unsolved crime decline. *Scientific American*, 82-89.

Rosenfeld, Richard. (2006a). Patterns in adult homicide: 1980-1995. In Alfred Blumstein and Joel Wallman (Eds.), *The crime drop in America* (revised ed.). New York: Cambridge University Press.

Rosenfeld, Richard. (2006b). Connecting the dots: Crime rates and criminal justice evaluation research. *Journal of Experimental Criminology, 2*, 309-319.

Rosenfeld, Richard. (2007a). Explaining the divergence between UCR and NCVS aggravated assault trends. In James P. Lynch and Lynn A. Addington (Eds.), *Understanding crime statistics: Revisiting the divergence of the NCVS and the UCR*. New York: Cambridge University Press.

Rosenfeld, Richard. (2007b). Transfer the Uniform Crime Reporting Program from the FBI to the Bureau of Justice Statistics. *Criminology and Public Policy, 6*(4), 825-833.

Rosenfeld, Richard, and Robert Fornango. (2007). The impact of economic conditions on robbery and property crime: The role of consumer sentiment. *Criminology, 45*(4), 735-769.

Rosenfeld, Richard, Robert Fornango, and Eric Baumer. (2005). Did Ceasefire, Compstat, and Exile reduce homicide? *Criminology and Public Policy, 4*, 419-450.

Rosenfeld, Richard, Eric Baumer, and Steven F. Messner. (2007). Social trust, firearm prevalence, and homicide. *Annals of Epidemiology, 17*, 119-125.

Rosenfeld, Richard, Robert Fornango, and Andres Rengifo. (2007). The impact of order-maintenance policing on New York City robbery and homicide rates: 1988-2001. *Criminology, 45*, 355-383.

Sheley, Joseph F., and James D. Wright. (1995). *In the line of fire: Youths, guns, and violence in urban America*. Hawthorn, NY: Aldine.

Spelman, William. (2006). The limited importance of prison expansion. In Alfred Blumstein and Joel Wallman (Eds.), *The crime drop in America* (revised ed.). New York: Cambridge University Press.

Thornberry, Terrence P., Marvin D. Krohn, Alan J. Lizotte, Carolyn A. Smith, and Kimberly Tobin. (2003). *Gangs and delinquency in developmental perspective*. New York: Cambridge University Press.

U.S. Census Bureau. (2006). *Statistical abstract of the United States: 2007*. Washington, DC: U.S. Department of Commerce. Available: http://www.census.gov/compendia/statab/2008edition.html [accessed October 2008].

Weisburd, David, Shawn Bushway, Cynthia Lum, and Sue-Ming Yang. (2004). Trajectories of crime at places: A longitudinal study of street segments in the city of Seattle. *Criminology, 42*, 283-321.

Wilson, James Q. (2002). Crime and public policy. In James Q. Wilson and Joan Petersilia (Eds.), *Crime: Public policies for crime control* (pp. 537-557). Oakland, CA: ICS Press.

Zimring, Franklin E. (2006). *The great American crime decline*. New York: Oxford University Press.

3

Gender and Violence in the United States: Trends in Offending and Victimization

Karen Heimer and Janet L. Lauritsen

There has been increasing attention in social science to the recent U.S. decline in violent crime, which followed a period of large increases in violence (e.g., Blumstein and Wallman, 2000; Zimring, 2006). Interestingly, almost all of the analyses of crime trends over the past few decades have been silent on the issue of gender (for an exception, see Rosenfeld, 2000). While it is true that female offending accounts for a relatively small percentage of very serious violent offending, such as homicide and robbery, women accounted for roughly 25 percent of arrests for simple assaults and 21 percent of arrests for aggravated assaults in 2004, according to the FBI's Uniform Crime Reports (UCR). Moreover, by 2004 women accounted for 44 percent of simple assault, 34 percent of aggravated assault, and 33 percent of robbery victimizations, according to the National Crime Victimization Survey (NCVS) (Bureau of Justice Statistics, 2006). The experiences of women and girls therefore are important for understanding crime in the United States.

Some scholars suggest that an examination of changes in crime over time does not require attention to gender because the gender composition of the population does not change rapidly enough to affect aggregate crime rates substantially (Blumstein and Wallman, 2000, p. 10). However, this argument presumes that the "gender gap," or relative rates of female and male crime, remain constant over time. Perhaps it is reasonable to ignore gender in examinations of short-term trends, but research on long-term trends reveals important gender differences in both victimization (Lauritsen and Heimer, 2008) and offending (O'Brien, 1999). Moreover, most researchers would argue that examining long-term trends is essential for contextualizing shorter term spikes and drops in crime rates. Understanding crime trends in the United States would therefore seem to require consideration of female as well as male experiences with crime over a substantial period of time.

In addition, a full understanding of crime trends necessitates attention to victimization as well as offending. Focusing on female and male experiences with violence highlights this point. Women consistently are less likely than men to be both violent offenders and victims. Yet the gender difference in rates of victimization is smaller than in rates of offending, for the most part. For example, women are much less likely than men to kill or rob. They are also less likely than men to be killed or robbed, but the difference between female and male rates is smaller in the case of victimization.

This emphasizes the need for research addressing female as well as male trends and offending as well as victimization. Shifts in female victimization and offending may be of little unique significance if they simply mirror male shifts. Thus, a National Academies report on violence against women concluded that careful research comparing long-term trends in female and male violence is a priority (National Research Council, 2004).

This chapter seeks to broaden knowledge of offending and victimization trends in the United States by reporting and examining changes in (1) female and male violent offending, (2) female and male violent victimization, and (3) gendered patterns of victim-offender relationships in violent incidents. We produce estimates of annual rates of female and male violent offending and victimization for 1980 through 2004 by pooling the National Crime Survey (NCS) and NCVS data. We also examine gendered patterns of violence across victim-offender relationships.

There is no published study to date that examines all three of these aspects of gendered crime trends because research has relied heavily on arrest data from the UCR, which do not include information on victims. Using the pooled NCS-NCVS data, we estimate and report trends that have not been published previously and are free from potential criminal justice system bias. In addition, the NCS-NCVS data allow for important disaggregations that are not possible with UCR arrest data on nonlethal violence, such as by victim-offender relationships, and thus can be used to reveal factors that may be associated with crime trends. Our assessment of the data uncovers similarities and differences between gendered trends in victimization and offending. The detailed examination of these trends is a necessary first step toward better understanding violence in the United States.

GENDER, VIOLENCE, AND VICTIMS: PREVIOUS RESEARCH ON TRENDS

Two undisputed findings in criminology are that men are more likely than women to commit violent crime and, with the exception of rape, men are more likely to be the victims of violent crime. Although the gender gaps in violent offending and victimization are established, there is uncertainty about whether these gaps have changed in a meaningful way over time. Public perception seems to be that women are becoming more similar to men in terms of criminal violence. Over the past three decades, the popular press has warned periodically of a changing female criminal, who is more violent than her predecessors (e.g., Leach, 2004; Scelfo, 2005). The media and activist groups have highlighted the seriousness of violence against women (e.g., the National Organization for Women), and the increased attention to the problem has helped to bring this issue into public awareness. Indeed, the federal government responded by passing the Violence Against Women Act of 1994, reauthorized in 2005.

But media treatment of women, violence, and victimization—as well as some scholarly and textbook treatments—tend to blur the critical distinction between two very different questions. The first is "Has violence by and against women increased over time?" The second question is "Has the gender gap in violent offending and victimization narrowed over time?" Of course, the answers to these questions can differ. For example, female rates of violent offending and victimization could have increased (or decreased) at a time when male rates changed similarly. When this occurs, the gender gaps in violent offending and victimization would be constant, and the changes in female trends would not be unique. By contrast, female rates of violent offending and victimization could have increased more or decreased less than the corresponding male rates, which would result in a narrowing of the gender gaps, with women accounting for an increasing portion of violent offending and victimization over time. In other words, women's and men's patterns of victimization and offending would differ over time, which would highlight the importance of seeking gender-specific explanations of offending and victimization trends. The distinction between the two questions is critical and illustrates the importance of examining both shifts in female rates of violent offending and victimization as well as replacing and comparisons of female and male rates.

Yet some may ask whether decreasing gender gaps in violent offending and victimization are important in the current context of declining crime trends. In other words, would it be practically significant if female rates of offending and victimization remained stable while male rates declined, or if female rates decreased more slowly than male rates? The answer clearly seems to be "yes." In the first scenario, the finding that women's offending and victimization holds steady at prior levels when male offending or victimization declines undoubtedly would be of both scientific and policy importance. This pattern would indicate that social forces affecting men's exposure to violence seem to have little impact on women's experiences with violence. In short, women's lives do not improve as men's do in this regard.

The second scenario similarly highlights a situation that should be of both scientific and policy relevance. In it, women's exposure to violence (in the form of either offending or victimization) is reduced, but to a lesser extent than men's exposure. Interestingly, this situation is analogous to current trends in death from heart disease in Western nations. Women have lower rates of mortality from heart disease than men, and the rates for both sexes have been declining over time. Yet there has been a narrowing in the gender gap over time in the United States and other nations because female rates have not been dropping as quickly as male rates (Lawlor, Ebrahim, and Smith, 2001). This has been identified as an issue of concern; men's health is improving at a faster rate than women's health. The same logic applies to the case of female and male exposure to violence. If the gender gap in violent offending and victimization is narrowing—even during a period of declining crime—this would suggest that social environmental changes have benefited men more than women.

Research on long-term trends in the gender ratio of violent offending has produced mixed findings. Moreover, there has been a paucity of research on long-term trends in gender ratios of violent victimization. In the remainder of this section, we review existing research on trends in female-to-male offending and victimization, with an eye to limitations of previous research and unanswered empirical questions. Later in the chapter, we present data on these trends.

Gender and Trends in Violent Offending

Some studies of changes in gender ratios of offending report that women have accounted for an increasing proportion of all arrests over time (e.g., Heimer, 2000; O'Brien, 1999; Simon and Landis, 1991), but other studies report little change in gender rate ratios (e.g., Steffensmeier and Allen, 1996; Steffensmeier and Cobb, 1981). One reason for these seemingly disparate findings in the case of violent offending may be that trends in gender rate ratios of arrest vary depending on the years under investigation. Studies of the 1960s through the early 1980s tend to report little meaningful change, while studies including more recent years are more likely to find significant increases in gender rate ratios of arrests (Heimer, 2000; O'Brien, 1999). More specifically, recent research that includes the crime decline since the mid-1990s reports that the gender gap in arrests for violence (namely aggravated and simple assault) continued to narrow because female rates either remained stable or dropped more slowly than male rates (Steffensmeier et al., 2006).

Most researchers, however, have considerable concerns about relying exclusively on arrest data in studies of gender ratios of offending. It is possible that the relative violence of women and men changed little over time, and the increasing gender rate ratios (i.e., narrowing of the gender gap) instead reflect changes in policing. For example, the increasing equality of the genders may have shaped the way that police view female offending over time. In the past, police may have viewed women's violence as less serious or as less in need of criminal justice intervention. As time passed, however, police may have become more likely to view women's violence as problematic, and thus more likely to arrest female offenders. Or the criteria used in decisions about arrests for aggravated assault may have shifted over time, with police becoming more likely to "charge up" offenses that previously would have resulted in arrests for simple assault; this would disproportionately inflate the figures for aggravated assault over time (see Blumstein, 2000; Rosenfeld, 2006). Furthermore, cases that in the past would not have entered the official system—particularly domestic violence cases—increasingly have resulted in arrests for aggravated assault (Blumstein, 2000, p. 17). Similar arguments can be made with regard to simple assaults. If shifts in police discretion in arrests for violence operate similarly for both female and male offenders, then the changes in gender gap or gender rate ratios of arrests for violence would not be biased. However, if police use their discretion in substantially different ways in arresting women and men, then the observed narrowing of the gender gap in arrests may be an artifact of changing police practices (Steffensmeier et al., 2005, 2006).

An assessment of whether recent reports of increases in the gender rate ratios of violent offending represent real change in women's and men's violent behavior can be answered by examining victims' reports of the gender of offenders in the NCVS. The NCVS is unaffected by criminal justice system policies and potential bias in arrest decisions, yet it has been used in only two studies of trends in gender ratios of offending (Steffensmeier et al., 2005, 2006). Part of the difficulty in assessing the comparability of arrest and victimization data on female and male offending over time has been that the NCS was redesigned in 1992, when it became the NCVS. The data can be used to create a single time series, but doing so requires specific computational procedures, which we describe in our data section (see Lynch, 2002).

Gender and Trends in Violent Victimization

At the time of this writing, there was almost no published research on long-term trends in nonlethal violent victimization against women. One exception is an early study by Smith (1987), which used the NCS over a 10-year period (1973-1982) and reported some increases in the proportion of all robberies that had female victims, but no appreciable change in the proportion of assaults with female victims. However, there are good studies of long-term trends in the homicide victimization of women (e.g., Batton, 2004; Browne and Williams, 1993; Dugan, Nagin, and Rosenfeld, 1999, 2003; LaFree and Hunnicutt, 2006; Rosenfeld, 2000; Smith and Brewer, 1995). Most studies use the UCR's Supplemental Homicide Reports and show that while homicide offenders and victims are disproportionately male, the magnitude of the gender gap is smaller for victimization than offending. Moreover, homicide victimization rates declined during the 1990s for both genders, with very little change in the gender gap. Indeed, a recent cross-national study of homicide victimization trends by LaFree and Hunnicutt (2006) shows little evidence that the gender gap changed significantly in the United States over the period 1950-2001, despite the broader changes in women's lives.

However, recent evidence suggests that there have been changes in the gender gap in victims of homicides involving intimate partners (e.g., Browne and Williams, 1993; Dugan, Nagin, and Rosenfeld, 1999, 2003; Rosenfeld, 1997). Although intimate partner homicide rates declined for both women and men, the declines were greater among men. Given that female rates of intimate partner homicide were consistently higher than male rates over the past 30 years, the greater decline among men resulted in a widening of the gender gap in intimate partner homicide (Lauritsen and Heimer, 2008). Of course, it is difficult to rule out competing explanations of these changes with national-level data; researchers have thus turned to city-level analyses to try to determine how various factors might explain gender-specific changes in intimate partner homicide (Dugan, Nagin, and Rosenfeld, 1999, 2003). These studies suggest that the declines in female and male rates were significantly related to falling marriage rates. In addition, the greater decrease in male rates relative to female rates may reflect the improved economic status of women, as well as the expansion of domestic violence intervention programs.[1] Yet it is unclear whether patterns in gender rate ratio of homicide can be generalized to other forms of violent victimization (see Lauritsen and Heimer, 2008).

In short, little is known about long-term changes in violence against women other than homicide. This gap in knowledge is attributed to poor integration between studies of violence against women and research on crime and violence more generally, as well as the difficulty of finding measures of violent victimization that are reasonably valid and reliable over

[1]However, this research examines female and male homicide as outcomes and does not analyze patterns in the gender rate ratio.

time (National Research Council, 2004). Researchers concur that police data are problematic for this purpose because much violence—especially violence against women—is poorly measured by police data (National Research Council, 2004). Rape and sexual assaults, nonstranger incidents, and intimate partner incidents against women are often the least likely crimes to be reported to the police (Catalano, 2006). Yet even if reporting rates were higher, police-based UCR data would be of limited use because, for victimizations other than homicide, the UCR data lack information about the sex of the victim.

The NCVS, by contrast, is designed to produce data that allow for the assessment of long-term trends in violent victimization, for crimes other than homicide. As mentioned above, the NCVS data can be pooled with the earlier NCS data to estimate a continuous series of violence rates by using specific weighting procedures. Indeed, these are the only available source of continuous information about violent victimization and details about violent crime incidents.

Generating Gender-Specific Estimates Using the NCS and the NCVS

The NCS and the NCVS are rich sources of information on gender-specific rates of both violent offending and victimization (U.S. Department of Justice, ICPSR Study Numbers 8608, 8864, 4276).[2] We use these data to create national-level estimates of gender-specific rates of aggravated assault, simple assault, and robbery offending using victims' reports of the gender of offenders. Similarly, we derive estimates of gender-specific aggravated assault, simple assault, and robbery victimization rates. We do not compare rates of rape in our analysis because preliminary analyses showed that almost all perpetrators of rape are male and almost all victims are female, and that there were no detectable changes in the gender gap in the rape offenders or victims over time.[3]

The NCS/NCVS has been used to gather self-report survey data about people's experiences with violence and other forms of victimization continuously since 1973. Using a nationally representative sampling frame, interviews are conducted with persons age 12 and older in each sampled household to determine whether respondents have been the victim of an attempted or completed violent crime.[4] Persons who report an incident of

[2]The NCVS by design does not include information on homicide.

[3]For example, about 96-97 percent of all rapes and sexual assaults since 1992 involve male offender(s) only.

[4]The annual sample size has varied over the years, ranging from approximately 248,000 interviews in 1980 to 148,000 interviews in 2004. Persons and households are selected for participation on the basis of Census Bureau information (rather than random-digit-dialing procedures, which may produce biased samples). Person-level response rates are very high, ranging

violence over the six-month recall period are then asked a series of questions about the incident, including the sex of the offender(s).[5]

In 1992, the NCS survey began using a redesigned questionnaire and henceforth became known as the NCVS.[6] The redesigned survey instrument was phased into the data collection process in a way that makes it possible to assess the effects of the new format on victimization or offending estimates (Kindermann, Lynch, and Cantor, 1997; Lynch and Cantor, 1996; Rand, Lynch, and Cantor, 1997). Prior analyses of data from the phase-in period showed that the new questionnaire significantly increased the reporting of victimization and the magnitude of the change varied according to crime type. Rape reporting increased most, followed by aggravated assault and simple assault. Robbery victimization rates were not significantly higher in the NCVS compared with the NCS.

Generating Gender-Specific Rates of Violent Offending

In order to use the NCS and NCVS data together, it is necessary to take into account this break in the series and weight the earlier NCS data in ways that are informed by research on the effects of methodological and content changes to the survey. Lynch (2002) details the appropriate procedures for estimating long-term offending trends using the NCS and the NCVS. We follow these procedures to generate gender-specific estimates of assault and robbery offending from 1980 through 2004.[7] Some recent

---

from 97 percent in 1980 to 86 percent in 2004. Census-created sampling weights are used to take into account possible differences in response rates according to the age, race, sex, and residential location of the respondent. Interviews are conducted in English and in Spanish.

[5]Following a series of cues and questions about the possible occurrence of a victimization event, detailed questions are asked about what happened during the incident. The answers to these questions are used to place the incident into crime type categories. Subsequent questions about the incident arise in the following order: the number of times it occurred, when and where the incident took place, the nature of the incident (threatened, attacked, completed), whether the offender had a weapon, the extent of injuries and subsequent medical care, victim protective actions during the incident, whether bystanders were present, whether the victim knows anything about the offender, the number of offenders, the sex and age of the offender, whether the offender was a member of a street gang, under the influence of alcohol or drugs, the victim's relationship to the offender, and the race of the offender.

[6]Key reasons for the changes in the survey were the difficulties of obtaining estimates of events that were not commonly thought of as "crimes" and discoveries about the extent of family, intimate partner, and sexual violence from other surveys about violence against women (Kindermann, Lynch, and Cantor, 1997). For the purposes of estimating violent victimization, the 1992 redesign was the only major methodological break in the NCS-NCVS series.

[7]We begin our analyses with data from 1980 because the victim-offender relationship measures in the NCS changed in the late 1970s. By starting with 1980, the same time series can be compared across consistently defined victim-offender categories. These years also correspond to the years addressed in two recent publications on gender and violent offending (Steffensmeier

research presents gender-specific estimates of adolescent and overall offending that depart from ours (Steffensmeier et al., 2005, 2006).[8] We therefore describe our estimation procedure in detail.

When an incident of attempted or completed violence is reported to an interviewer, respondents are asked a series of follow-up questions about the incident, including the number of offenders and the sex of those offenders. Estimates of the number of incidents involving female offenders depend on how one treats incidents involving single and multiple offenders.[9] Because of this, we created two sets of measures to study female offense involvement. Our estimate of female involvement in violence includes single-offender incidents in which the offender was reported by the victim to be female and multiple-offender incidents in which any of the offenders were reported to be female. We also replicate our analyses using a more conservative measure of female violent offending that includes only single-offender incidents to assess whether changes in female involvement might be only as secondary offenders.[10] For the 1992-2004 NCVS period, our annual gender-specific violent offending rates are defined as follows:

---

et al., 2005, 2006). Although the definitions of stranger and nonstranger offenders did not change during this period, the additional categories of boyfriend/ex-boyfriend and girlfriend/ex-girlfriend made it possible to distinguish such incidents from those involving other friends and acquaintances to better define incidents involving intimate partners.

[8]The estimation procedure used to produce gender-specific rates of offending by Steffensmeier et al. (2005) is described in a footnote 5, in which the authors state: "We use three years of data surrounding the transition to calibrate upwards pre-redesign surveys to account for the expanded range of behaviors measured by the revised survey. See Figure 2 for the formula" (p. 369). The formula in Figure 2 reads: "Multiplier = $(n_{92} + n_{93} + n_{94})/(n_{90} + n_{91} + n_{92})$" (p. 380). The same multiplier is noted in the later study (Steffensmeier et al., 2006, p. 87).

[9]We found a slight increase over time in the percentage of incidents involving a single offender. Over the 1980-2004 period, approximately 54 percent of robberies, 72 percent of aggravated assaults, and 80 percent of simple assaults involved a single offender. Incidents in which the victim did not report the sex of the offender(s) were rare and are excluded from our estimates. About 1 percent of single-offender incidents are missing such information, as are about 2 percent of multiple-offender incidents.

[10]Researchers must also decide how to treat series victimizations in their rate estimations. Victimizations of a similar nature that occur more than six times during a recall period and for which the victim cannot recall sufficient detail are referred to as series victimizations. (During the NCS period, series victimizations were defined by three rather than six incidents.) To reduce respondent burden, series victims are asked to report the details (including sex of the offender) for the most recent event of the series. Victims' estimates of the number of times the event occurred tend to be rounded approximations that can have substantial influences on overall rates (see Planty, 2006; Rand and Rennison, 2005) as well as gender-specific offending rates. Because of this, we decided to count series victimizations as one incident. While male and female offending rates would certainly be higher if series victimizations were counted as three (NCS) or six (NCVS) or more incidents, we found that counting these crimes as one incident will not bias our conclusions about the gender gap in offending. Preliminary analyses showed that the proportion of robbery, aggravated assault, and simple assault incidents

$$\text{Male offending rate} = \frac{\text{Number of violent incidents with male offender(s) only} * 1{,}000}{\text{Number of men ages 12 and above in the population}}$$

$$\text{Female offending rate} = \frac{\text{Number of violent incidents with any female offender(s)} * 1{,}000}{\text{Number of women ages 12 and above in the population}}$$

To estimate comparable offending rates for the 1980-1991 NCS period, we examined the data from the redesign overlap period and weighted the NCS data accordingly. Because the NCS and NCVS instruments were administered concurrently, estimates from the two surveys can be compared according to a variety of crime or victim characteristics. If the NCS/NCVS-ratio of the rate estimates from the overlap period are found to be statistically significant, that ratio is then applied to the NCS estimates to make them comparable to NCVS estimates.[11] We found that the gender-specific offending estimates did not differ significantly within crime type; therefore, we use the same crime-specific ratios developed in earlier analyses of the design change and used by the Bureau of Justice Statistics (Kindermann, Lynch, and Cantor, 1997). Thus, for the 1980-1991 period, the crime-specific offending rates were multiplied by w_c, where $w_c = 1.00$ for robbery, $w_c = 1.23$ for aggravated assault, and $w_c = 1.75$ for simple assault.

Of course the NCS and NCVS estimates of offending are not without limitations and two caveats should be noted. First, the sample excludes persons who are unattached to households, and thus the data exclude incidents that are experienced by homeless and institutionalized persons. We do not know whether men and women offend against these persons in proportions that are different from their offending against others. Second, the use of weights to adjust NCS data to make them comparable to NCVS data assumes that the effect of the methodological change is constant across the NCS years. Although it cannot be determined whether this assumption is true, Rand, Lynch, and Cantor (1997) and others (Lynch, 2002) argue that

reported to be series was low and declined slightly from 1980 to 2004, and that the proportion of series incidents with female offenders remained fairly stable over time.

[11]Although prior research suggests that additional adjustments beyond crime type may not be necessary (e.g., Lynch and Cantor, 1996), we assessed whether this was true for gender- and crime-specific rates of offending. We compared the gender-specific offending estimates of robbery, aggravated assault, and simple assault for the NCS/NCVS overlap period and found small but statistically insignificant differences in the ratio according to the gender of the offender. Thus the weights for our gender-specific offending estimates for the NCS period are the same for female and male rates, consisting of the crime-specific ratios developed in earlier analyses of the design change (e.g., Kindermann, Lynch, and Cantor, 1997). Lynch (2002) similarly found that the NCS adjustment rates for crimes involving juvenile offenders did not vary by gender but did vary according to crime type and the presence of adult co-offenders.

it is probably the case that any potential weighting error is correlated with time and that estimates for distant years may be more problematic than those for years closer to the redesign. While the first caveat warns that the rates will be underestimates, the second urges caution if conclusions about the gender gap are driven by data from the earliest years of the series.

Generating Gender-Specific Rates of Violent Victimization

We use similar procedures to create gender-specific estimates of aggravated assault, simple assault, and robbery victimization for the period 1980 to 2004.[12] We also assessed how the NCS data should be weighted for the purpose of comparing crime- and gender-specific victimization rates. As with the offending data, small gender differences were associated with the new design for some types of victimization; however, these differences were not statistically significant.[13] Therefore, the final weights for the victimization estimates in the NCS period consist of the crime-specific ratios used in our earlier analyses of the gender gap in offending.

An important second strength is that NCVS estimates of violence against women have been shown to be externally valid when compared with estimates from the 1995 National Violence Against Women Survey (NVAWS). Rand and Rennison found that the rape rate was higher in the NVAWS than in the NCVS, but that the difference was not statistically significant due to the large standard error for the NVAWS estimate. The difference in women's assault rates was also higher in the NCVS, and this difference was statistically significant (Rand and Rennison, 2005, pp. 278-280). Thus, despite important differences in sampling method and the use of alternative questions, cues, and prompts, estimates from the NVAWS suggest that the NCVS data provide valid and reliable information about violence against women.

Also, it is important to remember the key limitations of the survey data regarding the sampling frame, the potential correlation between weighting error and time, and the fact that series victimizations are treated as a single incident. For reasons discussed earlier, we think that these limitations will lead to underestimated rates but are unlikely to bias our estimate of the trend in the gender rate ratio of violent victimization. Of course, all crime rates include measurement error, and sampling error is a component of the NCVS estimates. Changes in sampling error will not bias our trend esti-

---

[12]The issue of how to treat single-offender versus multiple-offender incidents is not applicable in these analyses because the victim is a single individual.

[13]When gender- and crime-specific weights are used, the adjustments make the gender gap appear slightly larger during the NCS time period. The use of such weights would suggest greater decreases in the gender gap over time.

mates, but readers should consider such errors before drawing conclusions about the difference between specific rates.[14]

Data on Victim-Offender Relationships by Gender

The last set of results presented in this chapter goes beyond the examination of offenders and victims by gender to further disaggregate by the relationship between the victim and the offender. This allows further elaboration of how the nature of violent incidents has changed over time. To this end, we use NCVS data to estimate rates of stranger, nonstranger, and intimate partner violence committed *by* and *against* women and men. For these analyses, rape, robbery, aggravated assault and simple assault incidents are combined to create a measure of violence that allows us to produce reliable estimates of the above rates.[15] Rape and sexual assault are an important part of violence against women, so it is important to include rape in a composite measure of violent victimization.

TRENDS IN THE GENDER RATE RATIOS OF VIOLENT OFFENDING AND VICTIMIZATION

Offending

Figures 3-1 through 3-3 show the female and male trends in aggravated assault, simple assault, and robbery, as well as the trends in the gender rate ratios for each offense. Following the literature on trends in the gender gap in offending, we compute the gender rate ratio as the female population-adjusted rate over the male population-adjusted rate of offending for each violent crime type (e.g., Heimer, 2000; O'Brien, 1999). This measure intui-

[14]We do not present tests of statistical significance between specific rates because these would be quite numerous and thus would overwhelm the presentation of results. Rather, our focus is on the description of general patterns in the rates.

[15]As with our analyses of offending and victimization, the data from the NCS years were weighted according to crime type. NCS estimates of rape were weighted by a factor of 2.57 (Kindermann, Lynch, and Cantor, 1997). Incidents in which the victim was unable to provide information on the victim-offender relationship were necessarily excluded. Victimization estimates are based on all (multiple and single offender) incidents, and in multiple-offender incidents the relationship was coded stranger if all of the offenders are reported to be strangers. Multiple-offender incidents involving intimate partners were rare and were coded as intimate partner incidents. Offending rate estimates presented in this section are limited to incidents involving single offenders. This is because in multiple-offender incidents it is impossible to match mixed-gender groups of offenders with each person's relationship to the victim.

TABLE 3-1 Percentage Change in Female and Male NCVS Offending Rates

	1984-1994		1994-2004	
	Female	Male	Female	Male
Aggravated assault	+1	+11	–42	–67
Simple assault	+51	+8	–50	–57
Robbery	+66	+2	–78	–65

tively captures the relationship between female and male offending rates.[16] The general patterns reveal some similarities as well as differences across offense type.

Because male rates of both offending and victimization are higher than female rates, the variability in female trend lines cannot be fully appreciated from examining these figures alone. Indeed, there is substantial change in the female rates that is masked in figures that depict female and male offending and victimization trends together. To illuminate these patterns more fully, we present the percentage changes in the female and male rates during the decades 1984-1994 and 1994-2004 in Table 3-1. This allows us to compare periods of equal length over time and across gender. We chose these specific periods because, at the time of this research, 2004 was the most recent year of available data and 1994 is near the peak of the crime rates in our study. We recognize that any choice of years to estimate percentage change is somewhat arbitrary; we use this strategy only to reveal changes in the trends that are difficult to see through visual inspection of the figures (e.g., changes in female offending rates). To ensure that this procedure did not produce misleading findings, we examined alternative 10-year periods, varying the end points of the decades. This did not change our general conclusions about the patterning of female rates, male rates, or gender rate ratios.

Figure 3-1 and Table 3-1 show that, from 1984 to 1994, the rate of male aggravated assault offending reported in the NCVS increased by about 11 percent and then plummeted by about 67 percent between 1994 and 2004. The NCVS offending data show little consistent trend and an overall trivial change in aggravated assaults by women between 1984 and 1994;

[16] We used the gender rate ratio of offending rather than the female percentage of all offending. The "female percentage" must also be population adjusted and thus must be described not as the "female percentage of total offenses" but rather as "the population-adjusted percentage of offending incidents accounted for by women" because female and male populations (the rate denominators) are not equal for all years.

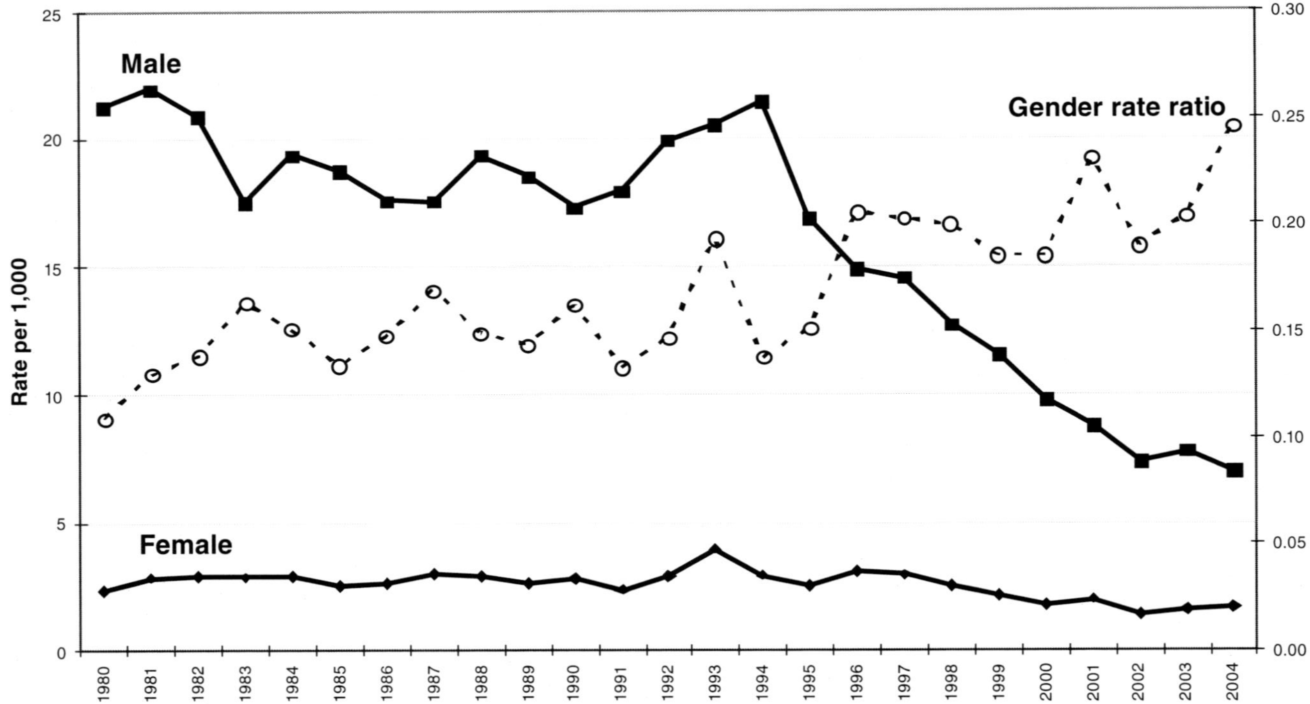

FIGURE 3-1 NCVS aggravated assault offending by gender, 1980-2004.

after 1994, the NCVS female offending rate dropped by 42 percent. (Note that because the female rate is so much lower than the male rate, fluctuations in the female rate are difficult to see in Figure 3-1.) Although the rate of aggravated assault offending dropped for both genders, the decline was more pronounced for men. The result is that the female-to-male rate ratio of aggravated assault offending increases from about .11 in 1980, to .15 in 1992, to .25 by 2004.[17] Female rates had reached 25 percent of male rates by 2004. It therefore appears that the NCVS data on offenders—which should be unaffected by potential bias in justice system processing—produces an upward trend in the gender rate ratio and therefore some decrease in the gender gap. Interestingly, this pattern parallels changes in the gender rate ratios of aggravated assault reported by analyses of UCR arrest data (e.g., Heimer, 2000; Steffensmeier et al., 2006).

Figure 3-2 and Table 3-1 show that, unlike in the case of aggravated assault, female rates of simple assault increased by a much larger percentage than did male rates between 1984 and 1994, by 51 percent among women and 8 percent among men. After 1994, the simple assault offending rates decreased for both genders. The male rates dropped by a greater percentage than the corresponding female rates, although the difference is not substantial (57 and 50 percent, respectively). These combinations of trends in female and male simple assault offending produce gender rate ratios that increases over time, from .19 in 1984, to .27 in 1994, and to .32 in 2004, with the largest increases occurring before the mid-1990s. The overall increase is sizable—whereas female rates were about 19 percent of male rates in 1984, they had grown to 32 percent of male rates by 2004.

The third offense that we examine, robbery, is well known to be the most male of crimes, with female robbery involvement being extremely low (Miller, 1998). Research on changes in the gender rate ratios of robbery arrests using UCR data has shown significant increases between 1960 and the middle 1990s (Heimer, 2000; O'Brien, 1999). Figure 3-3 and Table 3-1 indicate that there has been a similar upward shift in gender rate ratios of robbery offenders based on the NCS-NCVS data as well. Male robbery offending rates changed little between 1984 and 1994 (2 percent). As with simple assault, female robbery offending rates increased by a much greater percentage—about 66 percent—during this same time period. However, the female robbery offending rate dropped more (78 percent) than the male rate (65 percent) between 1994 and 2004, during the time of the great

[17]Our figures and tables present the victims' reports of the sex of offender in all victimization incidents, including those perpetrated by a single offender and multiple offenders. Replicating our analyses with the data from incidents with only a single offender, we found that the gender rate ratios did not change much and showed quite similar trends. We present the former measure because a substantial portion of violent incidents involves multiple offenders.

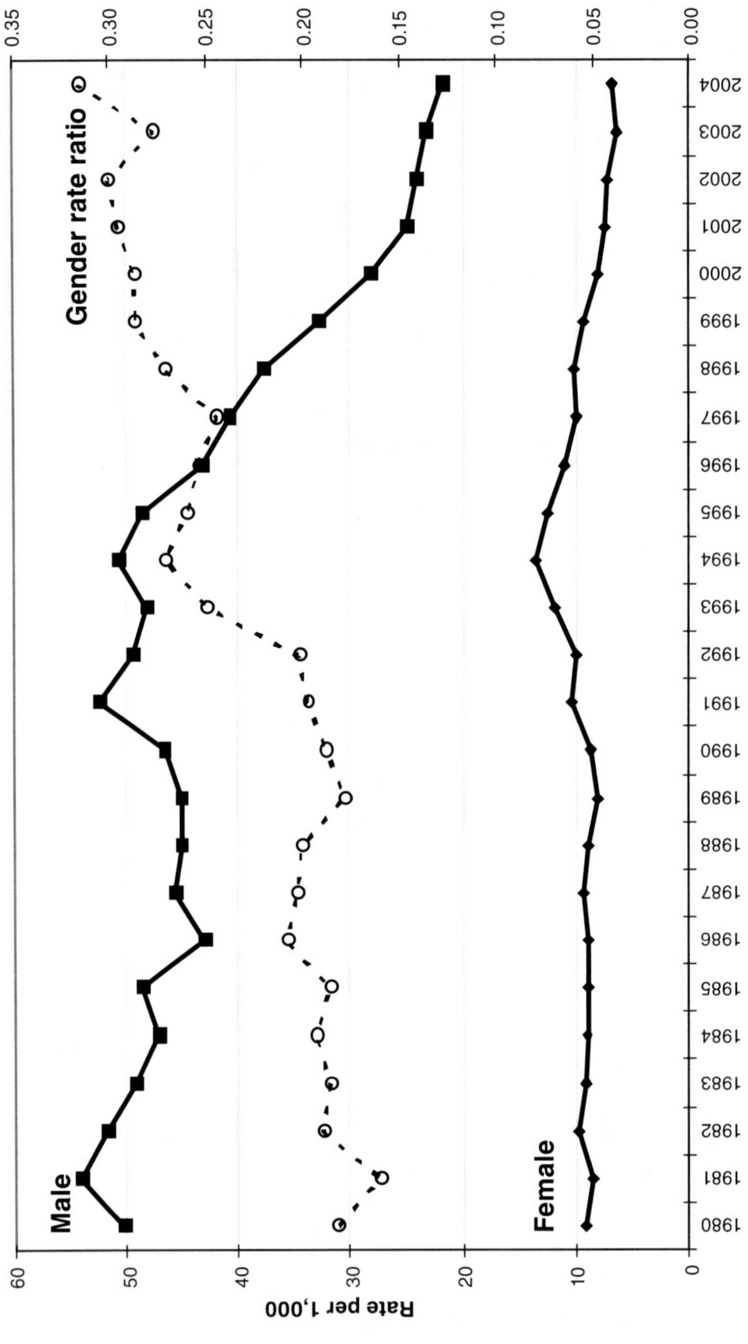

FIGURE 3-2 NCVS simple assault offending by gender, 1980-2004.

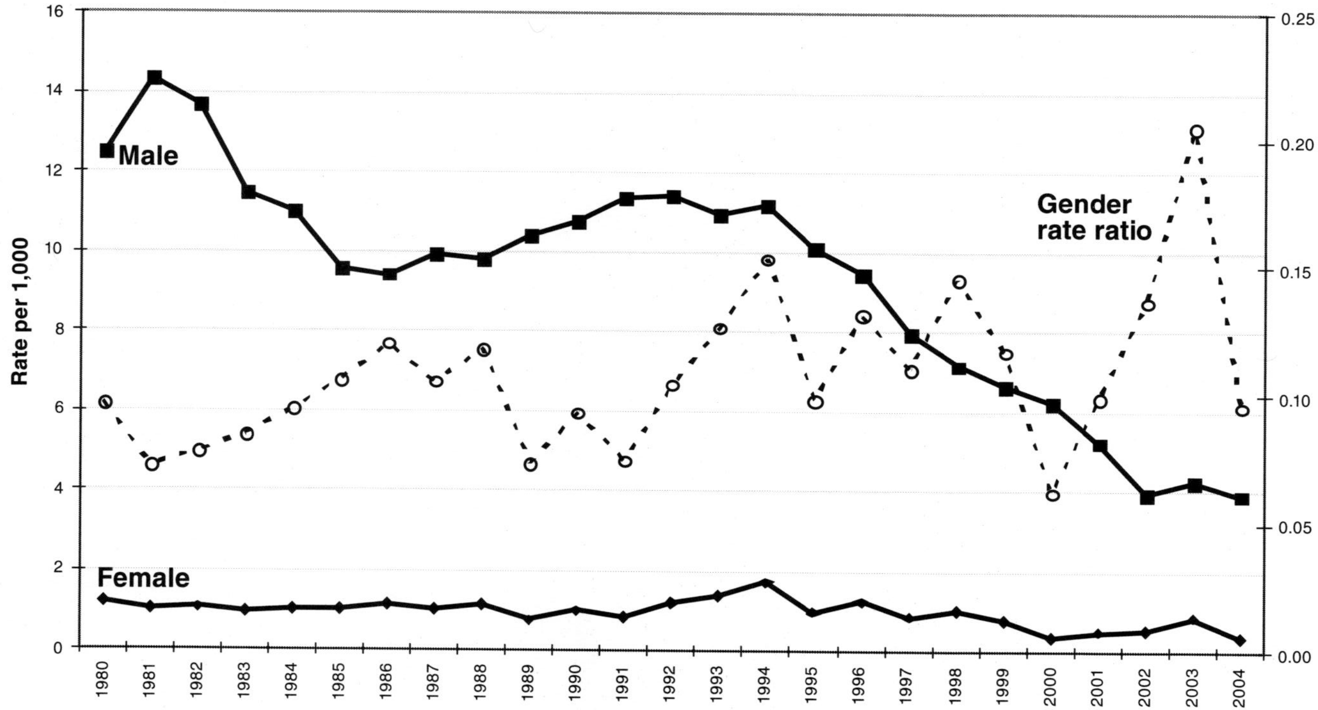

FIGURE 3-3 NCVS robbery offending by gender, 1980-2004.

crime decline. Yet Figure 3-3 shows a slightly increasing trend in gender rate ratios for robbery, growing from an average of .08 for the years 1980 to 1982 to an average of .15 for the years 2002 to 2004.

Overall, our data indicate that the gender gap in offending has narrowed over time, although violent offending has clearly declined among both genders since the mid-1990s. This parallels some previous findings, based on UCR arrest data. However, the NCVS data used here are unaffected by procedural shifts and gender bias in the criminal justice system. Comparing across the three offenses addressed here, one can see that in the case of simple assault and robbery, the narrowing of the gender gap stems in part from the greater increases in women's involvement in these offenses during the 1980s and early 1990s. In the case of aggravated assault, by contrast, the narrowing of the gap seems to stem from the more pronounced decline in male than female offending.

Victimization

This section focuses on change in the gender rate ratios in violent victimization from 1980 through 2004. As with offending, gender rate ratios are computed as female rates divided by male rates of victimization for each violent crime type. Figures 3-4 through 3-6 show gender-specific victimization rates for aggravated assault, simple assault, and robbery, as well as the gender rate ratios of these victimization rates. Table 3-2 presents the figures on the percentage change over time in female and male rates.

Figure 3-4 shows that there has been some narrowing of the gender gap in aggravated assault victimizations over time. Male rates declined some in the early 1980s and then increased slightly in the early 1990s. As Table 3-2 reports, male rates of aggravated assault victimization showed a net decline of about 4 percent between 1984 and 1994, but this was followed by a dramatic decline of about 62 percent between 1994 and 2004. By comparison, female rates did not decline in the 1980s, but rather were fairly stable until the early years of the 1990s when they increased. Thus, as

TABLE 3-2 Percentage Change in Female and Male NCVS Victimization Rates

	1984-1994		1994-2004	
	Female	Male	Female	Male
Aggravated assault	+22	–4	–65	–62
Simple assault	+23	+7	–54	–55
Robbery	+3	+4	–68	–64

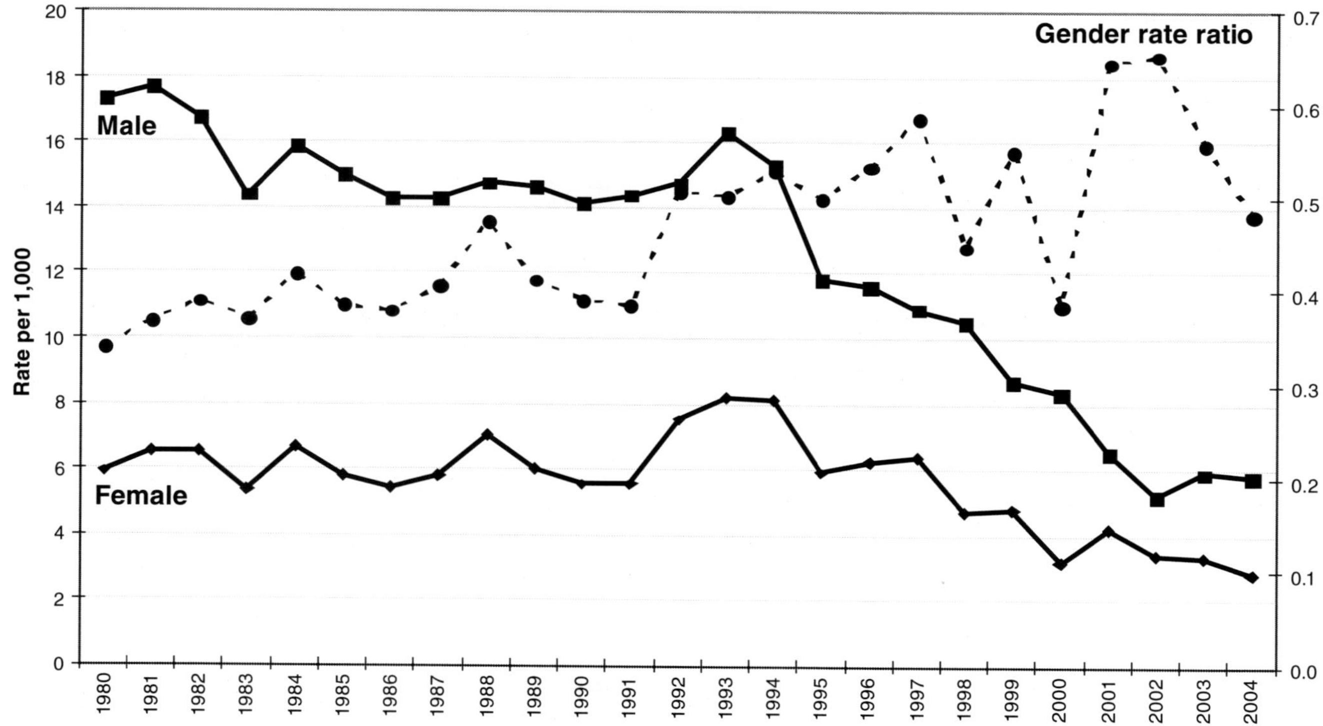

FIGURE 3-4 NCVS aggravated assault victimization by gender, 1980-2004.

Table 3-2 shows, female rates of aggravated assault victimization increased by about 22 percent between 1984 and 1994, whereas male rates showed only a small decrease. The decline in aggravated assault victimization following the middle 1990s, however, was fairly comparable among women and men. Overall, gender rate ratios increased showing that female rates of victimization escalated from about 34 percent of male rates at the beginning of the series to about 55 to 65 percent of the male rates by the early 2000s. As the patterns discussed above indicate, much of this change is traceable to the period before the great crime decline of the 1990s and early 2000s.

Figure 3-5 shows that compared with aggravated assault, rates of simple assault victimization are much higher for both women and men. The figure also shows that gender rate ratios of simple assault are much higher than the gender rate ratio of aggravated assault victimization. In terms of trends over time, there are some similarities to the patterns of aggravated assault victimizations. Specifically, like aggravated assault, male rates of simple assault declined somewhat during the 1980s, whereas female rates did not. Also like aggravated assault victimization, both men and women experienced increased simple assault victimization in the first few years of the 1990s, followed by subsequent declines. Between 1984 and 1994, male rates of simple assault victimization showed a net increase of about 7 percent (because of increases in the early 1990s following a period of decline in the 1980s), followed by a decline of about 55 percent between 1994 and 2004. Female rates of simple assault showed a net increase of approximately 23 percent between 1984 and 1994 (due to stability in the 1980s followed by the early 1990s increase) and, like male rates, declined by about 54 percent between 1994 and 2004 (see Table 3-2). Together, these patterns produce increasing gender rate ratios of simple assault victimization, from about .59 in the early years of the series to about .75 in 2004 (female rate was 75 percent of the male rate), with even higher ratios in years 2000 and 2001.

As in the case of aggravated assault, the increase in gender rate ratios for simple assault victimization appears to be the result of the stability (rather than decline) of simple assaults against women in the 1980s, coupled with larger percentage increases in female victimization rates in the early 1990s. The declines after the mid-1990s are similar in percentage across gender. This is an important finding, because it indicates that for both aggravated and simple assault victimizations, women's experiences have become increasingly like men's experiences mainly because of changes that occurred before the recent crime decline. Later we show that intimate partner victimization is an exception to this pattern.

The patterns of robbery victimization, perhaps not surprisingly, look quite different than assault victimizations. Figure 3-6 shows that the risk for robbery decreased substantially for both women and men between 1980

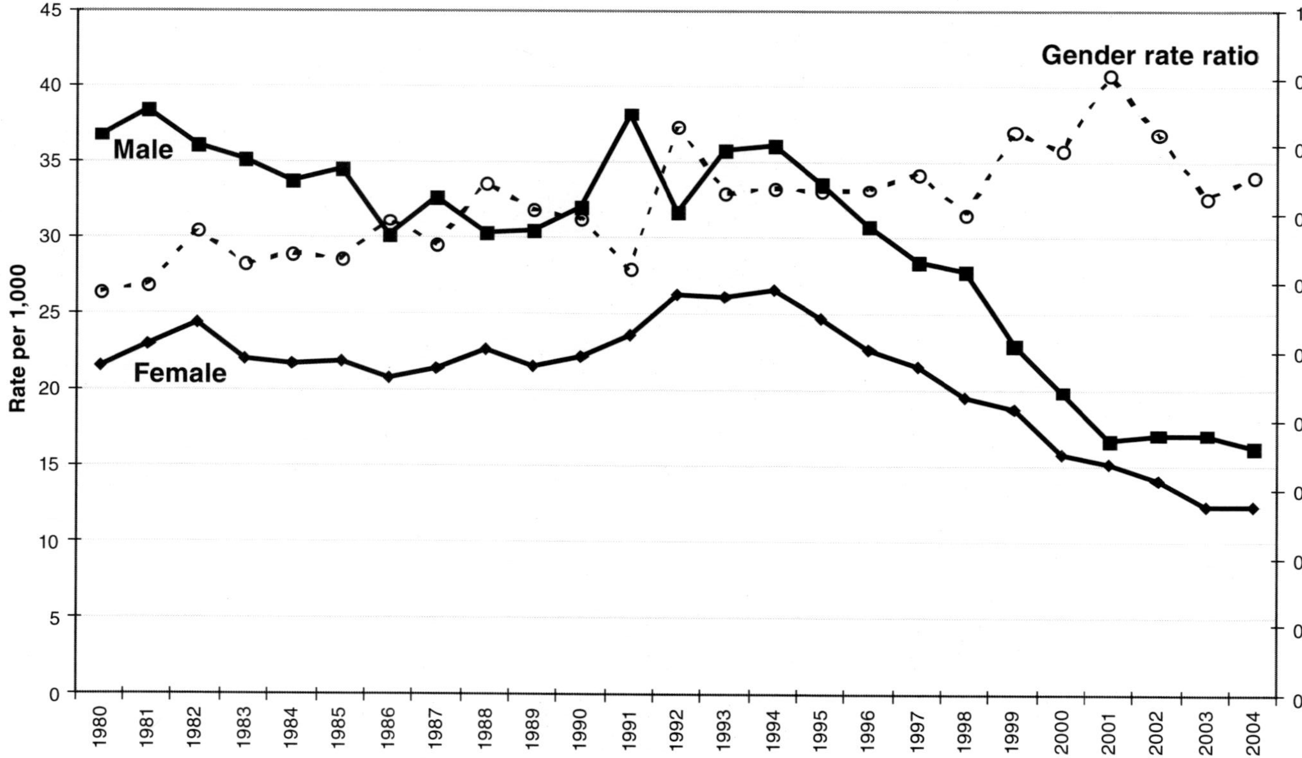

FIGURE 3-5 NCVS simple assault victimization by gender, 1980-2004.

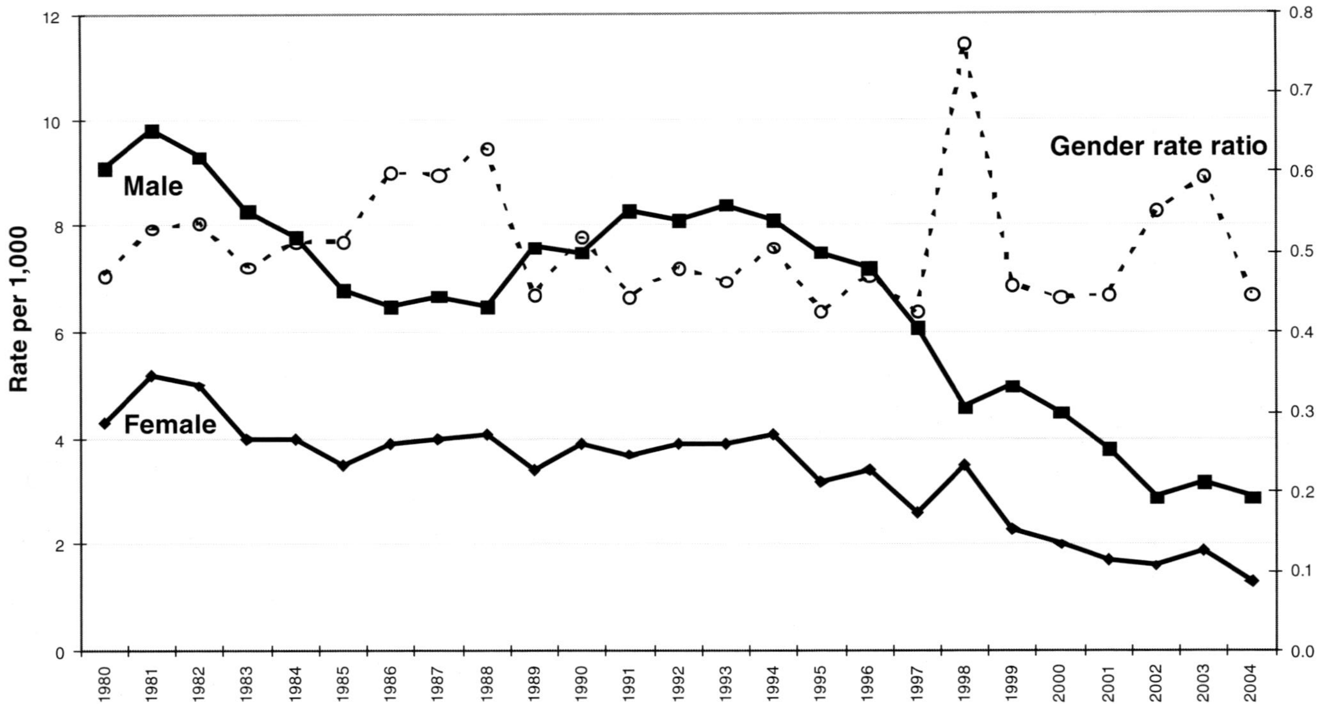

FIGURE 3-6 NCVS robbery victimization by gender, 1980-2004.

and 2004. Slight differences in the two trends can be found—for example, male rates increased somewhat in the early 1990s, whereas female rates did not. Beyond this, the trends are quite similar. Between 1984 and 1994, male rates of robbery victimization increased by about 4 percent, followed by a decline of about 64 percent between 1994 and 2004. Similarly, female rates of robbery increased approximately 3 percent between 1984 and 1994 and declined by about 68 percent between 1994 and 2004. Thus, the proportional changes over time are fairly similar for women and men. In the beginning of the series, the gender rate ratio was about .47; in 2004, it was about .45. Lauritsen and Heimer (2008) recently compared these patterns to those of homicide victimization and found little change in the gender rate ratios of either homicide or robbery. Gender differences in robbery victimization trends are similar to those of lethal violence but different from those of aggravated and simple assaults. This may reflect a gender difference linked to the use of guns, which is most common in robberies and homicides.

The female and male violent victimization findings lead us to conclude that the gender gap in assault victimization (but not robbery) has narrowed over the past several decades, with female victimizations constituting an increasing proportion of assaults.[18] The risks of victimization for simple assault became more similar for men and women in the late 1990s and into the early 2000s (see Figure 3-5). The risk for aggravated assault victimization also was more similar for women and men during this time (see Figure 3-4). This suggests that researchers must be careful not to assume that the factors that influence the aggregate trends necessarily apply equally to female and male violent victimization. Indeed, the factors influencing assault victimizations may have differed across gender or, if similar factors were at work, their impact may have varied across gender.

Comparing gender-specific trends in victimization with the trends in offending highlights several points. First, it appears that women have become more likely to encounter violent interactions over time, both as perpetrators and as victims. This is perhaps expected due to the fact that victimization and offending are correlated at the individual level and also share many of the same predictors when studied at the individual, situational, or community level (Sampson and Lauritsen, 1994). A second parallel across the victimization and offending trends is that the crime drop

[18]In earlier analyses, we found that these results are not due to the fact that intimate partner incidents are included in these trends. Those analyses showed that the trends in intimate partner violence against women closely match those for stranger violence against women and the crime-specific patterns shown here. We observed no declines in intimate partner violence against women until approximately 1993-1994. This issue is discussed later in the chapter.

of the late 1990s and 2000s appeared to affect women and men in fairly comparable ways.

While the most recent crime decline seemed to have a more or less similar impact across gender, a comparison of the percentage changes in Table 3-1 (offending) and Table 3-2 (victimization) suggests that, when narrowing of the gender gap occurs, it tends to be due to gender differences in the trends in the 1984 to 1994 period. More specifically, the data show either a greater proportionate increase in female than male rates (e.g., simple assault offending and victimization, robbery offending), or an increase in female rates while male rates show a net decrease decline (aggravated assault offending). These observations raise questions about how and why female and male violent offending and victimization may have been differently influenced in the 1980s and early 1990s. In the next section, the data are disaggregated by victim-offender relationships, as well as gender, to help shed light on what may have occurred.

Victim-Offender Relationships and Gendered Patterns of Offending and Victimization

It is possible that there may have been disproportionate changes over time in stranger, nonstranger, and intimate partner offending and victimization that would account for the shifts in the gender rate ratios in victimization and offending that we note above. Homicide research reports that men and women experience these types of violence in different proportions. For example, homicide offending and victimization rates vary by gender and by victim-offender relationship, and the gender gap is contingent on the victim-offender relationship in the homicide incident (Rosenfeld, 2000). We therefore disaggregate trends in female and male violent victimization as well as female and male violent offending by victim-offender relationship using the NCVS data, as described previously. Here we combine rape, robbery, aggravated assault, and simple assault incidents to create a measure of violence that allows us to produce reliable estimates of the above rates. Nonstranger violence includes incidents committed by intimate partners.

Figures 3-7a and 3-7b show the rates of female and male victimization disaggregated by victim-offender relationship for the period 1980 through 2004, and Figures 3-8a and 3-8b display the comparable trends in female and male offending. Table 3-3 summarizes these patterns across the same decades examined above, 1984 to 1994 and 1994 to 2004. These trends again show differences across gender in victimization risks in the earlier 1984-1994 period (see Table 3-3). During this earlier period, female risk of stranger violence increased by about one-quarter (24 percent) and male risk of stranger violence increased by 10 percent. Female risk of violent

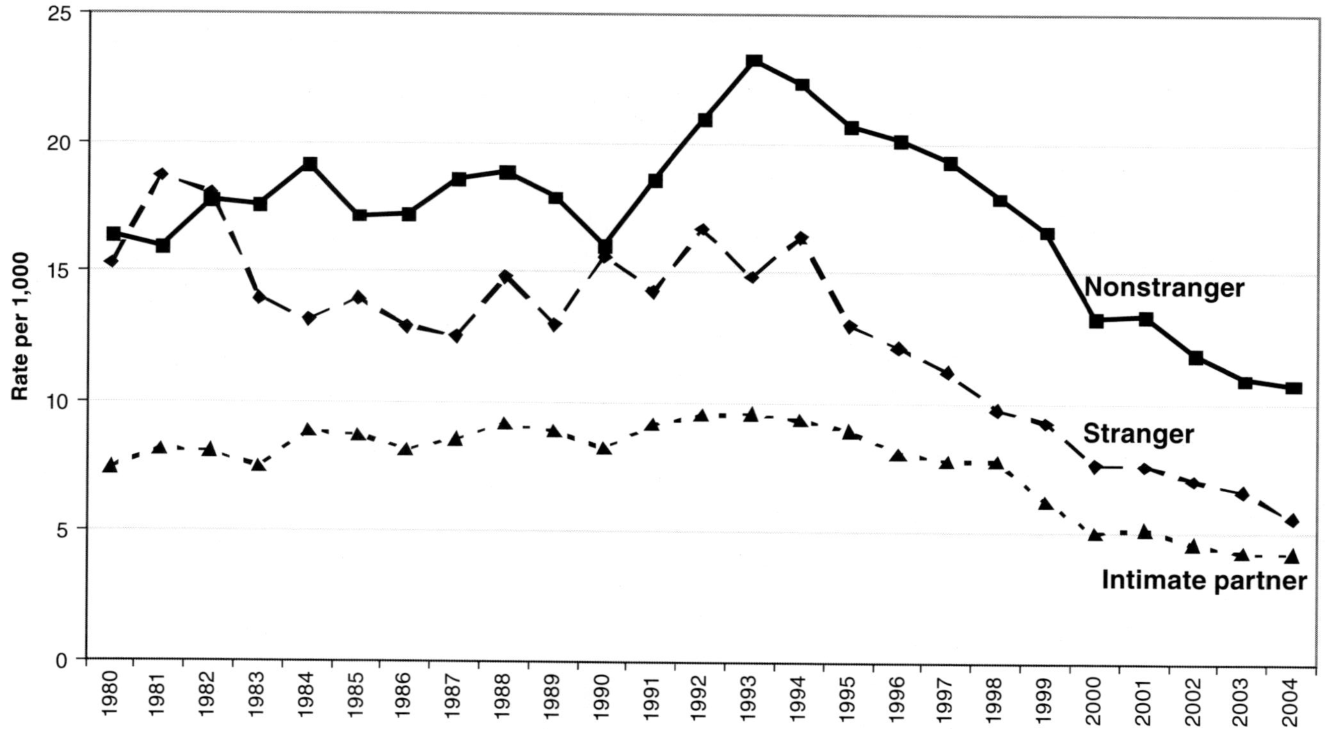

FIGURE 3-7a Female violent victimization by victim-offender relationship, 1980-2004.

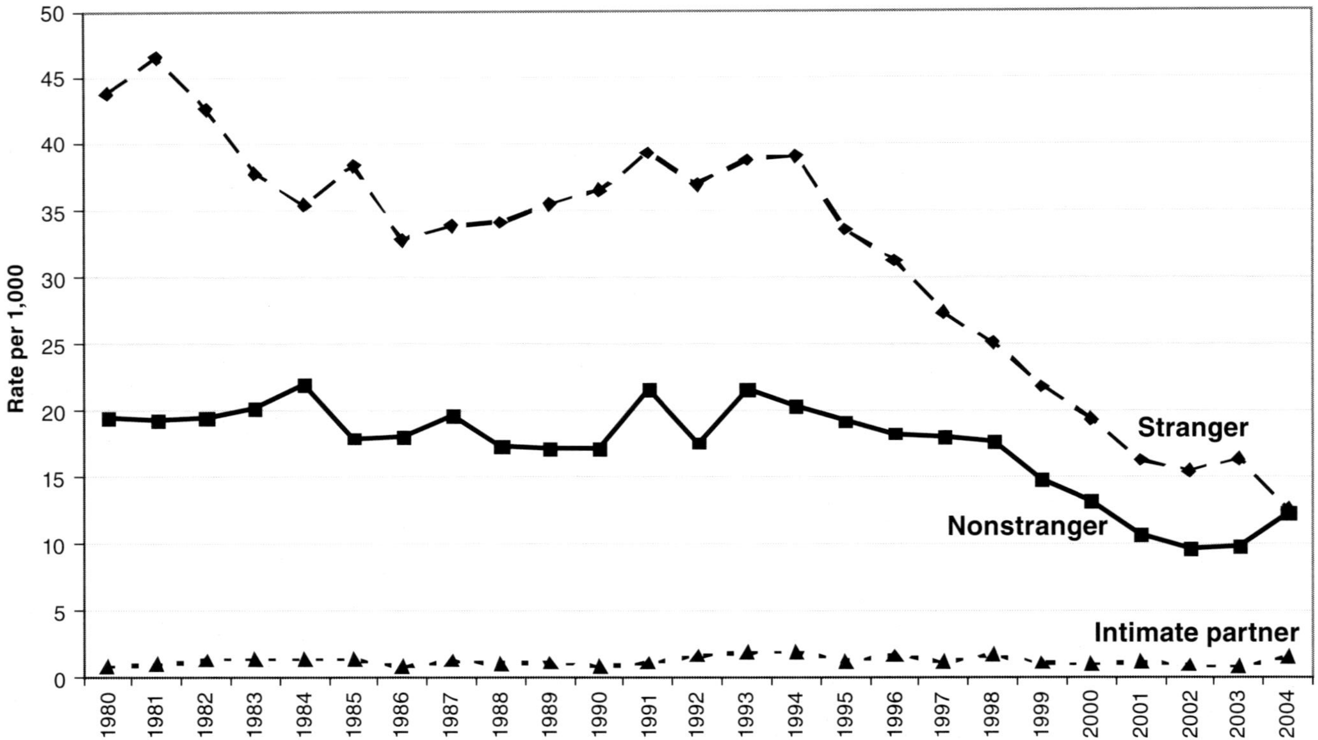

FIGURE 3-7b Male violent victimization by victim-offender relationship, 1980-2004.

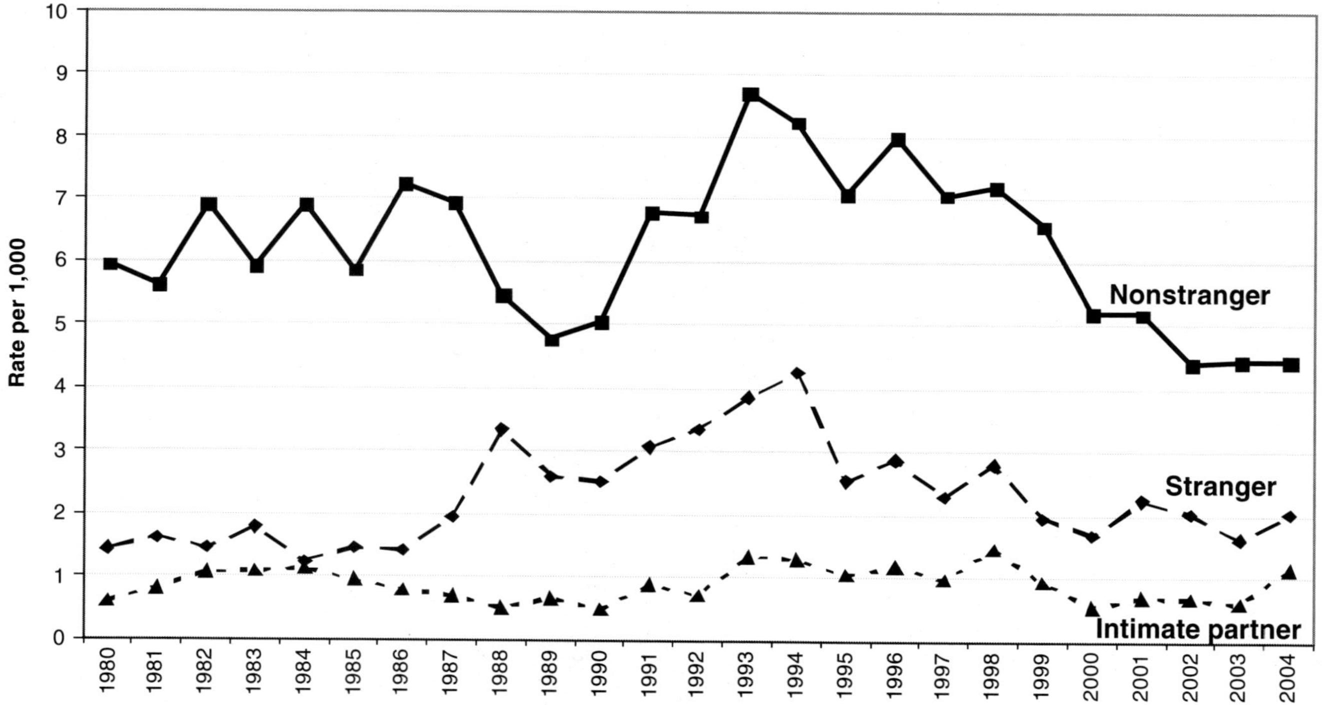

FIGURE 3-8a Female violent offending by victim-offender relationship, 1980-2004.

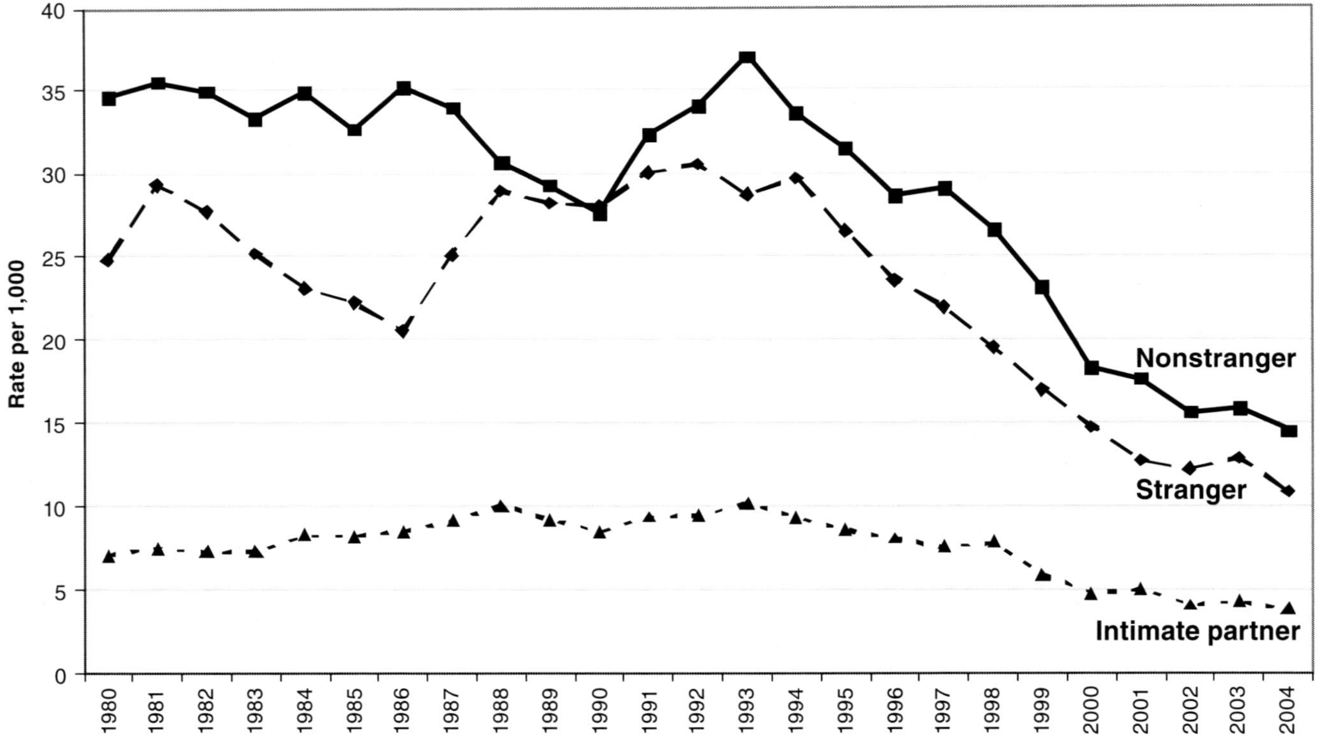

FIGURE 3-8b Male violent offending by victim-offender relationship, 1980-2004.

TABLE 3-3 Percentage Change in Female and Male Victimization and Offending Rates by Strangers, Nonstrangers, and Intimate Partners Across Decades: NCVS

	Victimization				Offending[a]			
	1984-1994		1994-2004		1984-1994		1994-2004	
	Female	Male	Female	Male	Female	Male	Female	Male
Stranger	+24	+10	−66	−68	+243	+28	−52	−63
Nonstranger	+17	−8	−52	−39	+20	− 4	−46	−57
Intimate partner	+5	+	−54	−	+	+13	−	−59

NOTE: Includes rape, robbery, aggravated assault, and simple assault.
[a]Based on single-offender incidents only.
+ = Rates too low to assess percentage change; however, data suggest increase.
− = Rates too low to assess percentage change; however, data suggest decrease.

victimization by nonstrangers and intimate partners also increased between 1984 and 1994 (17 and 5 percent, respectively), but at lower rates than the risk of stranger violence. Nonstranger victimization against men decreased only slightly between 1984 and 1994 (see Table 3-3), when the comparable female rates were increasing. This suggests that prior to 1994, female risks of violence increased more than male risks in all relationship categories, and the largest percentage increases among women occurred in violence by strangers.

After 1994, violent victimization declined for both genders across all relationship categories. The drop was quite sizable and comparable across gender in violence by strangers (66 percent for women, 68 percent for men). There was a less marked decline in nonstranger violence across gender, but women did experience a greater proportionate reduction in risk than men (52 and 39 percent, respectively). Women also experienced a sizable reduction in the risk of violence by intimate partners during this period (54 percent). We conclude from this that the crime drop of the late 1990s and early 2000s affected female victimization similarly across relationship categories, but it had relatively greater consequences for male experiences with victimization by strangers.

Table 3-3 summarizes similar disaggregated trends based on offending. Female offending against strangers increased between 1984 and 1994; then it declined at a rate similar to male offending against strangers between 1994 and 2004. While female violence against strangers has always been very low, Table 3-3 (and Figure 3-8a) show that it increased by 243 percent between 1984 (1.1 per 1,000) and 1994 (4.2 per 1,000). Female offending against nonstrangers increased by a smaller percentage (20 percent) during this period, from 6.9 per 1,000 in 1984 to 8.2 per 1,000 by 1994. The percentage increase in male violence against strangers was 28 percent between 1984 and 1994, and male violence against nonstrangers declined by 4 percent during this same decade (Figure 3-8b). Although the rates of female violence against strangers are very low and thus a small change in absolute numbers produces a very large percentage increase, the steeper upward slope in female stranger (Figure 3-8a) than male stranger (Figure 3-8b) offending would seem to flag a noteworthy change. We explore this further in the concluding section.

Turning to intimate partner offending and victimization, Table 3-3 shows that the decline in male intimate partner offending (and, equivalently, female intimate partner victimization) occurred between 1994 and 2004. In fact, the data suggest that male intimate partner offending increased slightly during the 1984 to 1994 period. Since these peak years, male rates of offending against strangers, nonstrangers, and intimate partners have all declined at similar magnitude, which could suggest that there may be some common causes of the declines in these types of offending during this period. We are unaware of any research that has assessed the factors associated with the decline in nonlethal intimate partner violence during the 1990s, but we suggest that future investigations of such trends should consider additional factors beyond changes in domestic violence policies and practices, which, along with women's economic and marriage rates, have been the focus of intimate partner homicide trends (e.g., Dugan, Nagin, and Rosenfeld, 1999, 2003).

The trends by gender of offender, type of violence, and gender of victim suggest a few basic conclusions. First, the modal category of violent crime in 2004 is not the same as it was in 1994 or 1984. Figures 3-7a and 3-7b show clearly that the risk for stranger and nonstranger violent victimization has declined substantially for women and men since 1993, but it also shows that these declines have been proportionately greater for stranger violence than for nonstranger violence. Indeed, while male victimization by strangers was by far the modal category of violence in the early 1980s, by 2004 it had decreased to the point at which it was no longer substantially higher than male or female victimization by nonstrangers. Second, despite the low base rate of female violence against strangers, the relatively large percentage increase between 1984 and 1994 seems to warrant further investigation. Third, Figures 3-7a and 3-7b show that, throughout the series, nonstranger violence against men and women has been at roughly comparable levels, but female rates came to exceed those of men by 1992.

DISCUSSION

This chapter uses pooled NCS-NCVS data to show that violence involving women has come to constitute a greater proportion of violent incidents over time and that gender clearly matters for understanding U.S. crime trends. First, we present empirical evidence from victims' reports of the gender of their assailants that shows meaningful changes in the gender rate ratios of violent offending over time, with some narrowing in the gender gap in aggravated assault, simple assault, and robbery. Second, we present data on the gender of victims that shows that the gender gap in violent victimization has narrowed for aggravated and simple assault. These findings are further illuminated by the changing patterns of female and male victimization and offending across stranger, nonstranger, and intimate partner relationships. The fact that gender rate ratios of offending and victimization have not remained stable indicates that there may well be something unique about gender during this time period. It also suggests that fully understanding crime trends requires consideration of variation across gender and victim-offender relationships. Furthermore, these findings clearly differ from those based on homicide data, which show no narrowing of the gender gap in victimization. This shows the need to go beyond homicide data to understand gender and violent victimization.

As noted at the outset, the goal of this chapter is to present data on long-term trends in female and male offending and victimization, as well as trends in the gender rate ratios. Examining long-term trends is essential for contextualizing shorter term fluctuations in crime rates, and to date research has not examined gender differences in long-term trends in both victimization and offending. In these conclusions, we compare the patterns in offending and victimization and illuminate them further using our findings of patterns across victim-offender relationships. We do not claim to explain the source of gender differences and similarities in these trends, as a time-series analysis that includes a full set of covariates would be questionable given the sample size of 25 years. Rather, because the first step in understanding any phenomenon is thorough description, we seek to highlight select comparisons and offer hypotheses to stimulate future research in this area.

A first observation that emerges from the data is that, with the exception of aggravated assault offending, a notable portion of the narrowing of the gender gap in violence can be traced to changing female-to-male ratios before the crime decline of the mid-1990s. Our findings show that large gender differences across the relationship categories occurred before the mid-1990s. During this time, there were increases in both offending against nonstrangers and victimization by nonstrangers among women, yet the corresponding male rates decreased. There also was a notable percentage increase in female violent offending against strangers and victimization by strangers before the mid-1990s, whereas male rates showed smaller percentage increases. This suggests that gender-specific social changes linked to victimization and offending may have occurred before the onset of the great crime decline of the late 1990s and early 2000s, and these changes appear to hold for both stranger and nonstranger crime.

It is interesting that the gender gap decreases not only across types of violence, but also for both victimization and offending. The fact that the largest increases in the gender rate ratios of offending and victimization occur at roughly the same time is not surprising, given research showing that involvement in victimization and offending are correlated and share many of the same predictors (Sampson and Lauritsen, 1994). Yet, because previous studies have not compared the gender gaps in offending and victimization over time, this correspondence has been ignored in the literature on crime trends and remains an important area for future research.

These shifts in the gender rate ratios of violence may have been associated with broad social changes due to enhanced social freedoms for women and gender equality that increased before and during the 1980s. For women, these changes may have been accompanied by higher levels of public interactions, in the labor force and elsewhere, thus expanding opportunities for violent victimization and offending.

However, changing gender roles may have had two very different consequences for violent victimization. On one hand, it may be that displays of interpersonal violence became increasingly less acceptable as women increasingly occupied the public sphere, thus helping to reduce male victimization. This comports with the long-term declines that we uncovered in violence against both men and women, by strangers as well as nonstrangers. On the other hand, women's increased presence in public life simultaneously created greater opportunities for nonfamilial victimization. Thus, although rates of violent victimization declined for both genders over the past 25 years, the decline for women was less than the decline for men for aggravated and simple assaults.

Viewing the trend data as an indicator of motivation for offending rather than opportunities for victimization suggests an alternative hypothesis: perhaps changing gender roles increased women's vulnerability to the effects of the economy. Although the feminization of poverty slowed in the 1980s for all ages combined, the youth of both genders felt the brunt of the decade's difficult economic times (Bianchi, 1999). The experience of economic stress may have combined with greater participation in street life by young women to produce relatively greater changes in women's than men's violent encounters.

Other hypotheses are certainly plausible. Perhaps increasing incarceration rates or changes in the policing of public spaces over the period studied had a more significant impact on male than female offending rates, thus contributing to the reduction in the gender gap in offending. Because men are more likely than women to be the victims of male-perpetrated violence, the large increases in the numbers of men incarcerated may have had a larger impact on male victimization than female victimization rates, thus contributing to increasing gender rate ratios of violent victimization. Similarly, increases in the policing of public places may have disproportionately decreased male victimization.

It is also important to understand why the crime drop after the mid-1990s affected women and men rather similarly. One hypothesis is that, perhaps by the 1990s, growth in social freedoms for women had slowed and the factors affecting female and male trends became more similar. So, for example, economic prosperity and the growth in imprisonment may have spurred decreases in female as well as male victimization and offending. Another hypothesis is that different factors were associated with the similar rates of decline in female and male violence. For example, the decline in female intimate partner victimization may have been related, in part, to successful policies and programs targeting violence against women, which became more widespread during the 1990s. Declines in other forms of violence against women, such as violence by strangers, and declines in violence against men may have been more associated with other contemporaneous policies targeting crime more generally, such as increased incarceration. Moreover, it could be that policies aimed at reducing violence against women had a spillover effect on other forms of male offending, by bringing men into the criminal justice system when they otherwise might have remained free to commit other types of offenses.

One final issue uncovered by our disaggregation of crime trends concerns the changing composition of violence over time. While male stranger victimization was by far the modal category of violence in the early 1980s, by 2004 it had decreased to the point at which it was no longer substantially higher than male or female nonstranger victimization. Why stranger violence has declined more rapidly than other forms of nonlethal violence is a challenging question for future research. Moreover, nonstranger violence against men and women had occurred at comparable levels, but female nonstranger victimization rates came to exceed male rates by about 1992. This means that nonstranger violence is now a critical part of violence in the United States, and women are now affected at levels similar to those of men. This presents a challenge to criminal justice policy, and it indicates that new efforts to reduce nonlethal violent crime are unlikely to have much effect unless they can affect violence by nonstrangers. If interventions to reduce violence against women have had some impact on violence by men both inside and outside intimate partner relationships, such strategies may offer a place to start the thinking about crafting policy to reduce violence.

We note that our analyses cannot speak to race, ethnicity, or age differences in these gender-specific patterns of offending and victimization. This is a very important issue that requires careful research attention to determine whether the patterns of gender rate ratios that we observed would hold across different race and age groups. Although the study of race and age differences in nonlethal victimization and offending cannot be addressed with UCR data, these important issues can be addressed with careful use of the NCVS data. However, disaggregating the data to address these patterns involves methodological complexities beyond those described here and therefore is beyond the scope of the present analysis. Our goal here has been to take a first step by focusing on long-term trends in the gender rate ratios of offending and victimization as measured by pooled NCS-NCVS data and to link the study of violence against women to the study of crime trends.

In conclusion, our findings highlight the complexities inherent in understanding trends in violence across crime types and gender. The trends that we present indicate that gender-specific trends in violence share similarities but also are sufficiently unique to indicate that female victimization and offending should be part of the consideration of crime trends in the United States. Given that the data reveal some reduction in the gender gap in violent offending and victimization, the situation is akin to that of a narrowing gender gap in mortality from heart disease. Even in a period of an overall decline in crime (or heart disease) the fact that women benefit less than men from the social changes affecting crime rates over the past 25 years signals the need for both scientific research and social policy to address the differences. Gender is therefore an important part of the story of violence in the United States and should not be excluded from analyses of crime trends.

REFERENCES

Batton, Candice. (2004). Gender differences in lethal violence: Historical trends in the relationship between homicide and suicide rates, 1960-2000. *Justice Quarterly, 21*, 423-461.

Bianchi, Suzanne M. (1999). Feminization and juvenilization of poverty: Trends, relative risks, causes and consequences. *Annual Review of Sociology, 25*, 307-333.

Blumstein, Alfred. (2000). Disaggregating the violence trends. In Alfred Blumstein and Joel Wallman (Eds.), *The crime drop in America* (pp. 13-44). New York: Cambridge University Press.

Blumstein, Alfred, and Joel Wallman. (2000). *The crime drop in America.* New York: Cambridge University Press.

Browne, Angela, and Kirk Williams. (1993). Gender, intimacy, and lethal violence: Trends from 1976 through 1987. *Gender and Society, 7*, 75-94.

Bureau of Justice Statistics. (2006). *Criminal victimization in the U.S., 2004.* Statistical tables. Washington, DC: U.S. Department of Justice.

Catalano, Shannan. (2006). *Intimate partner violence in the United States.* Bureau of Justice Statistics. Washington, DC: U.S. Department of Justice.

Dugan, Laura, Daniel S. Nagin, and Richard Rosenfeld. (1999). Explaining the decline in intimate partner homicide: The effects of changing domesticity, women's status, and domestic violence resources. *Homicide Studies, 3*, 187-214.

Dugan, Laura, Daniel S. Nagin, and Richard Rosenfeld. (2003). Exposure reduction or retaliation? Effects of domestic violence resources on intimate partner homicide. *Law and Society Review, 37*, 169-198.

Heimer, Karen. (2000). Changes in the gender gap in crime and women's economic marginalization. In Gary La Free (Ed.), *The nature of crime: Continuity and change* (pp. 427-483). Washington, DC: National Institute of Justice. Available: http://www.ncjrs.gov/criminal_justice2000/vol1_2000.html [accessed August 2008].

Kindermann, Charles, James Lynch, and David Cantor. (1997). *The effects of the redesign on victimization estimates.* (Bureau of Justice Statistics Technical Report Series.) Washington, DC: U.S. Department of Justice. Available: http://www.ojp.usdoj.gov/bjs/pub/pdf/erve.pdf [accessed August 2008].

LaFree, Gary, and Gwen Hunnicutt. (2006). Female and male homicide victimization trends: A cross-national context. In Karen Heimer and Candace Kruttschnitt (Eds.), *Gender and crime: Patterns in victimization and offending* (pp. 195-229). New York: New York University Press.

Lauritsen, J.L., and Karen Heimer. (2008). The gender gap in violent victimization, 1973-2004. *Journal of Quantitative Criminology, 24*(2), 125-147.

Lawlor, Debbie, Alnoor S. Ebrahim, and George Davey Smith. (2001). Sex matters: Secular and geographical trends in sex differences in coronary heart disease mortality. *British Medical Journal, 323*, 541-545. Available: http://www.pubmedcentral.nih.gov/picrender.fcgi?artid=48158&blobtype=pdf [accessed August 2008].

Leach, Susan Llewelyn. (2004). Behind the surge in girl crime. *Christian Science Monitor*, September 15. Available: http://www.csmonitor.com/2004/0915/p16s02-usju.html [accessed August 2008].

Lynch, James. (2002). *Trends in juvenile violent offending: An analysis of victim survey data.* Office of Juvenile Justice and Delinquency Prevention. Washington, DC: U.S. Department of Justice.

Lynch, James, and David Cantor. (1996). *Models for adjusting the NCS trend to account for design differences between the NCS and NCVS.* Memorandum to the American Statistical Association Committee on Law and Justice Statistics.

Miller, Jody. (1998). Up it up: Gender and the accomplishment of street robbery. *Criminology, 36*, 37-66.

National Research Council. (2004). *Advancing the federal research agenda on violence against women.* Steering Committee for the Workshop on Issues in Research on Violence Against Women, Candace Kruttschnitt, Brenda L. McLaughlin, and Carol Petrie (Eds.). Committee on Law and Justice, Division of Behavioral and Social Sciences and Education. Washington, DC: The National Academies Press.

O'Brien, Robert. (1999). Measuring the convergence/divergence of serious crime arrest rates for males and females: 1960-1995. *Journal of Quantitative Criminology, 15*, 97-114.

Planty, Michael. (2006). Series victimizations and divergence. In James Lynch and Lynn Addington (Eds.), *Understanding crime statistics: Revisiting the divergence of the NCVS and UCR* (pp. 156-182). New York: Cambridge University Press.

Rand, Michael, and Callie Marie Rennison. (2005). Bigger is not necessarily better: An analysis of violence against women estimates from the National Crime Victimization Survey and the National Violence Against Women Survey. *Journal of Quantitative Criminology, 21*, 267-291.

Rand, Michael, James Lynch, and David Cantor. (1997). *Long-term trends in crime victimization.* Bureau of Justice Statistics. Washington, DC: U.S. Department of Justice.

Rosenfeld, Richard. (1997). Changing relationships between men and women. *Homicide Studies, 1*, 72-83.

Rosenfeld, Richard. (2000). Patterns in adult homicide: 1980-1995. In Alfred Blumstein and Joel Wallman (Eds.), *The crime drop in America* (pp. 130-163). New York: Cambridge University Press.

Rosenfeld, Richard. (2006). Explaining the divergence between UCR and NCVS aggravated assault trends. In James Lynch and Lynn A. Addington (Eds.), *Understanding crime statistics: Revisiting the divergence of the NCVS and UCR* (pp. 251-268). New York: Cambridge University Press.

Sampson, Robert, and Janet Lauritsen. (1994). Violent victimization and offending: Individual-, situational-, and community-level risk factors. In National Research Council, *Understanding and preventing violence: Social influences on violence* (pp. 1-114, vol. 3), Albert Reiss and Jeffrey Roth (Eds.), Panel on the Understanding and Control of Violent Behavior. Washington, DC: National Academy Press.

Scelfo, Julie. (2005). Bad girls go wild: A rise in girl-on-girl violence is making headlines nationwide and prompting scientists to ask why. *Newsweek*, June 13. Available: http://www.newsweek.com/id/50082 [accessed August 2008].

Simon, Rita James, and Jean Landis. (1991). *The crimes women commit and the punishments they receive*. Lexington, MA: Lexington Books.

Smith, M. Dwayne. (1987). Changes in the victimization of women: Is there a "new female victim?" *Journal of Research in Crime and Delinquency, 24*(4), 291-301.

Smith, M. Dwayne, and Victoria E. Brewer. (1995). Female status and the gender gap in U.S. homicide victimization. *Violence Against Women, 1*(4), 339-350.

Steffensmeier, Darrell, and Emilie Allan. (1996). Gender and crime: Toward a gendered theory of female offending. *Annual Review of Sociology, 22*, 459-487.

Steffensmeier, Darrell, and Michael J. Cobb. (1981). Sex differences in urban arrest patterns, 1934-1979. *Social Problems, 29*(1), 37-50.

Steffensmeier, Darrell, Jennifer Schwartz, Hua Zhong, and Jeff Ackerman. (2005). An assessment of recent trends in girls' violence using diverse longitudinal sources: Is the gender gap closing? *Criminology, 43*(2), 355-405.

Steffensmeier, Darrell, Hua Zhong, Jeff Ackerman, Jennifer Schwartz, and Suzanne Agha. (2006). Gender gap trends for violent crimes, 1980-2003. *Feminist Criminology, 1*, 72-98.

Zimring, Franklin E. (2006) *The great American crime decline*. New York: Oxford University Press.

4

Crime and Neighborhood Change

Jeffrey Fagan

There is broad agreement in both popular culture and social science that rates of crime and delinquency vary across neighborhoods. Yet researchers and citizens disagree on whether these differences are attributable to characteristics and relationships among of persons who live in neighborhoods, or if there are factors about the neighborhoods themselves that influence crime rates independently of the persons who live there. The question becomes further complicated as neighborhoods change over time, since both the composition of the neighborhoods and the broader features of those neighborhoods are changing simultaneously. The challenge in this chapter is to assess research on the influence of neighborhood *change* on changes in crime rates and to determine the unique knowledge that neighborhood studies contribute to the understanding and control of crime.

Accordingly, this chapter reviews research on factors that influence changes in crime rates between and within neighborhoods in cities over time. First is a brief review of local area studies of neighborhood and crime, focusing on neighborhood "effects": the structures and processes in neighborhoods that are thought to affect trajectories of crime over time. Next the chapter identifies challenges in theory, measurement, and analysis that affect estimates of why and how neighborhood crime rates change, including size and definition of spatial units, mutual and reciprocal relations between units, the endogeneity of criminal justice enforcement and neighborhood ecology, the influences of macro-changes (i.e., the political economy of cities) on local crime rates, constraints of observational and administrative data, theoretical specifications of neighborhood and measurement and analytic strategies. Illustrations from recent research on crime trends in New York City highlight the challenges of estimating neighborhood influences on crime trends.

INTRODUCTION

For several decades, research on neighborhood and community variation in crime and delinquency focused on identifying cross-sectional between-area differences in rates of violent or property crime. Often constrained by data limitations, these studies have adopted a static view of community or neighborhood, assuming that differences in crime rates *between* neighborhoods were stable over time, and that these differences reflected differences in the characteristics of communities that were stable over time (see, for example, Bursik, 1984). Shaw and McKay (1943), for example, showed that crime rates were predictably higher in socially disorganized communities, independent of the residents of those areas. More recently, Land, McCall, and Cohen (1990) suggested that the social and economic correlates of crime were stable over time and across different spatial aggregations.

More recent studies have adopted a dynamic, developmental perspective to the study of social and economic behaviors in communities and neighborhoods. Recent interest in neighborhood effects has produced new research on small-area variations in child development and child maltreatment, teenage sexual behavior and childbearing, school dropout, home ownership, and several indicators of health, suicide, disorder, drug use, and adolescent delinquency (see, e.g., Brooks-Gunn et al., 1993; Coulton, Korbin, Su, and Chow, 1995; Crane, 1991; Gould, 1990; Gould et al., 1990; Harding, 2003; Wilkinson and Fagan, 1996).

These studies make strong claims that growing up in neighborhoods characterized by concentrated socioeconomic disadvantage has enduring consequences on child and adolescent development. These disadvantages are thought to affect adults as well, attenuating their access to decent housing, job networks that provide access to stable family-sustaining wages, and quality education to prepare them for changing labor markets (Jargowsky, 1997; Massey and Denton, 1993; Wilson, 1987).[1]

But fewer studies have recognized that neighborhoods are dynamic

[1]Not everyone agrees, however, citing weak evidence that there are neighborhood effects independent of the consequences of growing up in poor families on individuals that are net of the aggregate effects on poor people concentrated in poor places (Jencks and Mayer, 1990; see, generally, Raudenbush and Sampson, 1999). Indeed, just how important neighborhoods are can be gauged by the relative contributions of neighborhood effects and individual factors in multilevel studies of covarying change over time (Raudenbush and Sampson, 1999). Recent work by Harding (2003) suggests that after adjusting for the selection biases that produce the concentration effects of poor people in specific neighborhoods, there are important negative effects of growing up in a low-poverty neighborhood on school dropout and teen pregnancy.

entities that change over time (like people), and that these transformations are likely to produce complex and changing outcomes in several indicators of social and economic life, including crime (see Sampson, Morenoff, and Gannon-Rowley, 2002, for a review). This perspective reflects a large body of research that recognizes that rates of social and health behaviors vary in communities over time and that the characteristics of communities influence those rates. That is, communities have natural developmental histories that parallel changes in social behaviors of persons over the life course. And while it naturally follows that neighborhood effects would also influence crime, there has been less attention in recent studies to the question of how *changing* neighborhood contexts influence crime (see, for exceptions, Bellair, 2000; Fagan and Davies, 2004).

The few studies thus far on crime and neighborhood change point to complex interactions and (nonrecursive) feedback processes between crime and the social dynamics and compositional characteristics of neighborhoods (Bellair, 2000). Other studies (e.g., Fagan et al., 2007; Morenoff, Sampson, and Raudenbush, 2001) suggest that processes of diffusion and contagion explain changes over time in homicides and violence as neighborhoods change (see, also, Ludwig and Kling, 2007). Taylor and Covington (1988) examined crime rates in Philadelphia neighborhoods to show how neighborhood change, including gentrification, increased both relative deprivation in stable but poor areas and created new crime opportunities that raised the risks of crime in the improving adjacent ones. Schwartz (1999) linked changes in housing prices to declines in violent crime across New York City police precincts, net of changes in social indicators, and Tita, Petras, and Greenbaum (2006) tied violent crime to weaker housing prices. And some researchers discount the importance of changes in social ecology, whether citywide or in specific neighborhoods, in explaining recent changes in crime (Zimring, 2006).

But these studies are relatively rare data points that offer limited answers to the larger question of the relationship between neighborhood change and crime. The science of studying crime and neighborhood change is still developing, both conceptually and methodologically. Since the early Chicago School work (described below), few studies have applied a developmental perspective to chart the natural history of neighborhood change and crime in different areas of modern cities. While neighborhood change is not a necessary condition to produce changes in crime, the broad fact of differences within and between neighborhoods in crime rates over time challenges theories that are built on cross-sectional, time-limited differences in violence rates from one area to the next.

This chapter reviews research on neighborhood change and crime and identifies challenges in theory, measurement, and methods. The study of neighborhoods over time has created a rich body of sociological theory to conceptualize space and its effects on people, both individually and as collectives or aggregates. But studies of neighborhood change have been rare and usually limited to a few neighborhoods in single cities. Most rely on one of two types of research enterprises: qualitative methods that focus on social organization and exchanges between persons and groups, or observational data on social, economic, or health indicators. Few have been prospective, and most have limited their theoretical questions to social structure. Analytic methods that model within-person change can be applied to neighborhoods, but the translation is not simple, and it may be the case that methods have not yet developed to address the complicated questions of endogeneity of crime and area change, the spatial dependence of neighborhoods and the shared and diffused processes of change across natural or administrative borders, or the simultaneity of crime changes and neighborhood changes. After a review of studies on crime and neighborhood change, the chapter discusses five challenges that confront research in this area. These challenges are illustrated with data from a panel study of violent crime in New York City neighborhoods for the period 1985-2000. The chapter concludes by outlining an agenda for building an infrastructure of data that will sustain research on neighborhood differences in crime.

CRIME AND NEIGHBORHOOD CHANGE

Interest in neighborhood change as a predictor of changing crime rates can be traced to the Chicago School traditions of studying "natural social areas" whose identities are the products of complex social and economic factors, sometimes endogeneous (Park, Burgess, and McKenzie, 1925) and sometimes imposed from the outside by political economic dynamics (Logan and Molotch, 1988; Suttles, 1970). Despite this interest, there have been surprisingly few longitudinal studies of neighborhood change and changes in crime rates. The good news is that these few studies converge in several areas to inform theory and research.

Physical and social deterioration is a persistent theme of neighborhood change in these studies. Taub, Taylor, and Dunham (1984) used survey and archival data and physical observations to weave a story about crime and neighborhood change in eight Chicago neighborhoods. They report on a reciprocal dynamic in which crime experiences—both direct and vicarious victimization—degrade residents' investments in social control and upkeep. These visual cues of deterioration, together with subjective evaluations about the likelihood of crime and other adverse events, in turn cued citizens that the neighborhood had approached a racial "tipping point" that would trigger a sharp spike in crime, motivating some residents to move away. Schuerman and Kobrin (1986) also implicated physical deterioration in the shift of a neighborhood from low to high crime. They used a series of cross-sectional analyses to identify three distinct stages of neighborhood change—emerging, transitional, and enduring—that characterized the natural history of neighborhood evolution from a stable low-crime area into a high-crime area.[2] Harrell and Gouvis (1994) also used a residual change analysis over two decennial censuses to predict increases in crime associated with changes in neighborhood ecology. Their predictions weakened in areas where residential mobility increased, a response to deterioration similar to the narratives voiced by respondents in the Taylor et al. (1984) survey.

A second thread in these studies is the reciprocal influence of adjacent neighborhoods to increase crime rates. Taylor and Covington (1988) used residual change scores in census variables (1970 and 1980) to assess two indicators of violence (aggravated assault, murder, and nonnegligent manslaughter) in 277 Baltimore neighborhoods. Their study used two time points, not the 10 between the decennial censuses. The two most salient neighborhood changes during the decade were the emergence of a large number of gentrifying neighborhoods and the descent of several older, minority neighborhoods into an "underclass" status. They focused on the process of gentrification, located neighborhood change in both relative deprivation and social disorganization theories, and identified components of violence attributable to each process. As neighborhoods became more homogeneously poorer and socially isolated, they experienced increasing violence. In the gentrifying neighborhoods, violence increased as their status and stability increased relative to the increasingly poor adjacent neighborhoods.

Morenoff and Sampson (1997) also examined this dynamic, focusing on violent crime over three decades in Chicago's 862 census tracts as a function of population loss and the concentration of socioeconomic disadvantage. Using residual changes in the decennial census to measure neighborhood ecology, they identified a dynamic process in which homicide animated population loss, and the replacement process induced higher rates of spatially concentrated homicide and patterns of diffusion to other neighborhoods experiencing similar changes. They identified race-specific effects in homicide, spatial proximity to homicide, and socioeconomic disadvantage associated with African American population gains and white population loss. Heitgerd and Bursik (1987) also examined neighborhood change from 1960-1970 and analyzed juvenile court referrals to show that even stable,

[2]Changes signaling neighborhood deterioration and rising crime rates include a shift from single to multiple-family dwellings, as well as increases in residential mobility, unrelated individuals and broken families, the ratio of children to adults, minority group populations, women in the labor force, and nonwhite and Spanish-surname population with advanced education, structural domains long associated with social area theories of crime.

well-organized communities could have high rates of delinquency when the adjacent neighborhoods experienced rapid racial change.

Finally, several studies have analyzed neighborhood change to identify turning points in the natural history of neighborhood development to pinpoint when crime rates change and grow. Bursik and Webb (1982) updated Shaw and McKay's (1943) original data on juvenile court referrals Chicago's 74 local community areas to show that ecological shifts in neighborhoods were associated with deflections in a neighborhood's crime rates. Analyzing these data once again, Bursik (1984) identified correlates of neighborhood crime rates in each decade from 1940 to 1970. The sharp change in correlates in 1950 suggested an ecological shift that was linked to a turning point in neighborhoods' crime rates. Bursik and Grasmick (1992, 1993) used hierarchical linear models to estimate crime rate change from 1930 to 1970, again identifying an ecological shift in 1950 that preceded increases in crime.

More recent work has charted variation in trajectories of crime—specifically, homicide—in neighborhoods over time (e.g., Fagan and Davies, 2007; Griffiths and Chavez, 2004; Kubrin and Weitzer, 2003; Weisburd et al., 2004). The empirical solutions identify numerous patterns of rise and fall in homicide rates over time in neighborhoods in cities, using initial starting points of social structural characteristics of neighborhoods at the outset of the panel as predictors. But these studies don't link changes in homicide to changes in neighborhoods and are silent on the contemporaneous changes in neighborhood and crime.

Although each of these studies offers important clues about neighborhood change and crime, they also are limited in some important ways. First, most have used census tracts to bound and characterize neighborhoods. The older Chicago studies are an exception, but the 74 areas are large, heterogeneous aggregates of several smaller neighborhoods, a strategy that might mask important influences in smaller corners of these larger areas. For smaller areal units, there is no consensus whether census block groups or tracts or other boundaries—such as street segments in Weisburd's Seattle analysis—are either socially meaningful or theoretically appropriate to study either community structure or social processes (see Bursik, 1988). There are alternatives to using either administratively drawn boundaries or micro-units. For example, Fagan and Davies (2004), as well as Fagan, West, and Holland (2003), use boundaries drawn in New York that integrated residents' perceptions of the natural boundaries of their neighborhoods, proscribed by their attribution of shared belonging among residents, with census and other administrative boundaries that provide data conveniences for consistent measurement and comparability across studies (see Jackson and Manbeck, 1998). Research with these alternate social-spatial configurations may yield more accurate units to specify social processes, but these may run into other types of data problems and limit comparability between studies. Defining the appropriate space is a conceptual as well as empirical challenge, as illustrated later on.

Second, because census data are collected decennially, researchers interested in neighborhood change have limited their study periods to these fixed 10-year intervals. Other studies use much shorter time windows, limiting their analyses to shorter periods in which the window for estimating change may be artifactually short. Yet crime trends usually don't cooperate with the attributes and characteristics of the decennial censuses. Crime trends can be quite volatile within a decade or even span decades, and inferences about changes in crime rates at a decade apart can be quite misleading (see, for example, Fagan and Davies, 2004, and Fagan, Davies, and Holland, 2007, on the roller coaster of crime rates in New York from the early 1980s through 2000). The nonlinear patterns of these changes demand not only more frequent and disaggregated measurement of local conditions, but also more complex functional forms for analysis, including quadratic terms for time parameters to allow for curvilinear changes in crime rates as well as the predictors of crime.

Third, studies of neighborhood change in crime rates vary in the specificity of the crime form and the theoretical linkages that would predict changes in specific types of crime. Some studies specify linkages to violence based on carefully specified theories, and others measure changes in more global measures of crime without disaggregating crime into dimensions that might be differentially predicted by alternate theories. For example, Wilson and Kelling's (1982) theory of "broken windows" suggested that signs of disorder launched a contagious process that signaled to would-be criminals that there was no guardianship in an area, in turn leading to higher crime rates. Their general theory had no correspondence to any specific crime type, and subsequent empirical tests showed quite limited predictive power for any specific form of crime (Harcourt, 2001; Sampson and Raudenbush, 1999). In contrast, Taylor and Covington (1988) hypothesized and confirmed that the juxtaposition of contrasting trajectories of change may accelerate violence by creating targets of robbery opportunity in newly gentrified areas adjacent to chronically poor ones, but not necessarily other crimes.

These studies provide robust evidence of variation in the rates of change over time in crime between spatial units in cities, variation that cannot be explained simply by aggregating the social attributes and characteristics of individuals in these areas. They also contain lessons for theory and policy. Making ecological claims about factors that have variable effects risks theoretical error and possibly policy missteps. For example, cities experiencing steep crime declines may in fact have localized crime trends that either oppose the aggregate trend across areas, or that may mask more complex if not conflicting results in local areas, results that may challenge the broader citywide claim when viewed as a function of policy instruments (e.g., policing) or theoretically salient factors (e.g., immigration, the siting and form of public housing). Also, the benefits and burdens of declining crime in cities may not be shared by all citizens of a city. If the rise and fall in crime trends over time between neighborhoods varies by gender, age, or race, there may be local conditions that expose these population groups to—or inoculate them from—harm. Accordingly, these potential disparities raise the stakes in advancing the science of studying crime and neighborhood change, especially when crime rates are rising and falling at different rates and in different directions in neighborhoods in a city, and when other cities are experiencing similar volatility at the same time.

A parallel question is the extent of covariation between neighborhood change and crime trends. There is good evidence linking neighborhood differences in social structure and other ecological factors to differences in crime rates and, more recently, to the growth and contraction of crime (Fagan and Davies, 2004). But there is less evidence about whether structural or other types of changes in neighborhoods are causally linked to changes in neighborhood crime rates. And little is known about whether the pace of changes in neighborhoods itself can influence crime rates. So conceptualizing and measuring neighborhood change on these putative predictors of neighborhood crime trends also raise research challenges.

FIVE CHALLENGES

On both ends of this question, our understanding of patterns and trends in neighborhoods and crime trends is influenced by our choices of spatial units, crime specifications, theoretical perspectives, and analytic methods, as well as the limitations of measurement. These decisions influence both the substantive claims of research and their compatibility with other studies. There also are larger conceptual questions about how one thinks about space within cities and the interdependencies of these spatial units. Different spatial units matter in different way, depending on the question. In this section, these challenges are identified and illustrated.

What Spatial Resolution?

One simple empirical fact emerging from neighborhood studies is that the extent of observed heterogeneity in patterns over time in cities depends on the size of the spatial area studied. The size of the area and its spatial resolution depend on the question at hand, and the selection of a spatial unit thus becomes a theoretical question. But the variation of units in neighborhood studies begs the question of how area size affects the estimation of neighborhood effects. Bursik and Grasmick (1993) argue that findings are robust across units of different sizes, whereas Coulton, Korbin, Su, and Chow (1995) say that unit size makes a difference. Whether unit size matters because of aggregation biases or because of the theoretical question at hand is difficult to disentangle.

Weisburd et al. (2004, p. 291) analyzed changes in crime rates over 14 years in *street segments*, which are two or more faces on both sides of a street between two intersections. Using group-based trajectory modeling with a poisson distribution (Nagin, 2005; Nagin and Land, 1993), they identified 18 distinct trajectories of crime, using aggregate counts of crime incidents. No tests were reported to distinguish the 18 groups on dimensions of neighborhood social structure or social organization. Weisburd et al. (2004) also reported temporal heterogeneity among the street segments: Eight trajectories were stable (accounting for 84 percent of the total street segments), three were increasing, and seven were decreasing over time.

Although several factors may explain the high degree of heterogeneity in the Seattle study, two stand out. First, the fine resolution of the spatial unit and the use of general (multidimensional) crime categories yielded numerous and complex micro-trends over time. There were 29,849 street segments in Seattle, and over 2 million crime incidents over the 14-year period that were linked to specific geographic coordinates and "placed" on a block face. Nearly one in five was eliminated because they occurred at street intersections and could not be assigned to a street segment. With this many data points and observations, complex and diverse patterns are not surprising, especially over a lengthy period of observation. Whether these distinct patterns reflect real—theoretically meaningful—differences or noisy data is hard to sort out. Second, five crime categories were used to characterize incidents. The most frequent were Uniform Crime Reports index crimes (11.4 percent), and nontrivial traffic violations the least common (4.7 percent). If different neighborhood configurations and social ecologies are associated with different crime categories, the Seattle study captured four dimensions at once: time, ecological risk, temporal change, and crime type. Fine resolution in trends might be expected when the four dimensions are collapsed.

Weisburd et al. were interested in street segments because of their concern for identifying the "hot spots" of crime and the prevention potential for focusing limited legal resources on places where crime risks are highest. Other studies also are concerned with the effects of policing on crime trends but use larger spatial aggregations, such as police precincts in New York (Fagan, West, and Holland, 2003; Corman and Mocan, 2000; Rosenfeld, Fornango, and Rengifo, 2007) or smaller police units such as beats and districts in Chicago (Papachristos, Meares, and Fagan, 2007). These are administratively defined areas that reflect the units where police resources are allocated and managed and are conveniences for compiling data and examining variation in how police deploy resources. They also have the advantage of remaining stable over time.[3] While precincts may have had *social* meaning at one time, they now are socially and economically heterogeneous areas whose value for testing theories of social control is contested (see, e.g., Wooldredge, 2002). The limitations on administrative borders may be most important in studies that attempt inferences in administrative areas where distinct population subgroups regularly interact with legal actors.

Studies using police district aggregations often control for the differences in their social makeup by including both covariates for relevant population characteristics and fixed effects for the districts or precincts. For example, Papachristos et al. (2007) examined the effects of a gun violence suppression program using police beats in Chicago. Chicago police departments are organized into 28 police districts, and each district is then subdivided into beats. The beats were more homogeneous and socially meaningful than the larger districts, and Papachristos et al. were able to focus on specific areas where police efforts and crime both were concentrated. They examined crime trends over 84 police beats in 4 of Chicago's 28 police districts, showing strong downward trends for all beats but steeper slopes for the experimental group. They used propensity scores to identify treatment effects in a quasi-experimental design, controlling also for trends in other areas of the city. The use of beats struck a compromise between the artificiality of police boundaries and the scale of area that would be most likely to capture networked offenders in small social spaces. Papachristos controlled for the mutual influences of these spaces by including a measure of spatial dependence (Moran's I).

Fagan et al. (2003) and others (e.g., Corman and Mocan, 2000; Messner et al., 2007; Rosenfeld et al., 2007) examined the effects of policing policies—order maintenance policing, drug enforcement—on crime rates in New York's 75 police precincts. These precincts are large, with an average population of over 110,000 persons in 2000, and variable in size (standard deviation = 50,194). Some precincts are more racially and economically diverse than others and often include several smaller, more homogeneous neighborhoods. Other precincts include commercial areas that were virtually empty at night (Wall Street) or with different daytime and nighttime populations.[4] Police resources are allocated in precincts based on crime trends and patterns, and within precincts, specific beats are resourced in real time.

---

[3]However, New York City added a precinct in 1993, at the outset of the crime decline that lasted a decade.

[4]For example, the 22nd precinct is Central Park, where there is no population and little crime overall.

These differences matter. When Fagan et al. (2003) further disaggregated precincts into neighborhoods to reestimate local area affects of policing on crime, they reported different predictors of crime patterns in neighborhoods over time compared with the predictors at the precinct level.

Spatially smaller micro-trends, such as the ones detected by Weisburd et al. (2004) in Seattle, or the neighborhood models identified by Fagan et al. (2003) and Fagan and Davies (2004) in New York, may be masked in larger spatial aggregations, such as precincts or police districts. Covariates that control for compositional differences between precincts usually are computed from aggregations of census tract data. These aggregations of multiple neighborhoods in police districts raise risks of identification problems—if crime trends are a function of local social area or neighborhood effects (crime markets, population concentrations), these smaller area effects may be masked when heterogeneous, multineighborhood police districts or precincts are the unit of analysis.

The most common spatial unit used in analyzing crime trends (and many other neighborhood effects) is the tract (Hipp, 2007a,b; see also Sampson et al., 2002, for more detail). Tracts are smaller in both area and population and have the advantage of greater social homogeneity. But they also raise problems of spatial dependence since neighborhoods may span several tracts (this is discussed and illustrated in the next section). Tracts also change over time, multiplying as populations grow in a tract. Tracts in commercial areas have low populations, requiring the use of "journey" files that estimate the daytime and nighttime populations of tracts based on a complex algorithm using commuting times.

Other aggregations, such as planning districts in Chicago and neighborhoods in New York, solve these problems in terms of articulating "natural" boundaries that encompass areas with social meaning to their residents. For example, New York has defined neighborhood boundaries based on the work of Kenneth Jackson and John Manbeck (1998). Using historical data, tract boundaries, and interviews with local residents, they drew 330 neighborhood areas, each encompassing about 7 census tracts and between 25,000 and 45,000 people. Figures 4-1a and 4-1b show the relationship between neighborhoods and precincts and also precincts and census tracts.

These differences in area size and specification matter in the identification of crime trends. Figure 4-2 shows the results of semiparametric mixture (trajectory) models to identify trends in homicides over time in New York from 1985-2000. The top figure shows that we can identify four trajectory groups for neighborhoods, while three are identified for tracts in the bottom graph. The highest risks are concentrated in about one in nine neighborhoods, but one in five tracts. For neighborhoods, there is a second trajectory with more modest increases and declines. Each analysis shows stability in 45 per-

FIGURE 4-1a Shape file for New York City police precincts and census tracts.
SOURCE: Data obtained from http://www.infoshare.org.

cent of the units that are the lowest rate groups. Cross-tabulations of tracts and their neighborhood membership (not shown) show that these in fact are the same 45 percent. Although ANOVA tests using measures of social disorganization and economic deprivation showed similar predictors for the tract and neighborhood analyses, one difference did emerge—measures of spatial dependence (Moran's I) were not significant in the neighborhood models, but they were significant predictors in the tract models. The implications of this finding for conceptualizing "neighborhood" are discussed below.

Defining and Bounding Neighborhoods

The definition of "neighborhood" and the articulation of its spatial size and boundaries affect our estimates of crime trends. Definitions of neighborhood in sociology, geography, and criminology have varied over time, in part reflecting the process of development of the city itself. Definitions of

FIGURE 4-1b Shape file for New York City neighborhoods and police precincts.
SOURCE: Data obtained from http://www.infoshare.org.

"natural areas" over a century ago were based on the interplay of business competition and the growth of housing for workers near workplaces (Park, 1916; Park, Burgess, and McKenzie, 1925). Accordingly, neighborhoods included business, residences, and religious and social institutions that were part of the fabric that bound residents together. These areas also were connected to—and nested in—larger subdivisions of cities as well as to each other (Sampson et al., 2002; Shaw and McKay, 1943; Suttles, 1970). As cities grew and changed both commercially and demographically, the population composition of neighborhoods often changed, leading to changes in both its internal identity and cohesion as well as its relations to adjacent areas. At times, externalities imposed change, through the construction of public housing (Marcuse, 1995), or the replacement of slums with other housing reforms (Harcourt, 2005), or the construction of highways or other public works projects (Jacobs, 1961).

As a result, administrative boundaries sometimes became historical arti-

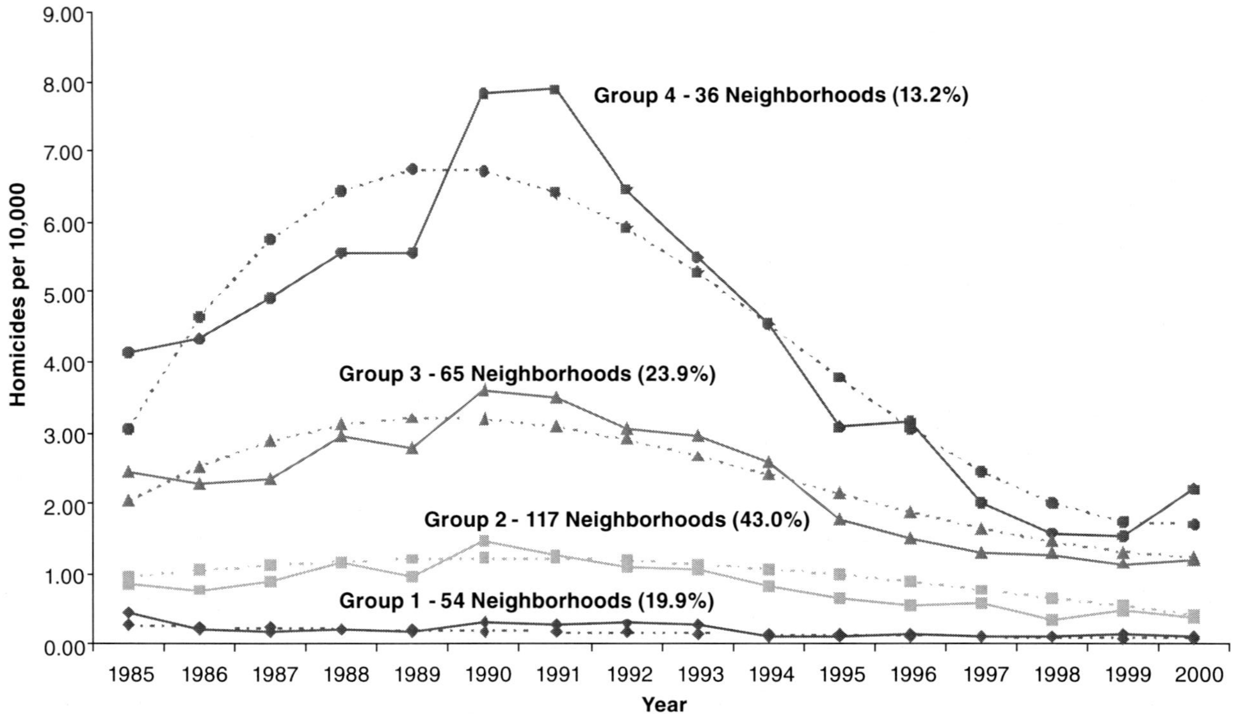

FIGURE 4-2a Trajectory models for homicides in New York City neighborhoods (N = 292), 1985-2000.

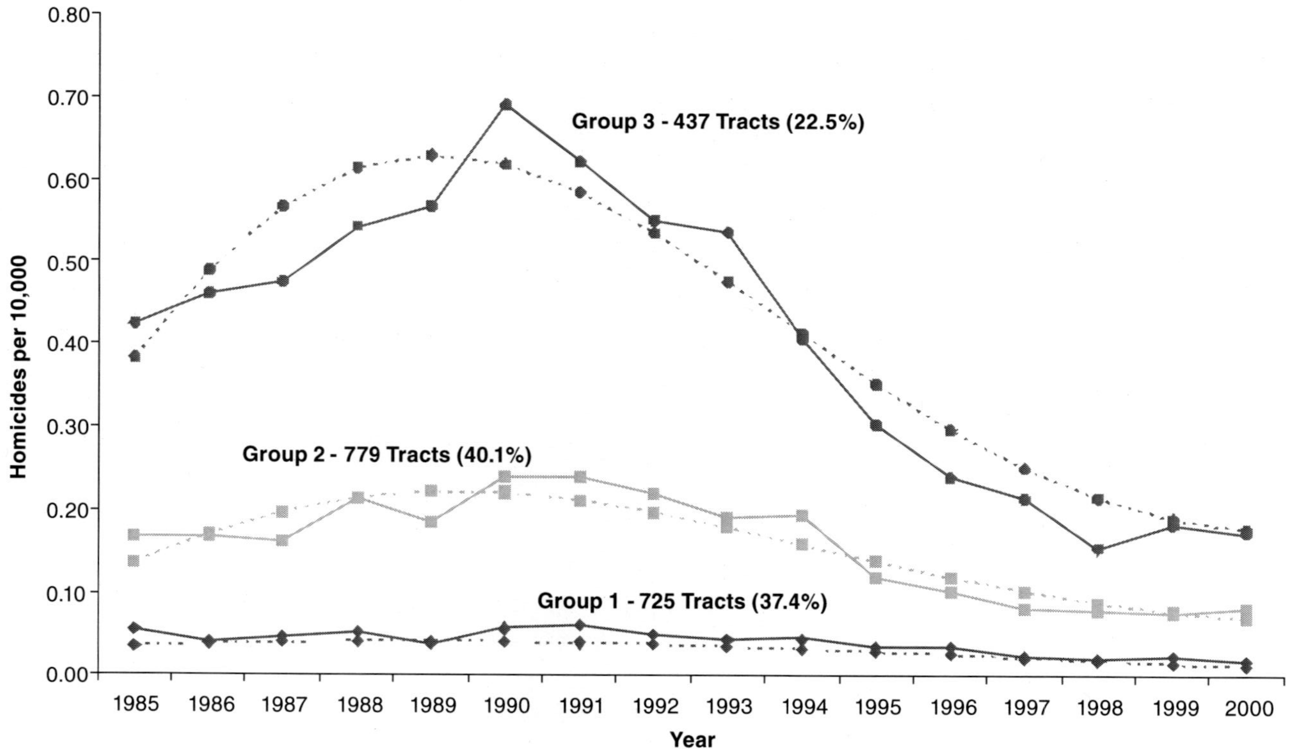

FIGURE 4-2b Trajectory models for homicides in New York City census tracts (N = 2,217), 1985-2000.

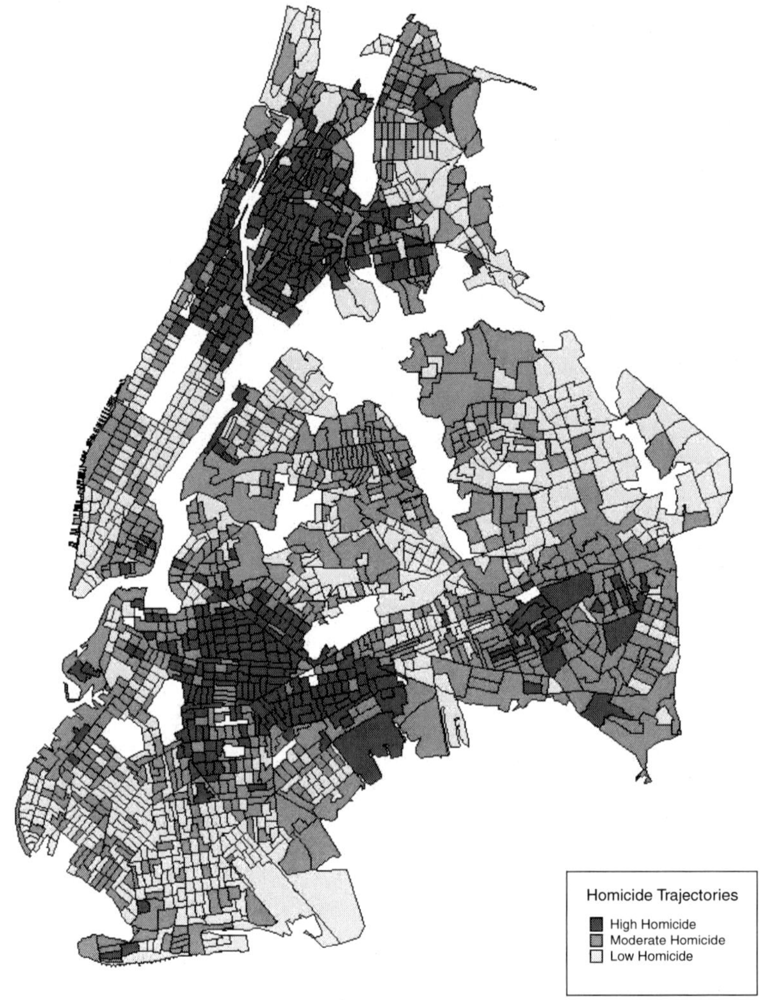

FIGURE 4-2c Homicide trajectory for New York City census tracts (N = 2,217), 1985-2002.

facts as neighborhoods changed. In addition to internal changes, concurrent changes in adjacent but administratively distinct areas could create social and economic ties that span those older boundaries and create cross-boundary social interactions or markets that complicate neighborhood analyses. So, a person's local environment may be influenced more by nearby locations that span administrative boundaries than by more distant locations in the same unit. A local environment thus needs to be defined as the proximity-weighted average of all surrounding locations in which a person interacts; in this formulation, proximity itself is a variable that needs both empirical and theoretical definition.

Accordingly, to understand what a neighborhood is and how it influences individuals, one needs to theorize the *relevant* contextual environment for a person or small local areas. For local social ties, the relevant context may be pedestrian-scale contexts (immediate block or blocks) (Grannis, 1998) or small location-based crime environments (Weisburd et al., 2004), which are most relevant for understanding neighborly interactions, social contact, etc. Or, if one conceptualizes relevant patterns of social interaction as based in economic or social institutions, then institutional-scale contexts (school attendance zones, shopping, churches, etc.) may be most relevant for the types of neighborhood (social) effects that are mediated through social institutions. Normalized or routinized economic activity also is defined in this context. Finally, these scales or contexts also are likely to have age-specific effects, so that the proscribed boundaries of child or adolescent interactions may differ in locus and scale from that which affects the social ties and behaviors of adults.

Figure 4-3 from Lee et al. (2008) illustrates these issues. Persons 2, 3, and 4 may share social ties, economic interests (either legal or illegal), and institutional affiliations. Yet they are separated for analytic purposes by the administrative boundary between Tracts A and B and (more important) are thought to be affected equally by either the structural or dynamic characteristics of their respective tract memberships. Person 6 in Tract C also shares Tract C characteristics with Persons 7 and 8, but the reality of her everyday interaction patterns is more likely to be influenced by the tract adjacent to the left (B). The difficulties of attributing in part or whole neighborhood effects equally to all three persons in Tract A or all three in Tract C are obvious. And, since no one in this example is living in Tracts D, E, and F, their influences may not be included analytically at all. Yet their proximity to Tracts A, B, and C suggests that its residents are likely to share economic, cultural, social, and institutional space with their neighbors, and have some influence on the behavior of nearby neighbors in adjacent tracts. Can spatial autocorrelation—either of dependent or independent measures—account for this? Not very well and only partially at best.

Lee et al. (2008), suggest an alternate strategy, in which each person's local environment is measured and aggregated across persons to estimate area effects as a continuous distribution that incorporates the shared influences of persons in "local communities" that span administrative boundaries. They suggest algorithms to estimate local area effects of relevant characteristics (e.g., policing, air quality, population density) in the local environment through careful aggregation of these characteristics in the

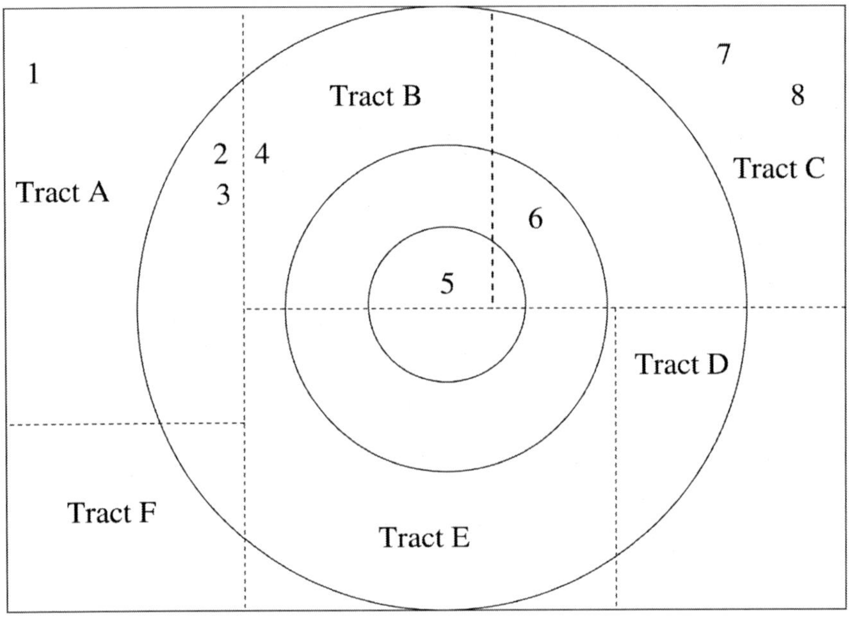

FIGURE 4-3 Proximity and local environments.
SOURCE: Lee et al. (2008).

surrounding areas weighted by proximity, density, or even network properties. This alternative rejects the notion of administrative boundaries to understand neighborhood and its effects, substituting both perceptions of persons in areas based on reciprocal influences on them and their neighbors who are in close proximity.

Grannis (1998) defined neighborhood by examined residential and street patterns and compared it with two measured dimensions of residents' lives: their social networks and cognitive maps of their areas. This approach is similar to the methods used by Jackson and Manbeck (1998) and Coulton, Korbin, and Chow (1995). Both of these fit well with Lee et al.'s notions of proximity, although Grannis focuses more closely on local residential interactions and their effects on micro-areas. Grannis's model produced good similarity in the boundaries drawn by the different individuals in the same areas and was especially efficient in explaining neighbors' efforts at social control.

Which, then, matters more: the perceived local environment, which may vary across developmental phases and particular social or economic contexts, or the structured environment, in which individuals cognitively structure their neighborhoods and each assigns contextual effects to those boundaries? Figure 4-3 shows the potential variability in the span of locational proximities. Estimates of neighborhood effects on crime may profit from using cognitively drawn boundaries to capture guardianship of specific areas as well as the allocations of formal (legal) and informal controls (see, for example, Sampson and Raudenbush, 2004). Developmental studies that track behavioral changes over the life course—whether in crime or other social interactions—may benefit more from capturing the multiple influences that shape behaviors and the varying combinations of influences at particular developmental stages.

The idea of direct measurement of neighborhood as a substitute for observational data is conceptually attractive but practically difficult. The methods to compute these effects are still developing, and such questions as the frequency of measurement, sampling frames, methods, and aggregation procedures require some experimentation. Because physical characteristics also are important features of neighborhood, direct measurement requires multiple methods, including social observation and interviews with residents. But the potential advantages of this strategy for understanding local crime trends and other social and institutional processes make a strong case for its importance as an alternative to the artificiality of current spatial thinking that often is a prisoner of arcane and incompatible administrative boundaries.

Theories of Change

Conceptualizing neighborhood is the central theoretical task in understanding neighborhood crime trends. A preliminary question is whether neighborhood change is implicated at all in changing crime trends. The answer depends, of course, on how one thinks about neighborhood. Until recently, studies of neighborhood effects—similar to city-level analyses—focused on the traditional characteristics of social disorganization, concentrated poverty and deprivation, segregation, and other social structural attributes and characteristics linked to the capacities of neighborhoods to exert social control. These characteristics were useful in differentiating which neighborhoods had higher risks of crime and violence over time, but they were less helpful in explaining change.[5]

One reason is that these characteristics may not change as quickly as changes in crime rates, or the scale of their changes may poorly match the rate or magnitude of changes in crime rates. Poverty, perhaps the most salient marker of neighborhood position, is stubbornly persistent over time (Sampson and Morenoff, 2006), and neighborhoods seldom change their ordinal ranking in disadvantage in a city even as their material conditions

[5]See, Bursik and Grasmick, 1993, for an exception.

may improve over time. Sampson and Morenoff (2006) show that the initial starting point for each place in a panel study of neighborhoods is the best predictor of where a neighborhood will rank over time. Thus, they characterize poor neighborhoods as poverty traps of "durable inequality" for which, beyond a tipping point, poverty will only ratchet up (Massey, 2007). For example, research on New York's crime decline typically controls for social structural attributes and characteristics at one time point (usually at the outset or midpoint of a panel) to isolate effects of neighborhoods or precincts on crime (Fagan and Davies, 2004; Rosenfeld et al., 2007). Others claim that the changes are too small and slow to account for sudden spikes or drops in crime (see Zimring, 2006) and that change need not be taken into account to understand crime trends.

That may be true for larger aggregates, such as police precincts or zip codes, perhaps because those aggregates are compositionally heterogeneous and smaller group-specific or small-area changes are hidden. But smaller units sometimes do change, usually in response to an external shock, such as deindustrialization (Galster and Mincy, 1993; Sampson and Wilson, 1995; Wilson, 1991), school desegregation (Weiner, Lutz, and Ludwig, 2006), or the passage of fair housing laws (Bursik, 1988). Recent studies show that the sudden influx of immigrants can also animate changes in crime. Saiz and Wachter (2006) suggest that housing prices grow more slowly in neighborhoods with higher rates of immigration, as a function of white flight and increased racial segregation. Sudden increases in numbers of immigrants can change the risks and rates of crime in either direction, often for the better (Massey, 1995, 2007; Massey and Denton, 1993). For example, MacDonald, Hipp, and Gill (2008) show that the succession of Mexican immigrants in poor neighborhoods in Los Angeles accounts for a significant portion of the crime decline in those areas. Martinez (2002) reports the same for Latino immigration and homicide in several cities.

But sudden increases in immigration also can destabilize neighborhoods, with crime increases following in short order. For example, the white population in the four census tracts in Washington Heights, in northern Manhattan, declined from 73 percent in 1970 to less than 25 percent in 1980, much of it replaced by Hispanic immigrants primarily from the Dominican Republic (Fagan, 1992). While crime rose across the city in this era, it rose more quickly in the Washington Heights neighborhood than in many other places where population characteristics were stable. The combination of rapid demographic change, access to transshipment routes, and a strategic location at the intersection of major highways connecting the city with the nearby suburbs from three states helped fuel the growth of a dynamic and violent drug market in this neighborhood that persisted for nearly two decades (Fagan, 1992). These rapid and significant changes, in a broader setting in which most areas change slowly and more modestly, show the need to decompose change and examine the effects of different levels and forms of change over time.

Beyond the pace and size of change the question remains as to what types of change to measure. A good starting point is to assume that the factors that typically explain neighborhood effects statically also will exert influences on crime rates as both crime and neighborhoods change. While the candidates are as broad as the literature on neighborhoods, one can identify three broad categories or domains of effects: social interactional mechanisms, political economy and institutional forces, and legal interventions. These three dynamics also may be reciprocal and over time become tightly wound in a social-institutional ecology of neighborhood.

Social Interactions and Social Organization

Social interactional mechanisms generally include the dynamic processes of what sociologists have traditionally termed informal social control. These include such factors as social ties, mutual trust, shared norms, social networks, and routine activities (see Sampson et al., 2002, for a review). These social processes and the forms of social organization that they influence or even produce become part of the dynamics of social regulation in neighborhoods, a process identified as collective efficacy by Sampson and colleagues (1997). The regulatory behaviors include willingness to intervene when wrongdoing takes place or to advocate for solutions to neighborhood problems, guardianship, and institutional participation (e.g., school boards, citizen groups) that can leverage services and resources. But adverse neighborhood change, such as increasing segregation and poverty concentration, can erode social control and social regulation, leading to a rejection of the social and moral norms underlying law and legal institutions (see Sampson and Bartusch, 1998, for an illustration in Chicago neighborhoods). The weaker social position of a neighborhood can also erode its leverage for essential services, launching a downward spiral in its social capital and regulatory efficacy. For now, there is limited evidence on whether changes in these mechanisms over time influence changes in crime rates, a product of the limited availability of neighborhood-level data on social interactions over sufficient periods to detect such effects.

Criminal groups and networks also are features of the social organization of neighborhoods that may exert strong influences on crime, and they may have variable presence and influence over time. The presence of gangs, for example, affects the developmental trajectories of adolescents and increases their risks for involvement in serious delinquency (Thornberry et al., 2004), sustain illegal markets in drugs (Levitt and Venkatesh, 2001; Venkatesh, 2000, 2006), and perpetuate lethal violence through recurring disputes (Papachristos, forthcoming). Like illegal markets, gangs are located in specific neighborhoods. Some gangs endure over time, others arise in specific eras and then dissipate (Klein, 1997). Drug-selling networks also are often location-based and themselves influence neighborhood social organization. They often are the targets of law enforcement, but they also exert their own brand of social influence and control on neighborhoods, a form of influence that can have the perverse effect of reducing crime to protect income-generating illegal activities (Fagan, 1992).

Political Economy

The broad category of political economy includes both institutional forces and the effects of physical structures in the neighborhood. Changes in the structure and composition of housing exerts an effect. For example, Schwartz, Susin, and Voicu (2003) linked changes in housing prices with changes in violent crime rates in New York; they show that in police precincts, declining crime rates through the 1990s stimulated a housing boom and increases in housing values. Fagan and Davies (2007) found the opposite: changes in housing prices stimulated changes in crime rates, and these effects were most salient in neighborhoods experiencing tipping points in crime. Looking back at Figure 4-1a, they show that the housing-crime relationship was strongest in Groups 3 and 4, while in wealthier areas, housing values rose while crime remained stable.

Other potentially important domains of housing include the locations of public housing and the potential leverage on crime either of policies designed to reduce collateral crime problems, such as drug dealing, or to aggressively monitor illegal occupancies. Construction of new housing and the replacement of dilapidated and condemned housing also can alter the social and economic landscape of communities by strengthening the social capital of local residents and increasing their capacities for local control (Saegert, Winkel, and Swartz, 2002).

In contrast, public housing developments maintain the concentration of poor families without altering the housing or social landscapes of their immediate social context. Public housing sites in New York are sited in the neighborhoods with the highest concentrations of homicides, regardless of whether the era was one with a high (1990) or low (2000) homicide rate (Fagan et al., 2007). Fagan and Davies (1999) illustrate the contagion effects of violence and other crime in and around public housing sites in New York. In a later analysis of the effects of drug enforcement in public housing, Fagan et al. (2007) show that policies targeting drug markets in and around public housing have crime reduction benefits for the surrounding neighborhood but limited benefits in the public housing projects. Accordingly, as housing and legal interventions improved in the areas surrounding public housing sites, the inability to transform either the physical features of public housing, to alter the mix of families and ameliorate concentration effects, or to change the perceptual frames of their residents, through either of these mechanisms, seemed to contribute to persistent crime problems over time.

What one sees, then, in such neighborhoods as the South Bronx and Red Hook in Brooklyn is that repairing or replacing poor housing with new developments potentially reduces the effects of physical disorder, and it may have a secondary effect on social disorder (Fagan et al., 2007; Geller, 2007). Physical disorder and social disorder are highly correlated, and "broken windows" theories posit that they combine to signal to would-be criminals that social control is weak. There have been several cross-sectional studies showing mixed results for this theory, but until recently there have been no panel studies to show whether changes in disorder lead to changes in crime. The few studies that do examine changes in disorder rely on observational data, including police-generated measures of disorder (e.g., Rosenfeld et al., 2007), which are less often based on citizen complaints of "violations," such as loud music or graffiti, than on police-initiated interventions.

The one panel design to test the influence of neighborhood disorder on crime was recently completed by Geller (2007), based on a longitudinal study of disorder in 55 subboroughs in New York from 1991 to 1999. Subboroughs (or subboros) are administrative boundaries designed by the Census Bureau to capture broad trends in housing. Geller used data from the Housing and Vacancy Survey (HVS), a survey conducted at three year intervals with subboros as the primary sampling unit. The HVS both replicates census variables for the person-level survey and measures housing characteristics for households. The HVS household data are used to index rent stabilization (i.e., rent control) rates in New York. Geller measured physical disorder using an index that includes housing conditions (broken windows, dilapidated walls and stairwells) and other neighborhood conditions (boarded-up buildings in the surrounding area) and compared it with crime rates in the subboros. Figure 4-4 shows a strong decline in crime, with the sharpest decline taking place in the most disorderly neighborhoods (in terciles). However, in a panel analysis in which she lagged disorder by one survey period and used fixed effects to account for unmeasured factors in the subboros plus a rich set of covariates, she found no effects of changing disorder on crime.

The inability to detect disorder effects on crime comports with the observations of Sampson and Raudenbush (2004) that disorder may be a social construction tied to the structural position of the residents of an area and their social position (Hipp, 2007). These studies raise doubts about whether physical and social disorder exerts an independent effect on crime that is separable from the poverty that almost always surrounds it. The most disorderly neighborhoods in New York also are the poorest (Fagan and Davies, 2000; Geller, 2007). If the links between disorder and crime

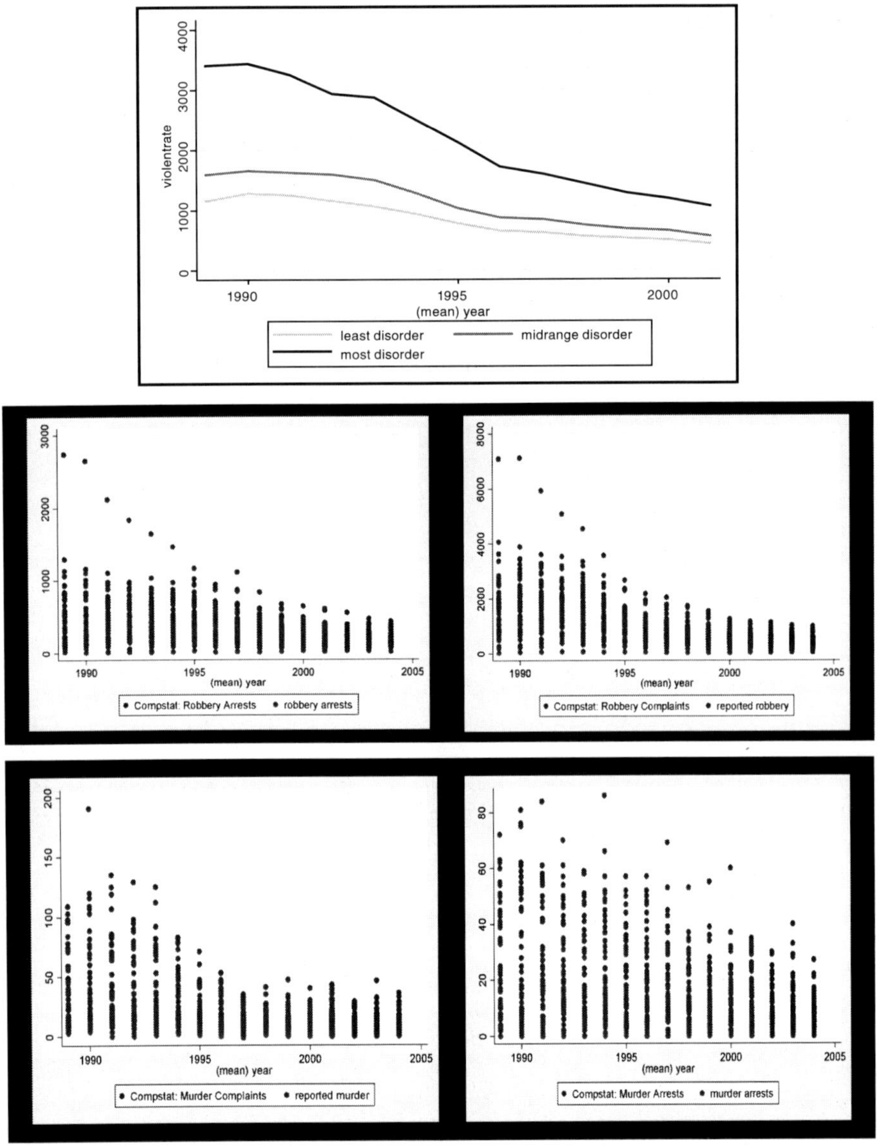

FIGURE 4-4 Physical disorder (broken windows) and felony violent crime rate per 10,000 persons, New York City subboros (N = 55), 1987-2002.
SOURCES: Geller, 2007; New York City Police Department, Statistical Report, Complaints and Arrests, various years; New York City Department of City Planning. Available: http://www.nyc.gov/html/dcp/pdf/census/cdsnar.pdf; New York City Housing and Vacancy Survey, various years, available: http://www.census.gov/hhes/www/housing/nychvs/nychvs.html.

are at best tenuous, then the decline in crime in these poorest—and most disorderly—neighborhoods may have less to do with disorder than with the forces impelling a broader and secular decline in crime that reflects more complex neighborhood changes in their social organization and political economy.

Immigration is one such change. The political economy and social organization of poor neighborhoods has been transformed by the rise in immigrant populations in New York's poorest neighborhoods (Fagan and Davies, 2006), and also in Los Angeles (MacDonald et al., 2008). Sociologists are now beginning to identify the secondary effects of the influx of immigrants on the social ties and economic activities in urban neighborhoods. In some cases, immigrants can increase risks of crime, as in the case of Washington Heights, discussed earlier. But there also is evidence from several cities, including Chicago, New York, Miami, and others, that the arrival of immigrants is associated with lower crime rates (Fagan and Davies, 2006; Martinez, 2002; Papachristos et al., 2007). Immigrants often seek neighborhoods that they can afford, and where people share racial or ethnic characteristics—that is, where people look like them. So they settle in areas that may have elevated crime risk, but their influence may alter that risk. They also may attract or develop commercial activity to provide essential services to newcomers, stimulating the creation of new institutions, such as churches and neighborhood self-help groups (Martinez and Valenzuela, 2006).

The causal mechanisms through which immigrants exert a protective effect on crime in neighborhoods that have concentrations of social structural risks are as yet unknown. Also, other studies of second and third generations of these immigrant families suggest that the protective effects may dissipate over time, with generational mixing and replacement that dilutes the selection effects of the first-generation settlers. But these processes vary by immigrant group. Smith (2005, p. 121) shows that most immigrants in the United Kingdom have low crime rates, but offending rates accelerate for second-generation Afro-Caribbeans but not among immigrants from South Asia. There is much that is not yet understood about this phenomenon, including its constancy across racial and ethnic groups, covariation with the characteristics of the landing neighborhoods, and the effects of human capital that new immigrants bring with them that advantages them in both in legal and informal workplaces.

Immigration illustrates a more general theoretical point: the movement of persons into and out of neighborhoods can alter the social composition, stability, and social organization of neighborhoods, affecting the social ties among neighbors and, in some cases, the networks of individuals through which crimes can occur or through which it is regulated and controlled. For example, exogenous shocks, such as court-ordered busing or economic downturns, have led to "white flight" in some places, producing sudden sharp and often adverse compositional changes. The churning effects of such population shifts tend to resegregate the abandoned neighborhoods as places where minority populations live in conditions of concentrated poverty, which tend to attenuate their life chances and the life chances of their children (see Frey, 1979, 1994). Such concentration effects sharpen the risk factors for crime (for a review, see Sampson and Wilson, 1995). Or, in the case of gentrification, these changes can homogenize neighborhoods but skew them toward less poverty. Gentrification draws better resourced persons who displace poorer long-term residents, often creating contrasts and tensions with surrounding areas that animate violent crime (see Taylor and Covington, 1988). Segregation and resegregation seem to be the rule; race and class integration of neighborhoods following population shifts are rare (Sampson and Sharkey, 2008; Sobel, 2006a).

Recent policy experiments tested the effects of housing vouchers as policy instruments to deconcentrate poverty and improve the well-being and safety of poor inner-city residents. Court-ordered desegregation of public housing in Chicago, for example, created the methodological conditions to test a different question: What are the effects on neighborhoods of moving disadvantaged persons living in poor neighborhoods with high crime rates to places that are more integrated, where poverty rates are lower and far less concentrated, and where schools and work opportunities are improved? These experiments and quasi-experiments produced inconsistent findings about the effects of such moves on individual families and on the neighborhoods to which they moved. Results from the Gautreaux program in Chicago, where 7,100 families used housing vouchers to relocate to private housing in Chicago and its suburbs, suggest positive effects on school outcomes and employment for the children in those families (Rosenbaum, 1995) and modest income and employment gains for the adults (Popkin, Rosenbaum, and Meaden, 1993). The Moving to Opportunities (MTO) program, a randomized experiment compared with the quasi-experimental design of Gautreaux, showed that many families moved to neighborhoods that were better off in terms of poverty, crime, and disorder (see, for example, Keel et al., 2005; Kling et al., 2004), but the effects on families were not as positive as in the Gautreaux program.

In comparing the outcomes of the Gautreaux and MTO initiatives and taking into account longer term neighborhood effects, including social ties, economic resources, and other services, Clampet-Lundquist and Massey (2008) show that neighborhoods exerted an independent and positive effect on the employment and earnings of MTO participants (but see Kling et al., 2004, and Ludwig et al., 2008). But the relocation of families from poor high-crime places raised the disturbing potential for criminogenic effects in the neighborhoods in which voucher recipients settled. Citing unpublished research by criminologists at the University of Memphis, Rosin (2008) claims that crime rates increased in the areas of that city in which families from high-crime neighborhoods relocated, while the neighborhoods they left experienced sharp drops in crime. No such effects were found in MTO, and Kling and Ludwig (2007) explicitly reject such "contagion" arguments.[6] Sampson and Sharkey (2008) suggest that when families relocate from poor places, there remains a stratification of incomes with virtually nonoverlapping income distributions and little exchange between minority and white areas. In other words, the interaction of selection effects and political economy produce racially configured hierarchies and equlibria of neighborhood inequality (Sampson and Sharkey, 2008). Crime patterns in new places reflect this inherent stability in reconstituted places, both neighborhood effects and their consequences endure, and these poverty traps appear to have their own perverse form of mobility.

Legal Interventions

The effects of policing and incarceration on crime have been examined in a variety of studies, and there is ample evidence that legal interventions can affect crime in both positive and negative ways. The question here is the relationship between legal interventions, neighborhood change, and crime. The few studies on this rely on observational data on both policing and crime, neither of which is unbiased. The usual research paradigm to estimate these effects is to examine a lagged measure of policing (arrests, expenditures, personnel) or incarceration rates (jail or prison admissions) on crime rates, with controls for the social structural conditions at the unit of analysis. Spatial dependence is not a factor, since most of these studies use larger spatial aggregates—such as police precincts—for which spatial dependence may be less influential on crime rates. The analyses may include fixed effects for both neighborhood units and time to isolate the effects of the policing or other legal variables.

The conceptual and analytic challenge in these designs is the identification of policing or other legal variables that interact with neighborhood structures or dynamics to shape the behavior of offenders or of neighbors who choose whether to participate in social regulation (see, for example, Fagan and Meares, 2008; Patillo, 1998). The "standard" paradigm is challenged to avoid the selection effects of how and where police and enforce-

---

[6]Ludwig and Kling find no evidence of contagion. Instead, Kling and Ludwig show that neighborhood racial segregation is the strongest predictor of variation between neighborhoods in arrests for violent crimes in the MTO sample. They speculate that factors such as drug market activity are more common in poorer neighborhoods with concentrations of minority residents.

ment are allocated. For example, Fagan and Davies (2000) showed that order maintenance policing in New York was concentrated in the city's poorest neighborhoods and that poverty and disorder were isomorphic in these analyses. One solution may be to use instrumental variables, but the selection of a valid instrument is difficult since many eligible candidates (e.g., health indicators, such as tuberculosis rates) are poorly measured over time locally. Also, changing neighborhoods may narrow the list of eligible instruments, since they also may be changing over time.

A second challenge in legal interventions is the relationship between policing and law enforcement generally and the reactions of local residents both to styles of policing and to the quality of interactions they and their neighbors have with police (National Research Council, 2004). Weitzer (2000) and Tyler and Fagan (2008) show that citizens react negatively to disrespectful policing and tend to withdraw from the social regulatory mechanisms that are an important of neighborhood controls on crime; they show that these effects are strongest in poorer neighborhoods and neighborhoods with high concentrations of minority citizens. These structural characteristics of policing, with the accompanying process dimensions, and the reactions of citizens are another type of neighborhood social interaction that is central to understanding neighborhood effects. Research has yet to capture these effects in panel designs to allow for tests over time of how changes in policing styles affect neighborhoods and crime.

Incarceration also affects neighborhoods (Clear, 2007). The movement of persons between prisons and neighborhoods is a dynamic process that unfolds over time and affects these areas in several ways. Returning inmates often place strains on their families and potentially weaken their participation in social control, both at home and among their neighbors. The concentrations of inmates in specific neighborhoods may attenuate property values, attract heightened surveillance by police, adversely affect child and adolescent development to increase risks of youth crime, and stigmatize the neighborhood and its residents in ways that could disadvantage them economically. If disenfranchised from electoral participation, for example, their political capital is weakened, and residents may have weaker influence and leverage to influence institutions and services in their areas. Returning prisoners also may bring with them mental health problems that can adversely affect the "psychological capital" of a neighborhood (Petersilia, 2003).

These processes may also reverse neighborhood fortunes at some tipping point. Crime may increase in response to changes in housing prices, for example, as neighborhoods change and newcomers come into conflict with long-time residents (Taylor and Covington, 1988). But crime may tip downward at some threshold of compositional change, even as prices continue to rise. The possibility of discrete eras separated by abrupt processes of neighborhood change suggests the need for analytic models that can account for contiguous but quite distinct ecological effects over time.

Endogeneity and Simultaneity

It is no surprise that neighborhood factors collapse into each other and into crime. That is, poverty, poor health, bad housing, weak social control, and other neighborhood deficits are highly correlated with each other and with crime, and their effects multiply to produce what Wilson (1987) termed "concentration effects." The interdependence of these factors in shaping the trajectory of neighborhood ecologies challenges researchers to identify or isolate specific effects of any single factor. These factors often are endogenous, meaning that they are linked in complex relationships where they affect each other reciprocally and simultaneously. Panel studies of neighborhoods further complicate endogeneity: the longer the time series, the more complicated the analysis, since different eras may experience different patterns and sources of change. Simultaneity raises parallel challenges in panel studies, with effects both sustained over closely spaced time intervals, and also exerting influences on other factors in the neighborhood ecology. Issues of endogeneity and simultaneity arise at the starting point of panels or time series and sustain over time (see, for example, Fagan et al., 2003, on the endogeneity of crime, neighborhood social structure, enforcement, and incarceration).

The social selection and self-selection of individuals to neighborhoods also raises the risk of aggregation biases that may affect our understanding of how these effects work in neighborhoods (Hipp, 2007; Wooldredge, 2002). Selection effects complicate inferences that might distinguish aggregation effects from structures and dynamic processes that are unique to neighborhoods, beyond the persons who live there (see Jencks and Mayer, 1990, for a discussion). Harding (2003) demonstrates a useful approach to resolving the problems of selection bias, confounding, unobserved heterogeneity, and omitted variable bias that complicate the estimation of neighborhood effects. Using a counterfactual causal framework based on propensity score matching and sensitivity analysis, he addresses the inherent endogeneity of adolescent development and neighborhood (see also MacDonald et al., 2007, on neighborhood contexts and citizen evaluations of police). The selection challenge is further complicated by the reality of changing neighborhoods, and these propensities must be recomputed periodically. And, there may be serial correlation or autoregression in the propensity scores themselves, due to relatively slow but measurable changes in neighborhood context.

Yet these problems are often ignored. Instrumental variables, or instruments, have some promise to address endogeneity (see, for an example,

Clear, 2007). Instruments can produce a consistent estimate of a causal effect when the predictors are correlated with the error terms. This often happens as a result of endogeneity (see, Levitt, 1998, for an example).

In panel designs of neighborhood change, there are risks with instruments: they too may change over time, and after a lengthy period of influence in a neighborhood, they may no longer be uncorrelated with the dependent variable at some tipping point. For example, crime may at the outset influence election cycles and put a more conservative party in office, but the relationship between crime and that party becomes endogenous over time. Or police may be assigned to high-crime areas, but they soon become part of the social fabric of the area and their presence endures over time. So instruments can be of help, but their selection is difficult and conceptually demanding. Also, the weaker the instrument, the larger the standard error and the more difficult it is to identify specific neighborhood effects.

One analytic solution is to use cross-lags, in which simultaneous regressions are estimated with reciprocal causal factors, each lagged simultaneously (Ferrer-Caia and McArdle, 2004). But the measurement constraints on cross-lag models—in terms of the number of predictors or covariates—are significant. Other solutions include using random effects for time to account for serial correlation or estimating (benchmark) endogeneity at the outset of a panel using simple ordinary least squares (OLS) regressions of the crime-neighborhood relationship. Returning to Harding, the counterfactual model offers a useful strategy for disentangling otherwise confounded effects produced by both endogeneity and simultaneity.

One final complexity in estimating the causal effects of neighborhoods is the inherent reliance on the stable unit treatment value assumption (SUTVA). Thinking about neighborhoods as a treatment for both individual and family, a basic neighborhood theory would demand homogeneity of treatment and no transference or interference among the residents—that is, one assumes that they are independently and identically distributed (Sobel, 2006a). This seems unreasonable, because of the network aspects of neighborhood life and the density of urban neighborhoods in particular, and also because of the complexity and heterogeneity of neighborhood components. But it is exactly that interference that may be the mechanism through which neighborhood acts (Sobel, 2006b), in turn making it inherently difficult to estimate neighborhood effects. When neighborhoods themselves are complex and changing contexts, the estimation of an average "treatment" effect becomes quite difficult. Sobel (2006b) warns that when interference is present among residents, there is a cross-level interaction of a structural or aggregate neighborhood effect that changes the meaning of the contextual effect estimate. Thus, one cannot empirically identify neighborhood effects when SUTVA is violated, but SUTVA is violated if one believes in neighborhood effects (Sobel, 2006a,b). This is a serious conundrum.

Data Limitations

Most studies use observational data to measure both crime and neighborhood characteristics, a matter of convenience and often necessity. Regression models with observational data can produce good fits, but they also risk biases in the regression coefficients models because of selection effects (Berk, Li, and Hickman, 2005).[7] While one compensates for the fact that people are not randomly assigned to neighborhoods nor are crime-control policies randomly distributed to neighborhoods, with propensity score models and other statistical accommodations, the success of these strategies depends on the nomination of, and data availability for, theoretically sensible components of a selection model. In considering neighborhood change, these complexities multiply.

Neighborhood data often are limited to observational measures representing compositional characteristics (e.g., income, ethnicity, unemployment rate, household structure, renter status) as proxies for the social mechanisms through which neighborhood effects are thought to operate (Pebley and Sastry, 2006). The Neighborhood Change Database (Tatian, 2003) illustrates the promise and limitations of neighborhood indicators that rely solely on structural features. Such limitations raise two important problems. First, neighborhood measures often are aggregated into administrative units that do not comport well with natural neighborhood boundaries or even with other administrative units. In New York, for example, precincts, tax collections, school districts, election districts, health service areas, mental health catchment areas, and census tracts are poorly aligned. The HVS sampling units (subboros) also are not aligned with any of the above, and census tracts often overlap the HVS units. The solutions to align and reconcile can be expensive and challenging. One solution is to obtain individual records by person or household, perhaps by student or recipient of key public services, and individually geocode each record. That would be prohibitively expense and raise privacy issues, particularly for children and in health settings. Another strategy is to use geographic information systems to generate comprehensive and compatible templates that can reconcile measures across bounded areas based on population weighting.

Second, compositional neighborhood data lack information on the neighborhood processes that connect structure to the moving parts of theory. For example, while many studies show a strong correlation between neighborhood poverty rates and crime, they rarely analyze data about the moving parts of a causal model of neighborhood effects to identify the mechanisms through which poverty influences neighborhood life: skewed

[7]In contrast, a very simple regression model for a properly implemented randomized experiment may not fit the data very well, but it is far more likely to produce unbiased estimates (Berk et al., 2005).

social networks, weak social organization, low levels of social ties and interactions among neighbors, levels of institutional participation, or the elasticity of social ties beyond the neighborhood's boundaries. Rarely are data available, either at a static point or in a panel design over time, to measure what Sobel (2006a) terms the *interference* of neighborhood effects (but see Grannis, 1998; Sampson and Raudenbush, 2004; Sastry, Ghosh-Dastidar, Adams, and Pebley, 2006). Causal modeling of neighborhood effects under these circumstances is analytically risky.

But the creation of these data is essential to developing a data infrastructure to study neighborhood dynamics and neighborhood changes over time. Data on residents' social interactions and networks within "natural" neighborhood boundaries require systematic data collection across neighborhoods on samples of residents (see, for example, Grannis, 1998; the Los Angeles Family and Neighbors Study in Sastry et al., 2006). These data can be combined with administrative data and resident surveys to develop rich datasets on the development of communities and their change over time. The frameworks suggested by Lee et al. (perceived environments) and Grannis (social interactional spaces) could be combined with observational (Sampson and Raudenbush, 1999) and administrative data to measure the types of densities and proximities to local institutions and networks that comprise the dynamic component of neighborhood effects. This would be a resource-intensive effort: the data must be collected by researchers themselves through interviews or direct observation (Pebley and Sastry, 2006; Sampson and Raudenbush, 1999).

Similar problems are evident in the measurement of crime and the availability of crime data. Not all cities make crime data available in a sufficiently flexible form to allow for spatial disaggregation in small units of resolution. In New York, for example, only complaints and arrests are reported, and only for precincts. Data on police beats or other data with spatial coordinates are not reported. Contrast this with the micro-data analyzed by Weisburd et al. (2004). Depending on the theoretical question, data on crime event locations and circumstances, together with victim and offender characteristics and residential information, are needed to answer important questions about neighborhoods and crime. Calls-for-service data also are indicators about crime and neighborhood. Calls for service reflect the propensity of residents in different neighborhoods to report crime to the police; they can represent social disorder or social disorganization, and they can address questions about the utilization of police services and the character of informal social control (Black, 1983, 1989) or the perceptions of citizens of the legitimacy of law and legal actors (Tyler and Fagan, 2008). Some researchers have analyzed call data to show crime hot spots to guide the allocation of police resources (Weisburd et al., 2004). There are some technical problems in calls data, including duplications (multiple reports of the same crime), errors (e.g., confusion of gunshots with a car backfiring, erroneous reports of weapons being brandished, cars that are used by one family member unknown to others who then report it as stolen), and inconsistencies in aggregation and reporting by type of crime (e.g., where the gunshot was heard may be some distance from where the gun was fired). These issues require data cleaning and quality checks to ready them for analysis of neighborhood effects.

Homicide records are the most stable measure over time and are available from multiple sources—both police and public health sources. The comparative validity of data from these two sources may vary from city to city and year to year. For example, there may be discrepancies in which fatalities are classified as homicide versus accidental deaths or unclassified deaths whose cause is not determined. Public health data on nonfatal injuries also has proven to be a valuable source as an alternative to subjective criminal legal categories, such as assault (see, for example, Zimring and Hawkins, 1997). For crimes other than violence, particularly property crimes, alternatives to criminal justice data are needed to capture crime trends that may be unreported to the police. In this regard, alternate sources, such as insurance records for theft and burglary losses, are important stopgaps to data gaps in administrative sources on crime. Insurance rate data also provide an alternate framework to assess neighborhood risk, particularly for property crimes, including residential burglary and property theft. The availability of these series over time is a distinct advantage for the measurement of neighborhood change.

CONCLUSIONS

Neighborhood influences on crime have been an enduring and central theme in criminological research for over a century. Theoretical and research attention on neighborhoods has been tied to broader interests in understanding how social influences contribute, either directly or in conjunction with individual influences, to the causes and control of crime. Interest in neighborhood influences transcends particular subareas in the study of crime, with important contributions to the study of crime causation or motivation, mechanisms of formal and informal social control, and now, at the conclusion of a full epidemic cycle of rising and falling violent crime rates, its influence on long-term temporal crime trends. In recent years, the study of neighborhood effects has evolved from static to dynamic effects: interest in life-course studies of individuals now parallels studies of neighborhood change, and the interaction of these two dynamics is the focus of this chapter.

The robust research activity on neighborhoods and neighborhood change has faced down serious challenges and continues to advance. We have now reached a tipping point in modern community research at which the evidence is more conclusive than it was in the Chicago era, nearly a century ago. And the methods and measures are much improved as well. Neighborhood studies and approaches have limitations, but the logical connections among them suggest a cumulative body of evidence that has made—and will continue to make—important contributions to theory and knowledge. The confluences among studies suggest new directions to disentangle the dynamics of neighborhood change and crime.

Accordingly, beyond responding to the challenges identified in this chapter, a research agenda to advance the study of dynamic change in neighborhoods and crime trends requires two separate streams of thought. One is a set of research questions that can establish basic facts about change and its importance. The other is the design of an infrastructure of data and analytic tools that can sustain the science of studying neighborhood change.

Essential Questions

Neighborhoods do change, some more quickly or slowly than others, apart from any changes in crime. And crime is part of the neighborhood landscape or ecology, and so crime change is, in fact, neighborhood change. This leads to several essential questions about crime and neighborhood change. First, what proportion of change in crime rates, up or down, is attributable to change in neighborhood contexts? Some portion or components of the variance in crime change is attributable to neighborhood change, but other parts of it may be part of secular trends or other unobserved exogenous factors. Understanding the leverage that neighborhoods have over crime rates is an important part of understanding both crime trends and neighborhood ecology.

Second, what are the causal paths? In other words, what is leading what? Since these changes may be closely spaced temporally, are the simultaneity problems insurmountable? Are there nonrecursive, reciprocal processes that make crime change and neighborhood change parts of a systemic process that perhaps is better understood not through multivariate models but through models and paradigms of equilibrium (see Persico, Todd, and Knowles, 2001, for an example)? Each of these causal arrangements raises difficult identification problems that will require analytic tools that are not part of the historically comfortable package of regression solutions.

Third, neighborhoods exist in conjunction with one another, as part of a larger urban ecology. At a minimum, they may be mutually influential, or the influence may be skewed, with one area dominating the other. What, then, is the reciprocity between neighborhoods? What are the processes of exchange and mutual influence or even unilateral influence? Why do some neighborhoods change faster or in a different direction than the adjacent areas, and is this important for a neighborhood that is relative stable but surrounded by dynamically changing areas? When policies target a specific area, can one isolate mutual or spatial influence of the surrounding areas from the effects of external shocks or policy instruments? And at some point in the evolution of neighborhoods, do those shocks eventually become internalized into neighborhood ecology?

Another domain of questions focuses on between-neighborhood differences. Crime trends in cities are very local: the largest changes, whether up or down, are limited to a relatively small group of neighborhoods within the larger city landscape (see, for example, Figures 4-2a and 4-2b). Even with rapid change and sharp crime declines, the relative position of most neighborhoods at any point in time remains the same (Sampson and Morenoff, 2006), suggesting that neighborhoods themselves exist in a larger political economy of the city. The enduring nature of their relative poverty in the face of material neighborhood improvements (including better housing and lower crime rates) raises a particular challenge: there is little chance that poor neighborhoods will change places with their wealthier counterparts. Given the spatial dependence of poverty concentrations, positive neighborhood change may in fact be fragile and at risk for reversing if broader social and economic conditions worsen (Sampson and Morenoff, 2006, p. 200). Thus, change can be curvilinear, with neighborhood fortunes improving and declining at different points in their life cycle. An important research question, then, is where the tipping point is for positive neighborhood change to be sustainable, and when it might be more fragile and reversible. Card, Mas, and Rothstein (2007) suggest that the tipping point for racial segregation is between 5 and 20 percent white (see Sampson and Morenoff, 2006), with predictably adverse consequences in terms of rents, housing prices, and other neighborhood characteristics.

Thus, neighborhoods have trajectories of change, which are likely to vary among neighborhoods (see, for example, Figures 4-2a–c). Research should test various theoretical propositions about factors that distinguish neighborhoods in the magnitude of increase and decline in their crime rates, and why these factors do not lead to more extensive changes in the social position of neighborhoods relative to the whole. In other words, what is it, when crime rates decline, that maintains the social order of neighborhoods, leaving the same ones vulnerable to crime epidemics in subsequent eras?

The final set of questions addresses the policy levers that induce neighborhood change in a way that can influence crime trends. In some cases, these policies were designed to alter conditions with no attention to crime, but their effects on crime, however incidental, can be salient and beneficial. Recent studies suggest, as discussed earlier, two domains of urban policy that can be analyzed in a search for effects on crime trends: housing and immigration. Other domains of urban policy, including family and child support or child care, public assistance experiments, and mental health interventions, can also be mined to see if there are unintended or collateral effects on crime. The design of these initiatives often falls short of the standards of social experimentation, yet there is much to be learned from a series of quasi-experiments that can be run on neighborhoods with different paths of change that have experienced one or more of these social interventions.

Building a Data Infrastructure for Understanding Neighborhoods and Crime

Research on neighborhoods and crime often begins anew with each project. Researchers reach into archives of existing data and approach agencies for updates and supplements to bring the measures up to date. Rarely is updating routinized in agencies unless there are institutional norms or legislative mandates to do so. (Crime may be an exception, based on both reporting mandates and needs for good data to support investigations.) Compiling reliable measures of the complex dimensions of neighborhoods over a period of time necessary to identify changes is a difficult challenge (see, for example, Tatian, 2003). Data are maintained separately by agency, rarely aggregated to similar spatial units, and (in the extreme) in languages that are better suited to administrative needs than for research. These difficulties are compounded by the diverse theoretical interests that are identified in this chapter.

An infrastructure for neighborhood data in cities is needed to support research on neighborhoods and crime, and such an infrastructure should be maintained in archives that are accessible to users with minimal administrative burdens. The Neighborhood Change Database is one such effort. Privacy concerns are limited in these proposals, since crime data often are aggregated administratively, as are data on attributes and characteristics of neighborhood ecology. Risks to human subjects are mitigated in neighborhood research that focuses on changes in rates of crime or social structural and other ecological parameters in areas over time. For example, neighborhood studies are likely to rely on observational data that often is deidentified to reduce risks from accidental disclosure. But privacy concerns may arise in the study of the social organization of neighborhoods and networks in them. Here, we can emphasize the importance of the regulatory functions in universities and research institutes that are charged with the protection of human research subjects from social risk and psychological harm.

Beyond these regulatory strategies, the social norms and ethical standards of researchers and their professional associations also can buttress respect for privacy and confidentiality. For example, the identities of distressed neighborhoods should be guarded whenever possible, to prevent stigmatization in the form of redlining or other deinvestments. Yet this raises a tension when spatial analyses of neighborhoods are employed, and the results are often displayed using maps.

One could argue plausibly that there is value in both national archives and local or regional ones. My preference is for the local. Archives of cross-city data are challenged to construct files with similar elements so as to avoid measurement errors arising from inconstancy in the underlying meaning of variables that may be based on different metrics across variable local contexts. Local data archives should feature data drawn from in the city or region and contributed by institutions and agencies under local working agreements and data-sharing arrangements. For example, within the Neighborhood Change Database project are more than 15 local supplemental archives. Locally designed archives have the advantage of building on national templates for both observational and survey data and then enriching these through measures that capture the texture of each city's neighborhoods. These additional elements could include direct observations of neighborhood interaction data that are coupled with surveys and local administrative datasets on compositional characteristics of neighborhoods as well as social outcomes across a range of behavioral dimensions (Raudenbush and Sampson, 1999).

A useful example of a dataset design that addresses both individual and neighborhood change is the Program in Human Development in Chicago Neighborhoods, in which the sampling design explicitly anticipates analyses of both individuals and neighborhood effects as well as their multilevel or hierarchical effects (Raudenbush and Sampson, 1999; Sampson, Raudenbush, and Earls, 1997). In Los Angeles, the Los Angeles Family and Neighborhoods Study is a similar effort that has produced a rich dataset paralleling the structure and interests of the Chicago study (Sastry et al., 2006; Pebly and Sastry, 2006), although with emphasis on developmental outcomes and less focus on antisocial behavior. In the Los Angeles study, neighborhood appears to have independent effects on child development net of individual and family characteristics, and the explained variance of neighborhood factors well outweighs the other effects (Pebley and Sastry, 2006).

There are a number of administrative datasets, ongoing surveys, and other data massing and integration projects that can be incorporated into these local archives or that can serve as templates for the design of a local archive. For example, the New York HVS, the Youth Risk Behavior Survey, the National Longitudinal Survey of Youth 97 (NLSY97), and others in progress all have local components that could be expanded and designed into local ongoing efforts. Surveys should also delve into the social interactions of neighborhoods to better understand the moving parts of neighborhood social control. In the health care system, vital statistics data in most cities and states provide addressable data on fatalities that can supplement police records. Most cities maintain zoning and housing indicators (sale prices, rent indices, etc.) to allow for measurement of the built environment in neighborhoods. School, health care, and public assistance records all can provide important information on composition that can supplement surveyed and observed data.

The final consideration is the pace of change and the schedule and spacing of data points. What are reasonable assumptions about neighborhood change and crime change that would determine the right frequency of observations? Some changes are slow, as in changes in the built environment, and others may be relatively quick, as in the case of the sudden population shift in Washington Heights reported by Fagan (1992). This pace itself can churn neighborhoods in a way to quickly change both patterns of social interaction and other neighborhood barometers such as crime rates. This would suggest more frequent observations, certainly more frequent than the decennial census and closer in timing to the Census Bureau's American Community Survey. A second consideration is the lag time that is theorized between change in a causal factor and the observed change in a social outcome. These lag times will vary by outcome domain: school test scores may improve more slowly than will changes in the crime rate.

The design of such archives and the infrastructure that is created will require both resources and political will to set institutional incentives for agencies to contribute. Crime data in particular may be a political question; there are risks in transparency that inelasticity in crime rates will be seen as political failure. What incentives are there for police to create stronger and more accessible crime data with local addressability, incentives that can offset the political risks that some departments may fear? There are two ways to address these requirements. Open records laws often provide the institutional aegis for the release of information on crime and neighborhoods to sustain research.[8] One way to address this is by shifting social and professional norms toward more open and transparent data systems to monitor changes in local crime rates that mirror changes in each city's neighborhoods.

[8]See, for example, Florida's Open Records Law, FL Statutes §119 (http://www.leg.state.fl.us/statutes/index.cfm?app_mode=display_statute&url=ch0119/ch0119.htm), describing the requirements and procedures for publicly available information while setting forth privacy restrictions that safeguard sensitive information about individuals.

REFERENCES

Anderson, Elijah. (1994, May). The code of the streets. *The Atlantic Monthly,* 81-94.

Anderson, Elijah. (1999). *Violence and the code of the street: Decency, violence and the moral life of the inner city.* New York: Norton.

Bellair, Paul. (2000). Informal surveillance and street crime: A complex relationship. *Criminology, 38,* 137-169.

Berk, Richard A. (2005). Knowing when to fold 'em: An essay on evaluating the impact of Ceasefire, Compstat, and Exile. *Criminology and Public Policy, 4*(3), 451-465.

Berk, Richard A., Azusa Li, and Laura J. Hickman. (2005). Statistical difficulties in determining the role of race in capital cases: A re-analysis of data from the state of Maryland. *Journal of Quantitative Criminology, 21*(4), 365-390.

Black, Donald. (1983). Crime as social control. *American Sociological Review,* 48(1), 34-45.

Black, Donald. (1989). *Sociological justice.* New York: Oxford University Press.

Blumstein, Alfred, and Joel Wallman. (2000). *The crime drop in America.* New York: Cambridge University Press.

Brooks-Gunn, Jeanne, Gregory J. Duncan, Pamela K. Klebanov, and Naomi Sealand. (1993). Do neighborhoods influence child and adolescent development? *American Journal of Sociology, 99,* 353-395.

Browning, Christopher R., Seth L. Feinberg, and Robert D. Dietz. (2004). The paradox of social organization: Networks, collective efficacy, and violent crime in urban neighborhoods. *Social Forces, 83*(2), 503-534.

Bursik, Robert J., Jr. (1984). Urban dynamics and ecological studies of delinquency. *Social Forces, 63*(2), 393-413.

Bursik, Robert J., Jr. (1988). Social disorganization and theories of crime and delinquency: Problems and prospects. *Criminology, 26,* 519-551.

Bursik, Robert J., Jr., and Harold G. Grasmick. (1992). Longitudinal neighborhood profiles in delinquency: The decomposition of change. *Journal of Quantitative Criminology, 8*(3), 247-263.

Bursik, Robert J., Jr., and Harold G. Grasmick. (1993). Economic deprivation and neighborhood crime rates, 1960-1980. *Law and Society Review, 27*(2), 263-283.

Bursik, Robert J., Jr., and Jim Webb. (1982). Community change and patterns of delinquency. *American Journal of Sociology, 88*(1), 24-42.

Card, David, Alexandre Mas, and Jesse Rothstein. (2007). *Tipping and the dynamics of segregation.* (NBER Working Paper No. 13052.) Cambridge, MA: National Bureau of Economic Research. Available: http://www.nber.org/papers/w13052 [accessed August 2008].

Clampet-Lundquist, Susan, and Douglas S. Massey. (2008). Neighborhood effects on economic self-sufficiency: A reconsideration of the moving to opportunities experiment. *American Journal of Sociology, 114*(1), 67-93.

Clear, Todd R. (2007). *Imprisoning communities: How mass incarceration makes disadvantaged neighborhoods worse.* New York: Oxford University Press.

Cook, Philip J., and John H. Laub. (1998). The unprecedented epidemic in youth violence. In Michael Tonry and Mark H. Moore (Eds.), *Youth violence.* Chicago: University of Chicago Press.

Cook, Philip J., and John H. Laub. (2001). After the epidemic: Recent trends in youth violence in the United States. In Michael Tonry (Ed.), *Crime and justice: A review of research* (pp. 1-37). Chicago: University of Chicago Press.

Corman, Hope, and Naci Mocan. (2000). A time-series analysis of crime, deterrence, and drug abuse in New York City. *American Economic Review, 90*(3), 584-604.

Coulton, Claudia J., Jill E. Korbin, M. Su, and J. Chow. (1995). Community-level factors and child maltreatment rates. *Child Development, 66*, 1262-1276.

Crane, Jonathan. (1991). The epidemic theory of ghettos and neighborhood effects on dropping out and teenage childbearing. *American Journal of Sociology, 96*(5), 1226-1259.

Donohue, John J., and Justin Wolfers. (2005). Use and abuses of empirical evidence in the death penalty debate. *Stanford Law Review, 58*(4), 791-845.

Eckberg, Douglas L. (1995a). Estimates of early twentieth-century U.S. homicide rates: An econometric forecasting approach. *Demography, 32*(1), 1-16.

Eckberg, Douglas L. (1995b). *What homicide epidemic? Long-term vital statistics trends.* Presented at the annual meeting of the American Association for the Advancement of Science, Atlanta, February.

Fagan, Jeffrey. (1992). Drug selling and licit income in distressed neighborhoods: The economic lives of street-level drug users and dealers. In George E. Peterson and Adelle V. Harrell (Eds.), *Drugs, crime and social isolation: Barriers to urban opportunity* (pp. 99-142). Washington, DC: Urban Institute Press.

Fagan, Jeffrey, and Garth Davies. (1999). Crime in public housing: Two-way diffusion effects in surrounding neighborhoods. In Victor Goldsmith, Philip G. McGuire, John Mollenkopf, and Timothy Ross (Eds.), *Analyzing Crime Patterns: Frontiers of Practice* (pp. 121-136). Thousand Oaks, CA: Sage Publications

Fagan, Jeffrey, and Garth Davies. (2000). Street stops and "broken windows": *Terry*, race, and disorder in New York City. *Fordham Urban Law Journal, 28*, 457-504.

Fagan, Jeffrey, and Garth Davies. (2004). The natural history of neighborhood violence. *Journal of Contemporary Criminal Justice, 20*(2), 127-149.

Fagan, Jeffrey, and Garth Davies. (2006). *Crime and immigration.* Presented at the annual meeting of the American Society of Criminology, Los Angeles.

Fagan, Jeffrey, and Garth Davies. (2007). *The political economy of the crime decline in New York City.* Presented at the annual meeting of the American Association for the Advancement of Science, San Francisco, February.

Fagan, Jeffrey, and Tracey L. Meares. (2008). Punishment, deterrence and social control: The paradox of punishment in minority communities. *Ohio State Journal of Criminal Law* 6(2), 173-229.

Fagan, Jeffrey, Franklin E. Zimring, and June Kim. (1998). Declining homicide in New York: A tale of two trends. *Journal of Criminal Law and Criminology, 88*, 1277-1324.

Fagan, Jeffrey, Juanjo Medina-Ariza, and Susan Wilt. (2002). *Social and ecological risks of domestic and non-domestic violence against women in New York City.* (Final Report, National Institute of Justice, Grant #1999-WT-VW-0005.) Washington, DC: U.S. Department of Justice.

Fagan, Jeffrey, Valerie West, and Jan Holland. (2003). Reciprocal effects of crime and incarceration in New York City neighborhoods. *Fordham Urban Law Journal, 30*, 1551-1602.

Fagan, Jeffrey, Garth Davies, and Jan Holland. (2007). Drug control in public housing: The paradox of the drug elimination program in New York City. *Georgetown Journal on Poverty Law and Policy, 8*(3), 415-460.

Ferrer-Caia, Emilio, and John J. McArdle. (2003). Alternative structural models for multivariate longitudinal data analysis. *Structural Equation Modeling, 10*, 493-524.

Frey, William H. (1979). Central city white flight: Racial and nonracial causes. *American Sociological Review, 44*(3), 425-448.

Frey, William H. (1994). The new white flight: New migration patterns are creating three separate, unequal Americas. *American Demographics, 16*(4), 1-40.

Galster, George C., and Ronald B. Mincy. (1993). Understanding the changing fortunes of metropolitan neighborhoods, 1980 to 1990. *Housing Policy Debate, 4*(3), 303-352.

Geller, Amanda B. (2007). Neighborhood disorder and crime: An analysis of *Broken Windows* in New York City. Ph.D. dissertation, School of Social Work, Columbia University.

Gladwell, Malcolm. (1996). *The tipping point*. Boston: Little, Brown.

Gostin, Lawrence. (1991). The interconnected epidemics of drug dependency and AIDS. *Harvard C.L.-C.R. Law Review, 26*(1), 113-184.

Gostin, Lawrence O., Scott Burris, and Zita Lazzarini. (1999). The law and the public's health: A study of infectious disease law in the United States. *Columbia Law Review, 99*(1), 59-64.

Gould, Madelyn S. (1990). Teenage suicide clusters. *Journal of the American Medical Association, 263*(15), 2051-2052.

Gould, Madelyn S., Sylvan Wallenstein, Marjorie H. Kleinman, Patrick O'Carroll, and James Mercy. (1990). Suicide clusters: An examination of age-specific effects. *American Journal of Public Health, 80*(2), 211-212.

Grannis, Rick. (1998). The importance of trivial streets: Residential streets and residential segregation. *American Journal of Sociology, 103*(6), 1530-1564.

Griffiths, Elizabeth, and Jorge M. Chavez. (2004). Communities, street guns, and homicide trajectories in Chicago, 1980-1995: Merging methods for examining homicide trends across space and time. *Criminology, 42*(4), 941-978.

Harcourt, Bernard. (2001). *Illusion of Order: The false promise of broken windows policing.* Cambridge, MA: Harvard University Press.

Harcourt, Bernard. (2005). *Policing L.A.'s skid row: Crime and real estate development in downtown Los Angeles (an experiment in real time).* Chicago: University of Chicago Legal Forum.

Harding, David J. (2003). Counterfactual models of neighborhood effects: The effect of neighborhood poverty on dropping out and teenage pregnancy. *American Journal of Sociology, 109*(3), 676-719.

Harrell, Adelle, and Caterina Gouvis. (1994). *Predicting neighborhood risk of crime*. Washington, DC: The Urban Institute.

Heitgerd, Janet L., and Robert J. Bursik. (1987). Extracommunity dynamics and the ecology of delinquency. *American Journal of Sociology, 92*(4), 775-787.

Hipp, John R. (2007a). Block, tract and levels of aggregation: Neighborhood structure and crime and disorder as a case in point. *American Sociological Review, 72*(5), 659-680.

Hipp, John R. (2007b). Income inequality, race, and place: Does the distribution of race and class within neighborhoods affect crime rates? *Criminology, 45*, 665-697.

Jackson, Kenneth, and John Manbeck. (1998). *The neighborhoods of Brooklyn*. New Haven, CT: Yale University Press.

Jacobs, Jane. (1961). *The death and life of great American cities*. New York: Random House.

Jargowsky, Paul A. (1997). *Poverty and place: Ghettos, barrios, and the American city*. New York: Russell Sage Foundation.

Jencks, Christopher, and Susan E. Mayer (1990). The social consequences of growing up in a poor neighborhood. In National Research Council, *Inner-city poverty in the United States* (pp. 111-186). Laurence E. Lynn and Michael G. H. McGeary (Eds.), Committee on National Urban Policy, Commission on Behavioral and Social Sciences and Education. Washington, DC: National Academy Press.

Kahan, Dan M. (1997). Social influence, social meaning, and deterrence. *Virginia Law Review, 83*(2), 349-395.

Keels, Micere, Greg Duncan, Stefanie DeLuca, Ruby Mendenhall, and James Rosenbaum. (2005). Fifteen years later: Can residential mobility programs provide a long-term escape from neighborhood segregation, crime, and poverty? *Demography, 42*(1), 51-73.

Kelling, George, and Catherine Cole. (1996). *Fixing broken windows*. New York: Free Press.

Kirk, David S., and Andrew V. Papachristos. (2007). *Legal cynicism and the framing of neighborhood violence: Implications for "neighborhood effects" research*. Available: http://ssrn.com/abstract=1081894 [accessed August 2008].

Klein, Malcolm W. (1997). *The American street gang: Nature, prevalence, and control*. New York: Oxford University Press.

Kling, Jeffrey R., Jeffrey B. Liebman, Lawrence F. Katz, and Lisa Sanbonmatsu. (2004). *Moving to opportunity and tranquility: Neighborhood effects on adult economic self-sufficiency and health from a randomized housing voucher experiment*. (Princeton University Department of Economics, Industrial Relations Section Working Paper #481.) Princeton, NJ; Princeton University. Available: http://ideas.repec.org/p/pri/indrel/860.html [accessed August 2008].

Kling, Jeffrey R., Jens Ludwig, and Lawrence F. Katz. (2005). Neighborhood effects on crime for female and male youth: Evidence from a randomized housing voucher experiment. *Quarterly Journal of Economics, 120*, 87-130.

Kling, Jeffrey R., Jeffrey B. Liebman, and Lawrence F. Katz. (2007). Experimental analysis of neighborhood effects. *Econometrica, 75*(1), 83-119.

Knowles, John, Nicola Persico, and Petra Todd. (2001). Racial bias in motor vehicle searches: Theory and evidence. *Journal of Political Economy, 109*(1), 203-229.

Kubrin, Charles E., and Ronald Weitzer. (2003). Retaliatory homicide: Concentrated disadvantage and neighborhood culture. *Social Problems, 50*, 157-180.

Land, Kenneth, Patricia McCall, and Lawrence Cohen. (1990). Structural covariates of homicide rates: Are there any invariances across time and social space? *American Journal of Sociology, 95*(4), 922-963.

Lee, Barrett A., Sean F. Reardon, Glenn Firebaugh, Chad Farrell, Stephen A. Matthews, and David O'Sullivan. (2008). Beyond the census: Patterns and determinants of racial segregation at multiple geographic scales. *American Sociological Review, 73*(5), 766-791.

Levitt, Steven D. (1998). Why do increased arrest rates appear to reduce crime: Deterrence, incapacitation, or measurement error? *Economic Inquiry, 36*(3), 353-372.

Levitt, Steven, and Sudhir Alladi Venkatesh. (2001). Growing up in the projects: The economic lives of a cohort of men who came of age in Chicago public housing. *American Economic Review, 91*(2), 79-84.

Logan, John R., and Harvey L. Molotch. (1988). *Urban fortunes: The political economy of place*. Berkeley: University of California Press.

Ludwig, Jens, and Jeffrey R. Kling. (2007). Is crime contagious? *Journal of Law and Economics, 50*(3), 491-518.

Ludwig, Jens, Jeffrey B. Liebman, Jeffrey R. Kling, Greg J. Duncan, Lawrence F. Katz, Ronald C. Kessler, and Lisa Sanbonmatsu. (2008). What can we learn about neighborhood effects from the Moving-to-Opportunity experiment? A comment on Clampet-Lundquist and Massey. *American Journal of Sociology, 114*(1), 114-188.

MacDonald, John M., John R. Hipp, and Charlotte Gill. (2008). *Neighborhood effects of immigrant succession on crime: Did immigrants cause the crime drop in Los Angeles?* Presented at the 2008 Annual Workshop on Crime and Population Dynamics, Population Research Center, University of Maryland at College Park.

Marcuse, Peter. (1995). Interpreting "public housing" history. *Journal of Architectural and Planning Research, 12*(3), 240-258.

Martinez, Ramiro, Jr. (2002). *Latino homicide: Immigration, violence, and community*. London: Routledge Press.

Martínez, Ramiro, Jr., and Abél Valenzuela (2006). *Coming to America: Immigration, ethnicity, and crime*. New York: New York University Press.

Massey, Douglas S. (1995). Getting away with murder: Segregation and violent crime in urban America. *University of Pennsylvania Law Review, 143*(5), 1203-1232.

Massey, Douglas S. (2007). *Categorically unequal: The American stratification system.* New York: Russell Sage Foundation.

Massey, Douglas S., and Nancy Denton. (1993). *American apartheid.* Cambridge, MA: Harvard University Press.

McArdle, J.J., and F. Hamagami. (2001). Latent difference score structural models for linear dynamic analyses with incomplete longitudinal data. In L. Collins and A. Sayer (Eds.), *New methods for the analysis of change* (pp. 139-175). Washington, DC: American Psychological Association.

Messner, Steven A., Sandro Galea, Kenneth J. Tardiff, Melissa Tracy, Angela Bucciarelli, Tinka Markham Piper, Victoria Frye, and David Vlahov. (2007). Policing, drugs and the homicide decline in New York City in the 1990s. *Criminology, 45*(2), 385-414.

Morenoff, Jeffrey. (2003). Spatial dynamics of birth weight. *American Journal of Sociology, 108*, 976-1017.

Morenoff, Jeffrey, and Robert J. Sampson. (1997). Violent crime and the spatial dynamics of neighborhood transition: Chicago, 1970-1990. *Social Forces, 76*, 31-64.

Morenoff, Jeffrey, Robert J. Sampson, and Stephen W. Raudenbush. (2001). Neighborhood inequality, collective efficacy and the spatial dynamics of homicide. *Criminology, 39*(3), 517-560.

Nagin, Daniel S. (2005). *Group-based modeling of development.* Cambridge, MA: Harvard University Press.

Nagin, Daniel S., and Kenneth C. Land. (1993). Age, criminal careers, and population heterogeneity: Specification and estimation of a nonparametric, mixed poisson model. *Criminology, 31*(2), 327-362.

National Research Council. (2004). *Fairness and effectiveness in policing: The evidence.* Committee to Review Research on Police Policy and Practices, Wesley Skogan and Kathleen Frydl (Eds.). Committee on Law and Justice, Division of Behavioral and Social Sciences and Education. Washington, DC: The National Academies Press.

Papachristos, Andrew V. (forthcoming). Murder by structure: A network theory of gang homicide. *American Journal of Sociology* (in press).

Papachristos, Andrew V., Tracey L. Meares, and Jeffrey Fagan. (2007). Attention felons: Evaluating Project Safe Neighborhoods in Chicago. *Journal of Empirical Legal Studies, 4*(2), 223-272.

Park, Robert. (1916). Suggestions for the investigations of human behavior in the urban environment. *American Journal of Sociology, 20*(5), 577-612.

Park, Robert, Ernest W. Burgess, and Roderick D. McKenzie. (1925). *The city.* Chicago: University of Chicago Press.

Patillo, Mary E. (1998). Sweet mothers and gang bangers: Managing crime in a black middle class neighborhood. *Social Forces, 76*(3), 747-774.

Pebley, Anne R. and Narayan Sastry. (2006). Neighborhoods, poverty, and children's well-being. In David B. Grusky and Szonja Szelény (Eds.), *The inequality reader: Contemporary and foundational readings in race, class, and gender* (pp. 165-178). Greenwich, CT: Westview Press.

Popkin, Susan, James E. Rosenbaum, and Patricia Meaden. (1993). Labor market experiences of low-income black women in middle-class suburbs: Evidence from a survey of Gautreaux program participants. *Journal of Policy Analysis and Management, 12*(3), 556-573.

Raudenbush, Stephen W., and Robert J. Sampson. (1999). Ecometrics: Toward a science of assessing ecological settings, with application to the systematic social observation of neighborhoods. *Sociological Methodology, 29*(1), 1-41.

Reardon, Sean F. (2007). *Measuring spatial context: Race, space, and scale in the metropolis, 1990-2000.* Presented at Workshop on Wealth and Inequality, Institute for Economic and Social Research and Policy, Columbia University, New York.

Reardon, Sean F. (2008). Beyond the census tract: Patterns and determinants of racial segregation at multiple geographic scales. *American Sociological Review, 83*(October), 771.

Reardon, Sean F., and David O'Sullivan. (2004). Measures of spatial segregation. *Sociological Methodology, 34*(1), 121-162.

Ridgeway, Greg. (2006). Assessing the effect of race bias in posttraffic stop outcomes using propensity scores. *Journal of Quantitative Criminology, 22*(1), 1-30.

Ridgeway, Greg, Dan McCaffrey, and Andrew Morral. (2006). *The TWANG package: Toolkit for weighting and analysis of non equivalent groups.* Unpublished technical report, RAND Corporation, Santa Monica, CA.

Rosenbaum, James E. (1995). Changing the geography of opportunity by expanding residential choice: Lessons from the Gautreaux program. *Housing Policy Debate, 6*, 231-269.

Rosenfeld, Richard, Robert Fornango, and Andres F. Rengifo. (2007). The impact of order-maintenance policing on New York City homicide and robbery rates: 1988-2001. *Criminology, 45*(2), 355-384.

Rosin, Hanna. (2008). American murder mystery. *Atlantic Monthly,* (July/August), 40-54.

Rowe, David C., and Joseph L. Rogers. (1994). A social contagion model of adolescent sexual behavior: Explaining race differences. *Social Biology, 41*, 1-18.

Rubinowtiz, Leonard S., and James E. Rosenbaum. (2000). *Crossing the class and color lines: From public housing to white suburbia.* Chicago: University of Chicago Press.

Saegert, Susan, Gary Winkel, and Charles Swartz. (2002). Social capital and crime in New York City's low income housing. *Housing Policy Debate, 13*(1), 189-226.

Saiz, Albert, and Susan M. Wachter. (November 2006). *Immigration and the neighborhood.* (FRB of Philadelphia Working Paper #06-22.) Available: http://ssrn.com/abstract=931733 [accessed August 2008].

Sampson, Robert J. (2008) Moving to inequality: Neighborhood effects and experiments meet social structure. *American Journal of Sociology, 114*, 189-231.

Sampson, Robert J., and Dawn Jeglum Bartusch. (1998). Legal cynicism and (subcultural?) tolerance of deviance: The neighborhood context of racial differences. *Law and Society Review, 32*, 777-804.

Sampson, Robert J., and Jeffrey Morenoff. (2006). Durable inequality: Spatial dynamics, social processes, and the persistence of poverty in Chicago neighborhoods. In Samuel Bowles, Steven S. Durlauf, and Karla Hoff (Eds.), *Poverty traps* (pp. 176-203). Princeton, NJ: Princeton University Press.

Sampson, Robert J., and Stephen W. Raudenbush. (1999). Systematic social observation of public spaces: A new look at disorder in urban neighborhoods. *American Journal of Sociology, 105*, 603-651.

Sampson, Robert J., and Stephen W. Raudenbush. (2004). Seeing disorder: Neighborhood stigma and the social construction of "Broken Windows." *Social Psychology Quarterly, 67*(4), 319-342.

Sampson, Robert J., and Patrick Sharkey. (2008). Neighborhood selection and the social reproduction of concentrated racial inequality. *Demography, 45*(1), 1-29.

Sampson, Robert J., and William Julius Wilson. (1995). Toward a theory of race, crime, and urban inequality. In John Hagan and Ruth D. Peterson (Eds.), *Crime and inequality.* Stanford, CA: Stanford University Press.

Sampson, Robert J., Stephen W. Raudenbush, and Felton Earls. (1997). Neighborhoods and violent crime: A multilevel study of collective efficacy. *Science, 277*, 918-924.

Sampson, Robert J., Jeffrey Morenoff, and Thomas Gannon-Rowley. (2002). Assessing "neighborhood effects": Social processes and new directions in research. *Annual Review of Sociology, 28*, 443-478.

Sastry, Narayan, Bonnie Ghosh-Dastidar, John Adams, and Anne R. Pebley. (2006). The design of a multilevel longitudinal survey of children, families, and communities: The Los Angeles Family and Neighborhood Survey. *Social Science Research, 35*, 1000-1024.

Schuerman, Leo, and Soloman Kobrin. (1986). Community careers in crime. In Albert J. Reiss, Jr., and Michael Tonry (Eds.), *Communities and crime* (pp. 67-100). Chicago: University of Chicago Press.

Schwartz, Alex. (1999). New York City and subsidized housing: Impacts and lessons of the city's $5 billion capital budget housing plan. *Housing Policy Debate, 10*(4), 839-877.

Schwartz, Amy Ellen, Scott Susin, and Ioan Voicu. (2003) Has falling crime driven down New York City's real estate boom? *Journal of Housing Research, 14*(1), 101-135.

Shaw, Clifford R., and Henry D. McKay. (1943). *Juvenile delinquency and urban areas.* Chicago: University of Chicago Press.

Smith, David J. (2005). Ethnic differences in intergenerational crime patterns. *Crime and Justice, 32*, 55.

Sobel, Michael E. (2006a). What do randomized studies of housing mobility demonstrate? Causal inference in the face of interference. *Journal of the American Statistical Association, 101*, 1398-1407.

Sobel, Michael E. (2006b). Spatial concentration and social stratification: Does the clustering of disadvantage "beget" bad outcomes? In Samuel Bowles, Steven S. Durlauf, and Karla Hoff (Eds.), *Poverty traps* (pp. 204-229). Princeton, NJ: Princeton University Press.

Suttles, Gerald. (1970). *Social order of the slum: Ethnicity and territory in the inner city.* Chicago: University of Chicago Press.

Tatian, Peter A. (2003). Neighborhood change database, data users guide. Washington, DC: The Urban Institute. Available: http://www2.urban.org/nnip/ncua/ncdb/NCDB_LF_DataUsersGuide.pdf [accessed October 2008].

Taub, Richard P., Garth D. Taylor, and Jan D. Dunham. (1984). *Paths of neighborhood change: Race and crime in urban America.* Chicago: University of Chicago Press.

Taylor, Ralph B., and Jeanette Covington. (1988). Neighborhood changes in ecology and violence. *Criminology, 26*, 553-589.

Thornberry, Terence P., Marvin D. Krohn, Alan J. Lizotte, Carolyn A. Smith, and Kimberly Tobin. (2004). *Gangs and delinquency in developmental perspective.* New York: Cambridge University Press.

Tita, George E., Tricia L. Petras, and Robert T. Greenbaum. (2006). Crime and residential choice: A neighborhood level analysis of the impact of crime on housing prices. *Journal of Quantitative Criminology, 22*(3), 299-317.

Tyler, Tom R., and Jeffrey Fagan. (2008). Legitimacy, compliance and cooperation: Procedural justice and citizen ties to the law. *Ohio State Journal of Criminal Law* 6(2), 231-275.

Venkatesh, Sudhir A. (2000). *American project: The rise and fall of a modern ghetto.* Cambridge, MA: Harvard University Press.

Venkatesh, Sudhir A. (2006). *Off the books: The underground economy of the urban poor.* Cambridge, MA: Harvard University Press.

Wallace, Roderick. (1991). Expanding coupled shock fronts of urban decay and criminal behavior: How U.S. cities are becoming "hollowed out." *Journal of Quantitative Criminology, 7*, 333-356.

Weiner, David A., Byron F. Lutz, and Jens Ludwig. (2006). *The effects of school desegregation on crime.* Unpublished working paper, University of Chicago. Available: http://www.aeaweb.org/annual_mtg_papers/2007/0107_1300_0303.pdf [accessed August 2008].

Weisburd, David, Shawn Bushway, Cynthia Lum, and Sue-Ming Yang. (2004). Trajectories of crime at places: A longitudinal study of street segments in the city of Seattle. *Criminology, 42*(2), 283-322.

Weitzer, Ronald. (2000). Racialized policing: Residents' perceptions in three neighborhoods. *Law and Society Review, 34*, 129-155.

Wilkinson, Deanna L., and Jeffrey Fagan. (1996). The role of firearms in violence "scripts": The dynamics of gun events among adolescent males. *Law and Contemporary Problems, 59*(1), 55-90.

Williams, Kirk R., and Robert L. Flewelling. (1988). The social production of criminal homicide: A comparative study of disaggregated rates in American cities. *American Sociological Review, 53*, 421-431.

Wilson, James Q., and George L. Kelling. (1982). Broken windows: The police and neighborhood safety. *The Atlantic Monthly*, March, 29-37.

Wilson, William J. (1987). *The truly disadvantaged.* Chicago: University of Chicago Press.

Wilson, William J. (1991). Studying inner-city social dislocations: The challenge of public agenda research. *American Sociological Review, 56*, 1-14.

Wooldredge, John. (2002). Examining the (ir)relevance of aggregation bias for multi-level studies of neighborhoods and crime with an example comparing census tracts to official neighborhoods in Cincinnati. *Criminology, 40*(4), 681-710.

Zimring, Franklin E. (2006). *The great American crime decline.* New York: Oxford University Press.

Zimring, Franklin E., and Gordon Hawkins. (1997). *Crime is not the problem: Lethal violence in America.* New York: Oxford University Press.

5

An Empirical Assessment of the Contemporary Crime Trends Puzzle: A Modest Step Toward a More Comprehensive Research Agenda

Eric P. Baumer

The main purpose of this chapter is to report findings from an original analysis that aims to add a heretofore missing element to the extant crime trends literature: a comprehensive assessment that includes most of the major factors that have been identified as potential keys to resolving the recent crime trends puzzle. I begin with an overview of the state of the existing research and then outline the ways in which the present study goes beyond previous efforts. I then describe the sample and data used in the empirical analysis, summarize the key empirical findings and assess them in comparison to conclusions drawn in other recent studies, and close with a call for additional research that can build on the analysis to help establish the kind of research agenda needed to make significant progress in developing a more definitive portrait of the determinants of recent crime trends.

THE CRIME TRENDS PUZZLE

The basic portrait of U.S. crime trends during the past three decades is now well known. There were steep increases in rates of robbery, motor vehicle theft, and overall homicide from the mid- to late 1980s through the early 1990s. The patterns for homicide during the 1980s varied by age and method, with youth firearm homicide rates following the trend shown for overall homicide, but adult homicide rates and nongun homicide rates falling modestly throughout the 1980s, much like the observed trends in burglary (e.g., Blumstein and Rosenfeld, 1998; Cook and Laub, 1998). Crime patterns were much more consistent across crime types in the 1990s, as all forms of crime declined considerably, a trend that showed signs of slowing only during the early years of the present decade (Blumstein and Wallman, 2006a; Zimring, 2006). In the past few years, attention has turned to increases in violence observed in some cities across the United States (e.g., Police Executive Research Forum, 2006).

What explains these recent shifts in crime rates? Are they the result primarily of modifications to the quantity and quality of policing and incarceration? Were shifts in abortion laws, demographics (e.g., age structure and immigration), or the economy (e.g., unemployment and wages) important? Have changes in illicit drug (e.g., crack cocaine) involvement or alcohol consumption played a role? Do these or other factors help explain the substantial degree of variability in crime trends observed across places? And, ultimately, which factor or set of factors has contributed most to shaping recent crime trends? These are the questions of primary interest in this volume and the ones that I have been asked to examine in this chapter. Addressing these questions is difficult but vitally important for shaping perceptions of public safety among citizens, informing public policy debates about how best to respond to crime, and identifying conditions that are most apt to produce or prevent major shifts in crime.

THE STATE OF KNOWLEDGE

Policy makers, the media, and other citizens have rightly pressed for answers to the puzzling changes in U.S. crime rates over the past three decades. However, the existing empirical research on recent crime trends is in the early stages of development and is not at the point of sufficient breadth or depth to provide definitive evidence on which factors mattered a lot, which mattered relatively little, and, importantly, which mattered the most. The research community appears to have been reluctant to admit this apparent fact, concluding instead that the available evidence supports either the conclusion that virtually all of the dozen or so factors implicated in the theoretical literature played some role in shaping recent crime trends or the conclusion that one or more specific factors were very important and others mattered little. In my view, neither of these conclusions is supported strongly by the available evidence, which consists primarily of inconclusive circumstantial patterns and empirical evidence based on limited data and models that, as elaborated below, simply do not permit strong conclusions one way or another. Despite bold claims about which factors mattered and which did not (e.g., Levitt, 2004), as Travis and Waul (2002, p. iii) summed up after a national forum on the subject, although a good deal has been learned from prior research, there are no "definitive answers to the questions raised by the recent crime [trends]—that would require more research, new data, and a sustained effort to reconcile every competing claim" (see also Blumstein and Wallman, 2006b; Rosenfeld, 2004).

The uncertainty associated with identifying more clearly the primary sources of recent crime trends is not due to a scarcity of ideas about why crime *probably* changed in the manner it has or to the absence of sophisticated empirical investigations. Within just the past decade, four books (Blumstein and Wallman, 2006a; Conklin, 2003; LaFree, 1998; Zimring, 2006), a National Institute of Justice (NIJ) symposium published in the *Journal of Criminal Law & Criminology* (Travis, 1998), a major NIJ intramural research project (Lattimore et al., 1997), and several articles and conference panels have been devoted to explaining the crime trends observed in the United States during the 1980s and 1990s. As illustrated in Figure 5-1, this attention has generated a rich and creative set of plausible hypotheses for recent crime trends. Surely, one or more of the factors identified in the figure was highly influential in shaping recent crime trends in the United States. But if the hypothesized causes have been identified, why

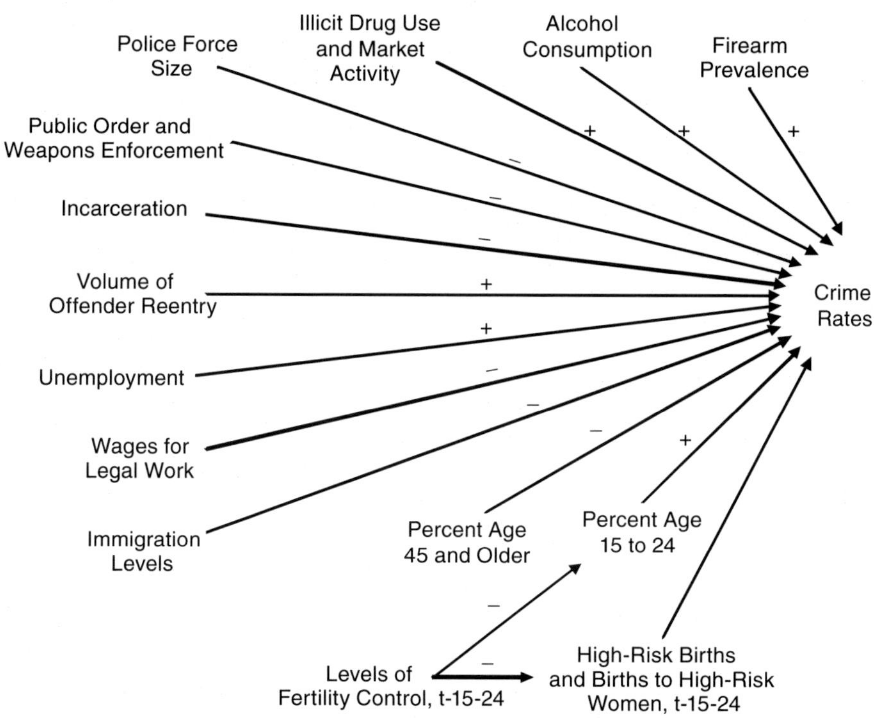

FIGURE 5-1 Heuristic model of hypothesized main effects on recent crime trends.

does one not know something more definitive empirically about the sources of recent crime trends, and specifically about which factors mattered or were most influential? When criminology and criminal justice scholars are asked why crime rates have taken their observed path since the early 1980s, why is the modal response something along the lines of "it is unclear, but probably several things worked together to bring crime down" (see, e.g., Tierney, 2007)?

In my view, there are two major impediments to providing definitive responses to key theoretical and policy questions associated with recent crime trends: There simply has not been a sufficient amount of empirical research on the matter, and the existing body of research is largely unsystematic along a variety of dimensions. In a vibrant research agenda, a diversity of data, measures, and methods brought to bear on a problem often are welcomed, because a high volume of research makes it is possible to see meaningful patterns emerge from a collective effort that helps to establish an overall sense of the issue at hand, net of the different ways in which the issue has been studied. But the volume of empirical research in this area does not seem sufficient at present to generate a landscape ripe for producing enough information to glean emergent patterns across the diverse approaches currently taken among those studying crime trends. What is more, the relatively barren landscape of crime trends research has provided fertile ground for advocates of the importance of particular factors (e.g., policing, incarceration, crack, abortion, immigration) to draw relatively strong conclusions in an empirical vacuum in which the various factors that also may have mattered (and possibly mattered more) are rarely considered simultaneously.

There are several excellent empirical papers on recent crime trends that provide persuasive evidence that a given factor was critical to shaping recent trends, yet most of the factors identified in Figure 5-1 have not been evaluated empirically very often or in systematic ways and, even when they are examined, the overall body of relevant empirical research on crime trends suffers from two major limitations that have served as impediments to establishing a more definitive body of knowledge on why crime rates have taken their observed path since the early 1980s: (1) a narrow research focus on only a few of the factors believed to be important for shaping recent crime trends and, consequently, a high degree of empirical misspecification and (2) substantial variability in the analytical methods applied across studies, including the explanatory variables considered, units of analysis employed, and the types of models estimated.

Regarding the first limitation, although most observers seem to agree that several factors probably coalesced to shape recent crime trends (e.g., Blumstein and Wallman, 2006a; Rosenfeld, 2004; Travis and Waul, 2002; Zimring, 2006), the empirical literature generally has focused narrowly on a small subset of the potentially relevant factors, most typically police force size, drug arrest rates, and incarceration. City- and county-level studies of recent crime trends (e.g., Baumer et al., 1998; Gallup-Black, 2005; Levitt, 1997; Lott, 1998; Ousey and Lee, 2002; Phillips, 2006) have focused on the first two of these factors, but they typically exclude time-varying indicators of nearly all of the other factors shown in Figure 5-1 and, perhaps most importantly, they rarely incorporate any indicators of incarceration or jail confinement rates, which have emerged as central in many other studies.

Similarly, although state-level studies of recent crime trends routinely include indicators of overall incarceration rates (e.g., Levitt, 1996; Liedka, Piehl, and Useem, 2006; Marvell and Moody, 1994, 1997), they have not considered age- or crime-specific incarceration rates, average sentence length, time served, or prisoner release rates, even though these factors have been highlighted as potentially important in theoretical discussions and are available as data elements in the public domain. It is also noteworthy that none of the existing studies of recent crime trends has included indicators of recent immigration flows and, surprisingly, only a few have incorporated direct indicators of changes in the nature of policing across multiple geographic units (MacDonald, 2002; Messner et al., 2007; Rosenfeld, Fornango, and Rengifo, 2007). A corresponding story emerges for many of the economic and demographic conditions emphasized as potentially important in the theoretical literature on recent crime trends. Although the occasional study examines wages (Gould, Weinberg, and Mustard, 2002), levels of "domesticity" (Dugan, Nagin, and Rosenfeld, 1999), and indicators relevant to assessing the role of abortion law changes (Donohue and Levitt, 2001, 2006), most studies do not consider these factors, despite evidence suggesting that they may be very important.

In short, a common theme in the extant research on recent crime trends is that most studies have a limited scope, focusing on a few select factors and ignoring many other potentially important ones. The high level of empirical misspecification makes the findings reported in much of the prior research on crime trends open to charges of spuriousness, including studies often cited as the primary regression-based evidence of a significant link between recent crime trends and such factors as crack cocaine involvement and incarceration (e.g., Baumer et al., 1998; Ousey and Lee, 2002; Stemen, 2007). Some studies minimize the serious omitted variables bias concern by incorporating "fixed effects," but this strategy does not say anything about the specific role of the omitted factors for which the fixed portions of the model are serving as a surrogate. Overall, despite much speculation about the explanatory potential of several factors, the limited scope of existing research and differences across studies in the variables considered make it difficult to draw definitive conclusions about the role of given factors, much less to make concrete determinations about the relative impact of specific factors.

A second major impediment to establishing from existing research a more definitive body of empirical evidence and knowledge about the factors that have shaped recent crime trends is the substantial variability in analytical methods applied across studies (see also Spelman, 2008). Beyond the significant differences in model specification already noted, the extant research also is hard to pin down systematically because of (a) the use of different units of analysis across studies and (b) the reliance on different types of statistical methods to estimate key parameters. With respect to the former issue, research on recent crime trends has been conducted across multiple units of analysis, most often states, counties, cities, neighborhoods, and police precincts. It is not necessarily important that a particular unit of analysis be identified, a priori, as superior for studying crime trends, for the reality is that each of these units has conceptual merit, and there are important trade-offs in the choice of unit. Nonetheless, it would be useful to know the empirical implications of using different units of analysis, something that cannot be deciphered easily from existing research.

There also appears to be little consensus on the type of methodological approach that is best suited for studying crime trends, especially in subnational (states, counties, cities, neighborhoods) studies, and consequently there is a tremendous degree of variation across studies in the methods applied. Some studies have used methods geared toward identifying classes of crime "trajectories" (e.g., Weisburd et al., 2004), while most have applied different versions of two suitable analytical strategies: pooled time-series cross-sectional panel models (e.g., Donohue and Levitt, 2001; Gould, Weinberg, and Mustard, 2002; Phillips, 2006) and multilevel growth curve models (e.g., Baumer et al., 1998; Kubrin and Herting, 2003; Ousey and Lee, 2004; Rosenfeld, Fornango, and Rengifo, 2007). The specific choice between the latter two approaches is not very important, for they can be made to be equivalent with proper modifications, but it is critical to recognize that the two approaches typically are implemented in ways that are likely to generate different findings and conclusions even when applied to the same data (see, e.g., Phillips and Greenberg, 2008).

It is also important to note that there are some important differences in how each of the two most common approaches is implemented. For instance, some studies of recent crime trends employ econometric panel models appropriately by testing for stationarity in the variables (e.g., Phillips, 2006), but most others do not do this (e.g., Donohue and Levitt, 2001; Gould, Weinberg, and Mustard, 2002). Some estimate models in both levels and differences (Moody and Marvell, 2005), while most focus on levels only (for a review, see Moody, 2007). And some include unit-specific trends (e.g., Raphael and Winter-Ebmer, 2001), while most studies do not.

In many instances there are legitimate disagreements about which of the many possible specifications is most appropriate under particular circumstances, but it is important to recognize that the different specifications used are likely to generate different results and conclusions even when applied to the same data (Spelman, 2008). Recognizing this is, of course, key to compiling a systematic body of knowledge that may or may not point to particular answers to questions about crime trends.

RESEARCH NEEDS AND THE PRESENT STUDY

Recent crime trends represent a major social phenomenon and a fundamental research issue for which criminological researchers should provide concrete answers. We should and can do better than "a lot of things mattered," but doing so will require a more vibrant research agenda that focuses on modeling recent crime trends in a much more comprehensive and systematic way. Ideally, this research agenda would incorporate a comprehensive set of measures that mirror as closely as possible the factors emphasized in theoretical and policy discussions of crime trends. It would also apply appropriate methodological techniques uniformly across multiple units of analysis (or a common unit) while attending to important econometric issues (e.g., stationarity, spatial dependence, endogeneity) that are critical for the inferences drawn from temporal data. As Spelman (2008) has recently demonstrated, attending to these issues even for a single crime rate covariate—incarceration rates—in a bivariate context is a highly complex enterprise, so extrapolating the effort to a larger scale will not be easy. Nonetheless, this kind of systematic effort is feasible and would help to better pinpoint empirical patterns in available data and minimize the degree to which conclusions are confounded by differences across studies in specification, unit of analysis, or method.

Developing the research agenda just described will take a concerted effort by a community of scholars who share data and ideas to build a knowledge base on crime trends incrementally and systematically. The goal here is to make a modest contribution to this effort by significantly broadening the scope of empirical research to incorporate not only the factors often considered (e.g., police force size, drug use and market activity, age structure, incarceration) in the literature, but also various others that have been highlighted in theory but only occasionally considered in empirical studies (e.g., immigration, wages, alcohol consumption, levels of domesticity, and youthful cohort "quality"). The main contribution, then, lies in an expansion of the empirical specification typically applied in research on recent crime trends—it is the first study of which I am aware that examines simultaneously each of the major factors shown in Figure 5-1 that have been emphasized in theoretical and policy discussions of recent crime trends.

This strikes me as a logical starting point for establishing a more definitive knowledge base about recent crime trends.

I must emphasize that the analysis described below is relatively modest and only an initial step in moving toward a more definitive knowledge base from which to draw answers to the important questions that have emerged about recent crime trends. As mentioned above and elaborated below, there are also several unresolved and complicated methodological issues that should be tackled in a comprehensive research agenda on crime trends. In an exhaustive analysis, for instance, the econometric properties of each of the variables considered should be evaluated (e.g., Are the variables stationary or nonstationary?) and appropriate transformations should be made to the data and estimation techniques (e.g., Should the variables be differenced? Are the variables cointegrated?). Furthermore, the many instances of possible endogeneity in models of crime trends should be addressed, spatial dependence should be assessed and, if necessary, modeled appropriately, and there should be a systematic approach to model selection so that one can make informed choices about the factors that emerge as most relevant. These matters are not merely statistical exercises; they have important implications for the inferences drawn about crime trends.

Although there is important work being done on these issues both in criminology and other disciplines, collectively they represent a challenging set of issues that is more complex than often portrayed in the literature and which cannot be addressed satisfactorily here given the space constraints of this volume.[1] Instead, although the present work expands on recent crime trends research by considering a much larger set of the factors most commonly emphasized in theoretical discussions, it applies the same econometric tools used in many existing subnational studies. Consequently, the conclusions that can be drawn must be viewed as tentative; the important methodological issues noted earlier will need to be addressed to assess the validity of the results reported below.

[1]National-level studies of crime and other social phenomena have addressed these issues, and some panel studies have entertained these issues as well, but in general they have not been dealt with effectively in the criminological literature. Among other things, most panel studies that employ panel unit root tests have used so-called second-generation tests that do not account for spatial dependence, which is likely to be present in most of the subnational data used to study crime trends and could bias results. Also, there are many questions about how to handle heterogeneous panels, some of which contain unit roots and others that do not, that have not been adequately resolved. Differencing is a common solution when nonstationarity is found in panel studies, but, without testing for cointegration, it is not clear whether this is an appropriate solution or one that produces valid results. Finally, assessments and corrections for endogeneity vary wildly in the literature, so its impact remains unclear, and there is little guidance from the literature about how best to approach such issues in practice.

BROADENING THE SCOPE OF CRIME TRENDS RESEARCH

This study expands the scope of research on recent crime trends by taking a more comprehensive approach to measuring and modeling effects of factors that have been well represented in prior research (e.g., such commonly considered factors as policing, incarceration, and illicit drug activity), by incorporating measures of factors that are irregularly included in the extant research (e.g., largely neglected factors, such as alcohol consumption, legal wages, levels of domesticity, immigration, and cohort quality indicators) and, more generally, by estimating models in which all of these factors are considered simultaneously. Many of these factors have been discussed extensively elsewhere, including prior chapters in this volume, so they do not need to be reviewed in detail here. But I elaborate on some relatively neglected issues and outline the ways in which I go beyond past work.

Reconsidering Commonly Addressed Factors

Two factors that have received a particularly high level of attention in public discourse on recent crime trends, and especially the 1990s crime decline, are changes in policing and incarceration. With respect to the former, Eck and Maguire (2006) provide an excellent treatment of the various changes in the quantity and quality of policing that have occurred in the past several decades, focusing especially on (1) increases in the number of police officers devoted to helping address crime problems and (2) enhancements to the manner by which police agencies have approached their work, particularly a move toward a targeted policing focus on behaviors thought to facilitate crime, such as levels of public disorder and the prevalence of weapon carrying. Several studies examining the link between crime trends and police size have generated inconsistent results (see Eck and Maguire, 2006, for an exhaustive review). A relatively large body of research also has examined the effects of different policing approaches on levels of crime (e.g., Sampson and Cohen, 1988; for a review, see MacDonald, 2002), but only a small handful of studies have assessed explicitly the role of recent changes in the nature of policing on contemporary crime trends.

Overall, the existing research suggests that policing efforts that targeted public order violations and weapon carrying may have had a modest effect on crime trends during the 1990s (Braga et al., 2001; Kennedy et al., 2001; Messner et al., 2007; Piehl et al., 2003; Rosenfeld, Fornango, and Rengifo, 2007), but the limited attention to this issue precludes more definitive conclusions being drawn. I build on existing work by examining whether a changing police focus on public order crimes and weapons offenses—as measured by the number of arrests per 100,000 residents for weapons violations, vandalism, prostitution, gambling, liquor laws, drunkenness, disorderly conduct, vagrancy, curfew violations, loitering, and suspicion (for similar measures, see Messner et al., 2007; Rosenfeld, Fornango, and Rengifo, 2007)—is associated with recent crime trends across a relatively large sample of cities.

The other major criminal justice factor emphasized in the literature on recent crime trends is the well-documented substantial increase in incarceration rates, which have more than tripled in the United States since the early 1970s (Zimring, 2006). There is a long history of linking incarceration to crime rates through incapacitation and/or deterrent processes (e.g., Zimring and Hawkins, 1973) and a relatively large and growing empirical literature. Yet, despite the substantial attention devoted in prior research to the role of overall incarceration rates and what appears to be some consensus on the overall impact of incarceration on crime trends (Stemen, 2007; but see Spelman, 2008), two aspects of the link between incarceration and crime have been neglected in prior work and warrant additional consideration: (1) the analysis of both "stock" (i.e., the overall number of persons per capita in prison at a given point in time) and "flow" (i.e., the number of persons per capita admitted to prison and released from prison in a given year) measures of incarceration and (2) the analysis of temporal variability and scale effects for incarceration.

Discussions of incarceration effects tend to emphasize the crime reduction that may result from relatively immediate sentencing actions, such as the recent removal from the street of each additional offender. Most studies of incarceration effects estimate how stock incarceration rates for a given year affect crime in that year or the next. However, during periods of sentence enhancements, such as the 1980s and 1990s, the stock incarceration rate may not be a very good indicator of how many offenders were removed from the streets and placed in prison in a particular year (it will reflect admissions in that year and many before it). Thus, modeling its contemporaneous or one-year lagged effect on crime rates may yield a misleading picture of the effect of recent incarceration practices on crime rates. Annual flow indicators of the number of persons admitted to prison (less the number of persons released), of course, are well suited for gauging such effects.

The present study therefore estimates models of crime for both stock and flow measures of incarceration to evaluate in a more comprehensive manner the role of incarceration in shaping recent crime trends. Considering the prison flow measures not only provides a more precise look at incarceration effects than relying solely on the stock incarceration rate, but it also permits an independent assessment of prison *releases* on recent crime trends. There has been a lot of attention recently to the consequences and challenges of a large volume of prisoners moving from prison back to their home communities (e.g., Travis and Visher, 2005) yet very little direct empirical investigation of whether and how trends in prison releases may have affected crime trends during the past few decades. Only one of the regression-based studies of recent crime trends has considered the quantity or quality of prison releases (Kovandzic et al., 2004). No significant impact of prison release rates was observed in that study, but the focus was exclusively on homicide, a relatively rare crime, and it is uncertain whether similar findings would emerge for more common offences.

Recent research on incarceration rates and crime trends also challenges the assumptions shared in most previous studies of linear and time-invariant incarceration effects. Some have argued that the elasticity of incarceration has changed over time, although there is disagreement about the direction of this change (see Liedka, Piehl, and Useem, 2006; Spelman, 2000). Spelman's (2000) research suggests that the effectiveness of prisons may have *increased* over time because of growth in the scale of imprisonment, the proportion of crime committed by adults, and the selectivity of law enforcement efforts (i.e., the degree to which serious offenders are imprisoned). More recently, Liedka, Piehl, and Useem (2006) suggest that the crime reduction benefits of incarceration are likely to be *reduced* as the scale of incarceration reaches very high levels and may even reverse, such that very high levels of incarceration may actually increase crime. Their state-level panel analysis of data of 1972-2000 reveals evidence consistent with this claim. Furthermore, although they do not examine the issue directly, they suggest that in contrast to Spelman's argument about the increasing effectiveness of incarceration over time, one implication of their findings may be that the elasticity of incarceration has probably *declined* (i.e., become less negative) as incarceration rates in many states have approached and surpassed an effective deterrent or incapacitation level.

These recent studies point to the need for additional refined analyses of incarceration effects that move beyond estimating elasticities under the assumption of temporal invariance and that are attentive to potential variability in elasticity by changes in scale and the composition of the prison-bound population. I explore some of these issues by examining not only the main effect of the overall prison admissions rate, but also the possibility of a nonlinear response for this variable and whether the estimated effects have changed over time.

The role of illicit drug use and market activity, especially with respect to crack cocaine, also has received a good deal of attention in the theoretical and empirical literature on recent crime trends. Although there are some doubters (e.g., Zimring, 2006), there seems to be a fairly strong consensus that the rise and fall of crack use and crack markets are important pieces of the crime trends puzzle over the past 25 years (Blumstein and Wallman, 2006a; Johnson, Golub, and Dunlap, 2006; Levitt, 2004). The central arguments provided for the link between crack and violence are logical and persuasive (Baumer et al., 1998; Blumstein and Rosenfeld, 1998), and the demographic features of recent homicide trends certainly fit well with the idea that crack use and crack markets were an important facilitator (Blumstein, 1995). However, the systematic empirical evidence in support of this hypothesis is not as abundant or definitive as one might suspect, and it is not clear precisely how important changes in drug market activity and drug use were during the rise in violence observed in the 1980s and the decline observed in the 1990s and beyond. The relatively few studies that have examined the issue generally show that cities with higher levels and greater increases in crack use and market activity experienced larger increases in violence during the 1980s (e.g., Baumer et al., 1998; Cork, 1999; Fryer et al., 2006; Grogger and Willis, 2000). However, these studies may overstate the magnitude of the link between crack and violence during the 1980s because they omit many other potentially important factors that changed over time and are thought to be connected to recent crime trends. The evidence is also mixed with respect to the role of changes in crack use and crack markets for the 1990s crime decline (see Corman and Mocan, 2000; Fryer et al., 2007; Messner et al., 2007; Rosenfeld, Fornango, and Baumer, 2005; Rosenfeld, Fornango, and Rengifo, 2007).

In short, while the rise and fall of the crack epidemic probably played an important role in recent crime trends, especially youth violence, there are several unresolved issues. Some of the evidence in support of the hypothesized connection can be criticized for being generated from empirical models that omit many of the other factors thought to be relevant to recent crime trends. Also, although some scholars have emphasized the possible interactive effects of drug markets and the legitimate economy on recent crime trends, aside from assessments of the contingent role of drug markets in areas with different *levels* of economic and social disadvantage (e.g., Ousey and Lee, 2004), this has rarely been examined systematically. Finally, one potentially important aspect of Blumstein's argument about the link between crack markets and violence has not been examined in previous work. Specifically, Blumstein (1995) suggests that a distinctive feature that made crack markets particularly violent in the late 1980s and early 1990s was their age composition, in particular the fact that they were dominated by younger people. As the demand for crack grew and the adult sellers who dominated markets were arrested and imprisoned, Blumstein notes that crack markets became staffed largely by young and inexperienced street sellers who, compared with their older counterparts, were more reckless and irresponsible. They lacked the necessary maturity and skills to resolve conflicts in nonphysical ways, stimulating them to use guns with little restraint (Blumstein, 1995, pp. 29-31). This suggests that recent crime trends may be linked to the degree to which drug markets are "staffed" by younger people, an issue that has not been examined directly. The present study contributes to the literature by examining multiple measures of crack cocaine involvement, including overall arrest rates for cocaine and heroin as well as an indicator of the age structure of crack markets and indicators of drug-related mortality, in a comprehensive empirical model that also incorporates other factors that might be relevant.

Attending to Some Neglected Factors

In addition to evaluating some expanded measures of commonly considered causes of recent crime shifts, I also examine several factors highlighted in theoretical and policy discussions but rarely examined systematically in the empirical literature. These include changes in alcohol consumption, legal wages, levels of domesticity, immigration, and birth cohort quality.

Alcohol has long been linked to violence, perhaps even more so than other drugs (Fagan, 1990; Parker and Rebhun, 1995), and national-level trends in alcohol consumption during the past several decades yield patterns similar to trends in homicide rates, especially the observed trends in adult homicide rates since 1980 (Parker and Cartmill, 1998). Although the available evidence suggests that alcohol consumption may play a significant role in shaping violence levels and trends at the national level and across states, metropolitan areas, cities, and neighborhoods (e.g., Fagan, 1990), most studies of recent crime trends have not considered this possibility. In fact, to my knowledge, there is not a single published study that has considered the link between trends in alcohol consumption and city or county crime trends using annual panel data. This is likely to be the case because data on alcohol consumption are not readily available for counties or cities.

In light of this, I evaluate the role of alcohol consumption on recent crime trends using a proxy measure—the percentage of fatal traffic accidents involving alcohol—that exhibits a strong temporal correspondence with alcohol consumption at the national level and that is available for cities and counties annually from the late 1970s to the present. Incorporating this measure into the analysis presented below not only provides a way to assess the independent effect of alcohol consumption on recent crime trends, but also may enhance the identification of other effects, including unemployment (see, e.g., Cook and Zarkin, 1985; Raphael and Winter-Ebmer, 2001).

A wide range of economic conditions have been mentioned in the literature on recent crime trends (see Rosenfeld and Fornango, 2007), but unemployment rates and wages have been the economic factors most often implicated as shaping the likelihood of offending directly as well as mediating the effects on crime of related variables, such as educational attainment (e.g., Blumstein and Wallman, 2006a). Wages are hypothesized to be negatively associated with crime rates, while unemployment is hypothesized to be positively related to crime. There is a voluminous empirical literature on the link between unemployment rates and crime rates using state- and national-level data; overall the evidence from this work reveals little, if any, effect of unemployment on violence rates but that property crime rates tend to decrease by about 1 to 5 percent with each percentage point reduction in unemployment rates (Levitt, 1996, 1997, 2001; Raphael and Winter-Ebmer, 2001). Much less empirical attention has been devoted to assessing the possibility that changes in legal wages are associated with recent crime trends. Gould, Weinberg, and Mustard (2002) have conducted the only aggregate-level study of which I am aware that examines the relationship between wages and crime rates. Overall, their results suggest that changes in real wages for unskilled men account for more than one-third of the increase in crime rates observed in U.S. counties during the late 1980s, but less than 5 percent of the decline in crime rates between 1993 and 1997.

The present study builds on recent research on the effects of unemployment and wages on recent crime trends in two ways. First, the key economic indicators are measured at a more local level in the present work, capturing economic conditions and crime at the county and city levels of analysis rather than the state or national level. This is potentially important given the high degree of local variability in both economic conditions and crime (Levitt, 2001), yet none of the existing city-level studies of crime trends includes a time-varying indicator of unemployment rates, and only a few county-level studies have done so (e.g., Phillips, 2006). Second, the present research explores interactions between unemployment and wage indicators and measures of the magnitude of the crack cocaine markets that characterize the large U.S. cities selected by the Committee on Law and Justice for examination—referred to here as "NRC cities." As noted above, several scholars have alluded to the possibility of this type of interaction (e.g., Blumstein and Rosenfeld, 1998; Fagan and Freeman, 1999; Grogger, 2006; Zimring and Hawkins, 1997), but it has rarely been examined systematically.

Although a variety of demographic features have been alluded to in the literature as potentially relevant to recent crime trends, the existing empirical literature has taken a relatively narrow approach to measuring the role of demography. This work adds to the literature by explicitly considering three demographic factors highlighted in theoretical and policy discussions of recent crime trends but that have received meager attention in the empirical literature: levels of domesticity (Rosenfeld, 2006), levels of immigration (Sampson, 2006), and the conditions under which the contemporary youth population was born (Donohue and Levitt, 2001; Sampson and Wilson, 1995).

Rosenfeld (1997) directs attention to a potentially important social change witnessed during the past few decades—the substantial retreat from marital unions (Amato et al., 2007)—and hypothesizes that the associated "declining domesticity" may be key to the observed reductions in adult homicide since the early 1980s and intimate partner homicide in particular. The rationale underlying this link is simple: when the fraction of the population that is married (or gets married) falls, so too does the overall number of reoccurring opportunities for lethal violence between intimates. Detailed analysis of adult spousal homicide trends (Rosenfeld, 1997; Blumstein and Rosenfeld, 1998) across groups that differ substantially on marriage and divorce propensities reveals evidence consistent with patterns one would expect if declining domesticity were an important contributor to the decline in intimate partner homicide. Dugan, Nagin, and Rosenfeld (1999) also provide support for the notion that declining domesticity is important for understanding declines in intimate partner homicide.

The present study, building on this earlier work, evaluates whether changes in levels of domesticity during the past 25 years are associated with changes in city crime rates. Like earlier work, the analysis examines the role of the decline in marital unions in shaping adult homicide trends. But I also extend prior work by considering whether recent changes in the prevalence of both marital unions and nonmarital cohabitation may help to explain changes in violence and changes in burglary rates since the early 1980s. Rates of nonmarital cohabitation have increased considerably during the past three decades (e.g., Amato et al., 2007; Casper and Cohen, 2000) and have substantially offset the decline in marriage rates. Given that cohabiting relationships have been shown to yield more violence than other types of relationship statuses (Brownridge, 2004; Shackelford, 2005), it is important to consider trends in cohabitation along with trends in martial unions, both because the former are interesting in their own right and because not doing so may bias estimates of the latter. It is also plausible that domesticity effects are relevant for burglary rates. From a routine activities perspective, for example, domesticity should be inversely associated with changes in burglary rates. I evaluate these predictions using annual state-level data on household composition from the Current Population Survey and testing whether cities located in states that exhibited greater changes in the proportion married or cohabitating experienced more substantial changes in rates of adult homicide, burglary, and other crimes.

Another demographic feature that has been linked to recent crime trends in the United States is the level of immigration. In a 2006 *New York Times* op-ed contribution, Sampson extrapolated from the findings revealed in recent individual- and multilevel studies of the role of immigrant status in shaping involvement in crime and violence (e.g., Butcher and Piehl, 1998; Sampson, Morenoff, and Raudenbush, 2005; for reviews, see Hagan and Palloni, 1998; Martinez and Lee, 2000) to suggest that recent increases in levels of immigration may be a major factor in the decline in crime during the 1990s in the United States as well as the leveling off of crime in the early part of the 2000s (see also, Sampson, 2008). The logic of his argument relies heavily on the relatively lower rates of offending exhibited by immigrants and the fact that, if additions to the population due to immigration are primarily nonoffenders, the crime rate will by definition drop. Increased immigration can affect aggregate crime rates in a variety of ways, however, beyond the criminal offending rates of new arrivals. Sampson has alluded to the possibility that the influx of immigrants in the 1990s may have reduced crime because immigration increased collective efficacy (Press, 2006). In addition, an influx of immigrants may bolster local economies and thus reduce pressures to engage in illicit conduct, or a large pool of immigrants may bring with them a value system that eschews violence as a means of settling interpersonal disputes (Reid et al., 2005; Sampson, 2008).

Sampson's speculation about an inverse association between changes in immigration and changes in crime rates is plausible, but what does the empirical evidence say about this possibility? Have changes in levels of immigration been relevant to recent crime trends, and, if so, have changes in immigration been associated with increases or decreases in crime? The circumstantial evidence is persuasive. Many U.S. border cities consistently exhibit relatively low crime rates (Martinez and Lee, 2000), and a cursory look at the cities that experienced the largest declines in crime during the 1990s (see, e.g., Zimring, 2006) reveals that many are places that routinely experience high levels of immigration. Also, at the national level, immigration grew substantially during the 1990s, and this growth accelerated right around the time (about 1994) when the crime decline accelerated (Simanski, 2005).

Yet there is relatively little systematic empirical evidence on the link between immigration and crime at the aggregate level, and only three studies of which I am aware consider empirically the role of immigration on recent crime trends (Butcher and Piehl, 1998; Rosenfeld, Fornango, and Rengifo, 2007; Sykes, Hangartner, and Hathaway, 2007). The weight of the evidence from aggregate cross-sectional research on immigration and crime appears to be that the relationship is either nonexistent or negative (Martinez and Lee, 2000; Reid et al., 2005), but findings are decidedly mixed in other types of studies, with the effects positive for some crimes or contexts and negative for others (e.g., Hagan and Palloni, 1998). Butcher and Piehl (1998) found no significant association between changes in crime rates and changes in the stock of foreign-born or the flow of new immigrants during the 1980s. Rosenfeld, Fornango, and Rengifo's (2007) analysis of 1990s crime trends for New York City police precincts shows that areas with a higher percentage of foreign-born residents experienced significantly greater declines in robbery rates, but they found no significant relationship between changes in percentage foreign-born and changes in crime. In contrast, a state-level panel analysis conducted by Sykes, Hangartner, and Hathaway (2007) reveals a significant negative association between changes in the percentage foreign-born and changes in rates of property and violent crime, which is consistent with Sampson's argument.

More research is needed to assess the merits of the idea that immigration flows are associated (negatively or positively) with recent crime trends. Admittedly, estimating the number of people who immigrate to the United States with precision in any given year is very difficult (Hagan and Palloni, 1998), but the present study builds on recent panel analyses of this issue by drawing on data from the Immigration and Naturalization Service to estimate annual figures on legal immigrants who reported an intended residence in the metropolitan areas in which the NRC cities are located. These data were used to estimate the annual number of newly admitted legal immigrants (per 100,000 current residents) intending to reside in the metropolitan statistical areas in which the NRC cities are located.

Perhaps the most controversial demographic argument that has emerged in discussions of recent crime trends is Donohue and Levitt's "abortion dividend" thesis. Although the details of this argument are somewhat complex, in essence Donohue and Levitt (2001) invoke a classic cohort theory argument (e.g., O'Brien, Stockard, and Isaacson, 1999) in suggesting that the legalization of abortion in the early 1970s in the United States served to reduce crime substantially during the 1990s because it resulted in smaller cohorts of teenagers and young adults (e.g., ages 15-24) in this period and, more importantly, because a smaller proportion of this age group had high-risk birth attributes and/or a smaller proportion were born to high-risk mothers, as indicated, for example, by maternal age, marital status, and educational and economic status at birth.

Much of the research attention on and discussion about the abortion dividend argument understandably has focused exclusively on the direct link between 1970s abortion law changes and recent crime trends. Although some observers have expressed skepticism about this link because the timing of abortion law changes and the beginning of observed declines in the 1990s do not coincide neatly (e.g., Blumstein and Wallman, 2006a; Fox, 2006; Rosenfeld, 2004), and others have raised concerns about questionable assumptions and empirical specifications associated with some of the initial findings presented by Donohue and Levitt (2001) (e.g., Foote and Goetz, 2005; Joyce, 2004; Sykes, Hangartner, and Hathaway, 2007; Zimring, 2006), the empirical evidence on the association between abortion law changes and contemporary crime trends presented by Donohue and Levitt (2001, 2006) has so far withstood the challenges. Moreover, others have reported results that affirm their core findings (Berk et al., 2003; Sorenson, Wiebe, and Berk, 2002), and the magnitude of the effects of abortion law changes implied in their work is substantial, accounting for perhaps half of the crime decline in the United States during the 1990s.

Nevertheless, the legalization of abortion is but one of many social changes that could yield the differential fertility outcomes posited by Donohue and Levitt (2001, 2006) to link abortion to contemporary crime trends. In my view, the key criminological and more proximate causal questions that emerge from their work are not whether abortion laws are associated with crime trends, but rather whether recent crime trends were significantly shaped by (1) the percentage of persons in high-crime-rate age groups (e.g., 15-24); (2) the relative number of persons in this age group who were born in high-risk family situations (e.g., unmarried mothers, teenage mothers, mothers with relatively little education or low economic status); and (3) the relative number of persons in this age group who experienced high-risk or suboptimal birth conditions (e.g., low birth weight, prenatal exposure to drugs and alcohol, neurological birth complications). The first of these issues has a long history in aggregate-level studies of crime, but the latter two rarely have been directly addressed in the crime trends literature.

Little is known about the possible role of high-risk births and births to high-risk women in the 1970s on shaping contemporary crime trends. The types of birth quality indicators most relevant to Donohue and Levitt's (2001) argument—parental age, marital and economic status, prenatal health, and such attributes as birth weight—have been linked to a heightened likelihood of involvement in delinquency and crime, but few studies have assessed their potential impact on aggregate crime trends. Research by O'Brien, Stockard, and Isaacson (1999) reveals strong evidence that a lagged measure of the percentage of births to unmarried mothers is significantly associated with contemporary trends in age-specific homicide arrest rates, which is consistent with the logic of Donohue and Levitt's (2001) argument (see also O'Brien and Stockard, 2002). I build on this work by more squarely evaluating whether recent city-level crime trends are associated with various features of the cohorts born 15 to 19 years earlier in the metropolitan area in which these cities are located, including the percentage born to unmarried mothers and teenage mothers and the percentage classified as low-weight births.

Summary of Prior Work and the Scope of the Present Study

There are many rich ideas about the factors that probably were responsible for the crime trends observed in the United States since 1980. These include changes in the quantity and quality of policing, incarceration, drug and alcohol use, drug markets, unemployment rates and real wages, the prevalence of firearms, domesticity, age structure, lagged birth cohort features, and immigration. Although the extant empirical research has contributed much to the understanding of what happened with respect to crime trends during the past 25 years, as well as why it happened, there are numerous questions that either have not been addressed or have not been addressed sufficiently. One of the significant omissions from the existing empirical literature is a simultaneous assessment of the many factors hypothesized to shape recent crime trends. The attempt here is to fill this gap by considering the effects on crime trends of each of the major factors emphasized in the literature and discussed above.

DATA AND METHODS

Units of Analysis and Sample

As explained in the first chapter of the volume, the Committee on Law and Justice of the National Research Council (NRC) selected the units of analysis and defined the sampling universe for this study. The units of analysis chosen were large U.S. cities, and the original database included 240 cities with populations of 100,000 or more based on the 2000 census.

In theory, the use of subnational units, like cities, provides a better chance of solving the contemporary crime trends puzzle than national-level studies. As Levitt (2001) points out, such an approach permits the estimation of panel time-series models, which can address a wider array of research questions and are much better suited for controlling for confounding temporal and spatial factors than national-level approaches. Cities also are a particularly sensible choice for studying crime trends given that most law enforcement agencies, and hence data on the volume of crime, are organized at the level of cities. And although decisions about crime policy often are influenced by state and county developments and politics, they are typically implemented by city personnel.

Although cities are a sensible unit of analysis for studying crime trends, there are two major drawbacks associated with this choice. First, very little of the requisite data one might use to measure directly key explanatory variables is collected for cities, or at least not on a regular basis. The original NRC city-level database supplied included only two time-varying city-level indicators as explanatory variables: police officers per capita and drug arrest rates. This was not an oversight. It is merely the reality of the current data infrastructure; many of the relevant time-varying indicators one might want for studying crime trends simply are not readily available for U.S. cities for most of the period under review. Given the importance of incorporating time-varying indicators in a study of crime trends and the desire to take a comprehensive approach, I therefore drew from a variety of sources to construct annual estimates that might be reasonably allocated to describe city conditions. In some instances, potentially relevant measures were available only for the counties, metropolitan areas, or states in which the NRC cities are located. It is arguably better to use county or metropolitan-area data to estimate annual trends for cities than to use nothing or to use city-level data from decennial censuses and simply assume a linear trend between decennial periods to estimate these conditions, which could introduce an artificial temporal relationship with crime rate trends. Nevertheless, the unit discrepancy between the NRC primary sample units (cities) and the lowest level of geography for which many potentially key indicators are available (counties) is a drawback of the present work, and future studies should evaluate its implications.

Second, one trade-off in attempting an inclusive assessment of contemporary crime trends is that the requisite data needed to do so could not be located or were very incomplete for many of the cities included in the original NRC sampling frame. Consequently, several of the cities were excluded from the analysis. Some of the cities became incorporated government units only in the late 1970s, which limits some of the data elements that can be gathered for them, and many of these cities and other areas did not report crime or arrest data consistently during the study period, especially during the early 1980s. Overall, I was able to locate complete data for 151 of the 240 cities in the original NRC sample frame. About one-third of the sample attrition arose because of the inclusion of disaggregated homicide rates in the study, which were available on a consistent basis across the study period for only 205 of the 240 original cities. Much of the remaining attrition was due to the inclusion of key explanatory variables, especially indicators of drug market activity and drug use, which contain a substantial amount of missing data.

I estimated models of contemporary crime trends for the full sample of 151 cities for which I could locate complete data, but the analysis reported below is based on a subsample of 114 of the cities with a population of 100,000 or more in 1980. As noted above, the NRC sample universe was defined as all large cities with populations of 100,000 or more based on the 2000 census. I modified this universe to use instead the 1980 census population counts to define large cities, retaining the 100,000 person minimum value. Doing so seemed sensible, given that the study focuses on crime trends from 1980 forward, since most of the extant city-level research on contemporary crime trends has used 1980 population counts to define large cities, and because using the 2000 census to define large cities would have resulted in a sample skewed toward newly emerging urban areas, especially in the western and southern regions of the United States (i.e., California and Texas), where recent population growth has been concentrated. Thus, the results presented below are based on the 114 cities in 1980 that had populations of 100,000 or more and for which data on all variables could be located.

Data and Measures

Variable definitions, sources, unit of measurement, and summary statistics for all variables included in the study are listed in Table 5-1. Subscripts in the table identify variables measured in lagged versus contemporaneous form. The original NRC database included annual rates of Uniform Crime Reports (UCR) homicide, robbery, burglary, and motor vehicle theft for large cities as well as annual indicators of city drug arrest rates and police force size, and state-level data on annual levels of incarceration. In addition, various demographic and economic indicators (age and racial composition, population size, family structure, poverty, unemployment, inequality, etc.) from the decennial censuses of 1980, 1990, and 2000 were included. To facilitate a more comprehensive analysis of contemporary crime trends, I modified the NRC database in three ways. First, given that prior research has shown that changes in youth homicide rates and gun homicide rates were distinct from other homicide trends during the 1980s and 1990s (e.g., Blumstein and Rosenfeld, 1998), I added data on these forms of lethal violence from the Supplementary Homicide Reports. Second, because the census data on social and economic attributes included in the NRC database were available for only 3 of the 25 time points examined in the study, I drew from a variety of additional sources to construct annual indicators of these conditions. Finally, some of the conditions emphasized in the literature as potentially important for understanding recent crime trends, such as the prevalence of firearms, levels of immigration, domesticity, alcohol consumption, birth cohort conditions, and wages received for legal work were not included in the NRC data, so I added measures of them to the data. As noted above, some of the factors emphasized in the literature as potentially relevant to shaping recent crime trends are not available for most cities, so in some cases the annual indicators used in the study describe conditions in the counties, metropolitan areas, or states in which the cities are located.[2]

[2]The wage data were deflated using the region-specific consumer price index for urban consumers published by the Bureau of Labor Statistics. Because annual data on age and race composition are currently not available for U.S. cities, annual county population estimates were used to compute year-to-year changes in the number of blacks and the number of persons between ages 15-24 and persons 45 and older in the counties in which the NRC cities fall. These county growth rates were applied to the available decennial (1980, 1990, and 2000) city-level estimates of population by race and age to compute city-level intercensal (1981-1989, 1991-1999, 2001-2004) values for percentage black, percentage 15-24, and percentage 45 and older for the NRC cities.

TABLE 5-1 Description of Variables Included in Analysis of Recent Crime Trends (N = 114)

Variable	Variable Definition and Source	Mean	Overall SD	Within-City SD
Dependent Variables				
Homicide rate	Homicides per 100,000 residents (UCR)	12.69	10.03	4.70
Gun homicide rate	Gun homicides per 100,000 residents (SHR)	7.78	7.29	3.63
Nongun homicide rate	Nongun homicides per 100,000 residents (SHR)	4.41	3.27	2.07
Youth homicide rate	Homicides involving a person ages 15-24 per 100,000 residents ages 15-24 (SHR)	22.23	20.71	14.04
Adult homicide rate	Homicides involving a person ages 25-44 per 100,000 residents ages 25-44 (SHR)	11.25	9.54	6.27
Robbery rate	Robberies per 100,000 residents (UCR)	395.57	301.66	138.98
Burglary rate	Burglaries per 100,000 housing units (UCR and Census Bureau)	4,144.75	1,951.18	1,410.78
Motor vehicle theft rate	Motor vehicle thefts per 100,000 motor vehicles (UCR and Census Bureau)	807.70	1,056.05	471.88
Explanatory Variables				
Criminal justice factors				
State stock incarceration rate$_{t-1}$	Persons incarcerated in state prison per 100,0000 residents (BJS)	308.59	157.79	134.85
State prison admission rate$_{t-1}$	Persons admitted to state prison per 100,000 residents (BJS)	174.96	97.06	74.84
State prison release rate$_{t-1}$	Persons released from state prison per 100,000 residents (BJS)	158.46	94.35	74.17
City police force size$_{t-1}$	Police officers per 100,000 residents (UCR)	207.67	76.50	23.62
City public order and weapons arrest rate$_{t-1}$	Number of arrests per 100,000 residents for weapons violations, vandalism, prostitution, gambling, liquor laws, drunkenness, disorderly conduct, vagrancy, curfew violations, loitering, and suspicion (UCR)	282.92	343.79	276.35
City serious crime arrest certainty$_{t-1}$	Ratio of arrests for murder, robbery, burglary, and motor vehicle theft to the number of murders, robberies, burglaries, and motor vehicle thefts known to the police (UCR)	14.32	6.39	3.38
Economic conditions				
City job availability	Ratio of jobs in city commuting zone to city residents ages 16-64 (BEA and Census Bureau)	14.53	25.19	12.09

City unemployment rate	% of civilian labor force unemployed (BLS)	6.33	2.55	1.58
County average real wages	Mean real annual wage across all industries (BEA)	19,358	3,313.59	1,790.81
Guns, drugs and alcohol				
County firearm prevalence	% of suicides committed with a firearm (NCHS)	53.35	14.23	7.71
City cocaine/heroin arrest rate	Number of arrests per 100,000 residents for sale or possession of cocaine/heroin (UCR)	112.35	184.09	123.40
City % cocaine arrests < 18	% of cocaine/heroin arrests attributed to persons under 18 (UCR)	7.72	11.78	10.67
County cocaine mortality rate	Cocaine-related deaths, per 100,000 county residents (NCHS)	1.04	1.76	1.57
City alcohol-related traffic fatalities	% of traffic fatalities that involved a drunk driver (NHTSA FARS)	35.93	16.26	14.53
Demographic characteristics				
State % married couple households	% of state households with a married couple (CPS)	38.96	3.33	2.09
State % cohabiting couple households	% of state households with two unmarried adults of opposite sex who share living quarters (CPS)	3.37	1.20	.95
City % ages 15-24	% of population ages 15-24 (Census Bureau and SEER)	16.96	3.82	2.19
City % ages 45+	% of population ages 45 and older (Census Bureau and SEER)	29.47	4.46	2.33
City population size	Total population (Census Bureau and SEER)	39,2342	78,6873	58,192
City % black	% of population who are black (Census Bureau and SEER)	19.12	16.31	2.27
MSA immigration rate	New immigrants intending to reside in MSA per 100,000 MSA residents (INS and Census Bureau)	171.51	173.23	58.50
MSA % of births to teenage $women_{t\text{-}15\text{-}19\ years}$	% of births in MSA to women ages 15-19, lagged 15-19 years (NCHS Natality Files)	15.85	3.69	1.75
MSA % of births to unmarried $women_{t\text{-}15\text{-}19\ years}$	% of births in MSA to unmarried women, lagged 15-19 years (NCHS Natality Files)	13.49	6.55	5.36
MSA % of births < 2500 $grams_{t\text{-}15\text{-}19\ years}$	% of babies born in MSA who weighed < 2,500 grams, lagged 15-19 years (NCHS Natality Files)	7.34	1.09	.496

NOTE: BEA = Bureau of Economic Analysis; BJS = Bureau of Justice Statistics; BLS = Bureau of Labor Statistics; FARS = Federal Accident Reporting System; INS = Immigration and Naturalization Service; MSA = metropolitan statistical areas; NCHS = National Center for Health Statistics; NHTSA = National Highway and Traffic Safety Administration; SEER = Surveillance Epidemiology and End Results; SHR = Supplementary Homicide Reports; UCR = Uniform Crime Reporting Program.

Methods

Given the research issues addressed here and various features of the data used to do so, the present study applies econometric panel modeling techniques to evaluate the effects of the factors outlined earlier on recent crime trends. A series of two-way fixed-effects panel models of crime rates are estimated and reported below. This specification includes fixed effects that control for stable unmeasured city attributes and temporal shocks that are shared across cities. Also, linear and quadratic trend variables are included in the models to account for unit-specific temporal shocks (Raphael and Winter-Ebmer, 2001; Worrall and Pratt, 2004). The annual crime data examined in the study exhibit significant serial autocorrelation, so the models include as an explanatory variable lagged forms of the dependent variable (Beck and Katz, 1995). Finally, preliminary analyses of the data used here indicate the presence of substantial cross-sectional correlation in disturbances across cities. Failing to account for these features of the data can lead to invalid inferences, so in the models shown below I report panel-corrected standard errors, which allow the disturbances to be heteroskedastic and contemporaneously correlated across panels (Wilson and Butler, 2007).[3]

Before presenting results, it is important to highlight two issues that warrant careful consideration while proceeding in a panel estimation of crime trends. First, although the issue of stationarity has been studied extensively with national-level crime data (e.g., Greenberg, 2001), it has largely been ignored in the literature on recent crime trends. In fact, only a few of the studies commonly included in overviews of the literature on recent crime trends even mentions this issue (see also Moody, 2007; Spelman, 2008). The typical subnational study of recent crime trends assumes stationarity in the variables and proceeds by estimating panel regression models in levels (for some exceptions, see McDowall, Loftin, and Wiersema, 2000; Moody and Marvell, 2005).

If crime rates and the explanatory variables are stationary, then this is an appropriate way to proceed. However, if crime rates and/or the explanatory variables are nonstationary, the specter of spurious regression emerges and traditional panel model estimation strategies in levels *may* be inappropriate (see also Bushway and McDowall, 2006). One approach often applied when nonstationarity is suspected or found is to difference the variables, which can induce stationarity, and to estimate panel models on the transformed variables. Although easy enough to implement, this seem-

[3]The results presented are robust to alternative specifications. Models were also estimated without the unit-specific trends and with autocorrelation modeled as a nuisance parameter in lieu of the lagged dependent variable (e.g., Beck and Katz, 1995; Wolfers, 2006). The results of these supplementary analyses were substantively identical to those reported below.

ingly easy and quick fix may not necessarily be a wise decision or produce more valid results, because differencing masks the stable long-run levels relationships that may exist between variables (i.e., cointegration), which raises a whole host of additional modeling issues that can be critical for the inferences drawn (see Baumer and Rapach, 2007, for a review). Overall, the preferred strategy would be to evaluate stationarity formally with appropriate tests (e.g., panel unit root tests that account for cross-sectional dependence), assess the implications of some of the imprecision that is likely to result from such tests (e.g., some units and some variables may exhibit stationarity while others do not), test for cointegration if necessary, and proceed accordingly with panel regression estimation based on the results of such tests. Spelman's (2008) recent analysis of state-level data on incarceration and crime exemplifies the kind of analytical approach needed, though the fact that his scope in doing so in a full paper was limited to a single relationship with few explanatory variables underscores the complexity of the issues that need to be addressed in subsequent research.

A second issue that deserves mention is simultaneity. Several of the factors thought to be instrumental in raising or lowering crime during the past two decades are also likely to be affected by crime rates. For example, increases in incarceration, police force size, and arrest rates may be important for determining subsequent crime levels, but probably also are to some large extent the consequent of rising crime rates (Greenberg, Kessler, and Logan, 1979; Levitt, 1996, 2002). Economic conditions (e.g., wages and unemployment rates), firearm prevalence, and levels of drug use also have been suspected of exhibiting a simultaneous relationship with crime rates (e.g., Fagan, 1990; Raphael and Winter-Ebmer, 2001; Rosenfeld, Baumer, and Messner, 2007). In short, many of the factors routinely mentioned as possible causes of recent crime trends also might plausibly be consequences of crime. If so, and if this possibility is not formally considered in the analytical approach to studying crime trends, the inferences drawn may be misleading.

There are a variety of ways to address endogeneity concerns, including Granger causality and instrumental variables analysis. None of the available strategies is ideal or fully satisfactory under typical conditions, but addressing this issue is critical for drawing more definitive conclusions about the factors associated with recent crime trends. Granger tests are useful for assessing whether simultaneous relationships are present, but it appears that the greatest strides in tackling the endogeneity problem in crime trends research will come in the form of identifying and incorporating valid and relevant instrumental variables that can help separate simultaneous effects (see also Spelman, 2008). This will not be an easy task, but a growing literature has documented potentially useful instrumental variables that yield better estimates of the effects on crime rates of firearms (Kleck, Kovandzic, and Schaffer, 2005; Rosenfeld, Baumer, and Messner, 2007), incarceration rates (e.g., Spelman, 2005), unemployment rates (Raphael and Winter-Ebmer, 2001), and police strength (e.g., Levitt, 2002). Additional efforts to locate alternative instruments for these and other crime predictors would be useful, and estimating models that attempt to account for endogeneity in key predictors should become standard practice in a comprehensive and systematic research agenda on crime trends.

Given the space constraints of the present volume and my chosen focus of expanding the typical set of factors considered in crime trends, it is not possible to deal satisfactorily with these two important methodological issues. Examining stationarity and cointegration in a panel setting raises a series of complex issues that warrant detailed attention, discussion, and analysis of issues that have yet to be fully resolved in the literature. Some of the appropriate panel unit root tests (e.g., those that account for cross-sectional dependence) have only recently been developed in econometrics, and it is unclear how they should be applied and interpreted in common crime panel data settings, which are likely to contain some variables and some units that are stationary and others that are nonstationary.

In short, addressing the issue of nonstationarity is not merely a matter of differencing the data and seeing what happens. Although a research agenda on dealing with these issues in a panel setting is developing and beginning to sort through some of the relevant issues (Baumer and Rapach, 2007; Moody, 2007; Spelman, 2008), this work is still in early stages, and incorporating the necessary procedures in the present study would require a substantial expansion of scope. Addressing the prospects of cointegration is even more complex, especially in the context of relatively large multivariate models, such as those developed here. I therefore proceed "as usual" for subnational crime studies and assume stationarity in the variables and estimate panel models in levels. Also, although there may be several instances of simultaneity in the models presented below, the general strategy adopted here is to follow the typical approach used in crime trends research and use lagged explanatory variables to minimize endogeneity concerns for attributes that theoretically are expected to have a delayed effect on crime. Although this is a common strategy, extensions of this research should assess its validity by incorporating instrumental variables as noted above.

In summary, the analysis presented below adopts methods that have been used in most of the extant research on recent crime trends, yet it extends that work by incorporating, to a much greater degree, indicators of each of the major factors emphasized in theoretical and policy discussions. These results represent an assessment of the role that these factors played in shaping city crime trends since the early 1980s, as well as their relative contributions, and can be compared meaningfully with much of the extant research on recent crime trends. Nonetheless, like all research findings, the validity of these results rest on the validity of the underlying assumptions. As noted above, drawing definitive conclusions from the findings reported below should await a more rigorous assessment of the assumptions of stationarity, lack of cointegration, and exogeneity, in particular. I therefore do not focus on illustrating specific results in detail, but rather emphasize the general implications of results based on an analysis that expands the typical specification employed and on comparing these results with existing research that is based on less comprehensive approaches.

RESULTS

Given the qualifications just noted, the analysis proceeds as follows. Results are first presented for two sets of regression models: the first set covers the full time frame covered in the NRC database (1980-2004) and includes all variables described above except immigration and lagged birth cohort features, which are not available for the full period; the second set adds these indicators and covers the shorter period (1984-2000) for which these variables are available. Results for a parallel set of models that consider alternative measures (i.e., incarceration flow measures), functional forms, and temporal interactions for state-level incarceration rates for the full period are also discussed. After providing an overview of the regression models, their overall implications for recent crime trends are compared with recent overviews based on previous research. Finally, the implications of the results for predicting subsequent crime rates are outlined.

A Comprehensive Model of Recent Crime Trends

Table 5-2 displays estimates for two-way fixed-effects panel regression models for the 114 cities included in the analysis for the full study period (1980-2004). Table 5-3 presents results for a set of models for a slightly shorter period (1984-2000) that are identical, save for the addition of the potentially important measures of immigration and lagged birth cohort attributes (unavailable for the full period). In each case, results are presented in tabular form both for the four crime types included in the NRC database (total homicide, robbery, burglary, and motor vehicle theft) and for four disaggregated homicide measures (gun homicide, nongun homicide, youth homicide, and adult homicide). With some notable exceptions, the results for common variables in the two sets of models (i.e., the analyses for 1980-2004 presented in Table 5-2 and the expanded specification for 1984-2000 presented in Table 5-3) are very similar, so I summarize the general conclusions that emerge across these analyses and highlight noteworthy differences when relevant rather than describing each table in detail sequen-

TABLE 5-2 Two-Way Fixed-Effects Models of Crime Rates, 1980-2004 (N = 114)

Explanatory Variable	Logged Homicide	Logged Robbery	Logged Burglary	Logged MV Theft
Once-lagged crime rate (logged)	.065	.722*	.775*	.856*
	(.057)	(.031)	(.031)	(.026)
State % households with cohabiting couple	.036	.021*	.012*	.006
	(.022)	(.007)	(.005)	(.006)
State % households with married couple	.007	.001	–.001	–.0001
	(.007)	(.002)	(.002)	(.003)
City % ages 15-24	.026*	–.0001	.002	.002
	(.006)	(.002)	(.002)	(.002)
City % ages 45+	–.021*	.002	.001	–.0002
	(.007)	(.002)	(.001)	(.002)
City population size (logged)	.118	.140*	.024	.180*
	(.125)	(.044)	(.034)	(.042)
City % black	.031*	.007*	.004*	.004*
	(.005)	(.001)	(.001)	(.002)
County firearm prevalence	.003*	.001	.0001	–.0001
	(.001)	(.001)	(.0003)	(.0004)
City cocaine/heroin arrest rate (logged)	.026*	.007*	–.001	.003
	(.010)	(.003)	(.002)	(.003)
County cocaine mortality rate (logged)	.012	.007*	.005*	.005
	(.010)	(.003)	(.002)	(.004)
City % cocaine/heroin arrests < 18	.003*	.001*	.002	.001*
	(.001)	(.0003)	(.002)	(.0002)
City % crashes with a drunk driver	–.001	–.0001	–.0002	–.0002
	(.001)	(.002)	(.0002)	(.0002)
City job availability	.001	.001*	–.0001	.0001
	(.0006)	(.0002)	(.0002)	(.0001)
City unemployment rate	.001	–.001	.002	–.011*
	(.007)	(.003)	(.003)	(.003)
County average real wages (logged)	–.504*	–.052	–.001	–.041
	(.237)	(.064)	(.052)	(.057)
State stock incarceration rate$_{t-1}$ (logged)	–.347*	–.112*	–.054*	–.089*
	(.076)	(.027)	(.026)	(.029)
City police force size$_{t-1}$ (logged)	–.095	–.069*	–.005	–.044
	(.109)	(.029)	(.021)	(.029)
City public order and weapons arrest rate$_{t-1}$ (logged)	.102*	.009	–.004	–.010
	(.035)	(.010)	(.006)	(.009)
City serious crime arrest certainty$_{t-1}$ (logged)	–.099	–.047*	–.014	.005
	(.058)	(.014)	(.009)	(.013)
R-Squared	.768	.965	.957	.950

continued

TABLE 5-2 Continued

Explanatory Variable	Logged Gun Homicide	Logged Nongun Homicide	Logged Youth Homicide	Logged Adult Homicide
Once-lagged crime rate	.113*	.085	.011	.026
	(.053)	(.051)	(.050)	(.052)
State % households with cohabiting couple	.067*	.038	.072	.070
	(.031)	(.025)	(.046)	(.037)
State % households with married couple	.002	–.002	–.007	.005
	(.009)	(.009)	(.016)	(.012)
City % ages 15-24	.027*	.009	–.025	.025*
	(.008)	(.008)	(.014)	(.012)
City % ages 45+	–.030*	–.009	–.016	–.010
	(.008)	(.007)	(.012)	(.009)
City population size (logged)	–.008	.139	.106	.332
	(.149)	(.173)	(.256)	(.213)
City % black	.027*	.039*	.033*	.029*
	(.006)	(.005)	(.010)	(.008)
County firearm prevalence	.006*	–.0003	–.001	.002
	(.002)	(.002)	(.003)	(.002)
City cocaine/heroin arrest rate (logged)	.015	.037*	.041*	.025
	(.012)	(.014)	(.024)	(.020)
County cocaine mortality rate (logged)	.006	.007	.041	.006
	(.015)	(.015)	(.024)	(.020)
City % cocaine arrests < 18	.003*	.003*	.008*	–.001
	(.001)	(.001)	(.003)	(.002)
City % crashes with a drunk driver	–.002	.0002	–.002	–.002
	(.001)	(.001)	(.002)	(.002)
City job availability	.002	–.0002	.002	–.001
	(.001)	(.001)	(.001)	(.001)
City unemployment rate	.028*	–.027*	.012	.015
	(.010)	(.010)	(.018)	(.014)
County average real wages (logged)	.220	–1.06*	–.789	–.515
	(.289)	(.268)	(.481)	(.407)
State stock incarceration rate$_{t-1}$ (logged)	–.348*	–.270*	–.512*	–.420*
	(.104)	(.094)	(.157)	(.145)
City police force size$_{t-1}$ (logged)	–.239	–.129	–.319	–.330
	(.151)	(.147)	(.298)	(.216)
City public order and weapons arrest rate$_{t-1}$ (logged)	.151*	.050	.254*	.098
	(.046)	(.041)	(.068)	(.057)
City serious crime arrest certainty$_{t-1}$ (logged)	–.085	–.095	–.131	–.065
	(.063)	(.064)	(.099)	(.073)
R-Squared	.716	.614	.545	.578

*p < .05

TABLE 5-3 Two-Way Fixed-Effects Models of Crime Rates, 1984-2000 (N = 114)

Explanatory Variable	Logged Homicide	Logged Robbery	Logged Burglary	Logged MV Theft
MSA immigration rate	–.055	.011	.038*	.021
	(.080)	(.025)	(.017)	(.021)
MSA % teenage births$_{t-15\text{-}19\ years}$	.023*	.001	–.003	.008
	(.013)	(.005)	(.004)	(.005)
MSA % nonmarital births$_{t-15\text{-}19\ years}$	–.002	–.001	–.001	–.002*
	(.003)	(.001)	(.001)	(.001)
MSA % low birth weight	–.083*	.019	.014	.016
births$_{t-15\text{-}19\ years}$	(.040)	(.015)	(.013)	(.018)
Once-lagged crime rate (logged)	.021	.661*	.706*	.755*
	(.079)	(.049)	(.051)	(.037)
State stock incarceration rate$_{t-1}$ (logged)	–.373*	–.154*	–.099*	–.151*
	(.116)	(.040)	(.041)	(.039)
City police force size$_{t-1}$ (logged)	–.073	–.114*	–.056*	–.122*
	(.133)	(.035)	(.028)	(.038)
City public order and weapons arrest	.130*	.018	–.006	–.024
rate$_{t-1}$ (logged)	(.047)	(.015)	(.029)	(.013)
City serious crime arrest certainty$_{t-1}$	–.152*	–.065*	–.036*	.005
(logged)	(.071)	(.017)	(.012)	(.017)
City job availability	.0002	.003	.0002	–.0001
	(.0007)	(.002)	(.0002)	(.0002)
City unemployment rate	.004	–.006	.003	–.007
	(.010)	(.004)	(.003)	(.004)
County average real wages (logged)	–.724*	–.050	.057	.004
	(.363)	(.111)	(.077)	(.087)
County firearm prevalence	.003	.0001	–.0001	.0002
	(.002)	(.001)	(.0004)	(.0006)
City cocaine/heroin arrest rate (logged)	.030*	.010*	.002	.009*
	(.012)	(.004)	(.003)	(.003)
County cocaine mortality rate (logged)	.010	.004	.003	.003
	(.012)	(.004)	(.003)	(.004)
City % cocaine/heroin arrests < 18	.004*	.001*	.0002	.001
	(.001)	(.0004)	(.0002)	(.0002)
City % crashes with a drunk driver	–.001	.002	–.0002	–.0001
	(.001)	(.003)	(.0002)	(.0002)
State % households with cohabiting	.046*	.022*	.017*	.007
couple	(.023)	(.009)	(.007)	(.008)
State % households with married	.008	–.001	–.001	.003
couple	(.008)	(.002)	(.002)	(.003)
City % ages 15-24	.026*	–.001	.0003	.002
	(.007)	(.001)	(.002)	(.003)
City % ages 45+	–.027*	.001	.001	–.002
	(.007)	(.002)	(.001)	(.002)
City population size (logged)	.128	.106	–.065	.725*
	(.228)	(.081)	(.055)	(.069)
City % black	.041*	.008*	.007*	.018*
	(.007)	(.002)	(.002)	(.002)
R-Squared	.781	.966	.951	.951

continued

TABLE 5-3 Continued

Explanatory Variable	Logged Gun Homicide	Logged Nongun Homicide	Logged Youth Homicide	Logged Adult Homicide
MSA immigration rate	–.053	–.035	.191	–.065
	(.115)	(.098)	(.129)	(.139)
MSA % teenage births$_{t-15\text{-}19 \text{ years}}$	.039*	–.012	.090*	–.004
	(.018)	(.022)	(.034)	(.026)
MSA % nonmarital births$_{t-15\text{-}19 \text{ years}}$	.002	–.001	.008	–.012*
	(.004)	(.003)	(.006)	(.006)
MSA % low birth weight births$_{t-15\text{-}19 \text{ years}}$	–.149*	–.026	–.127	–.089
	(.061)	(.070)	(.104)	(.091)
Once-lagged crime rate	.110*	.055	–.011	–.023
	(.071)	(.070)	(.066)	(.071)
State stock incarceration rate$_{t-1}$ (logged)	–.562*	–.197	–.668*	–.694*
	(.150)	(.120)	(.261)	(.187)
City police force size$_{t-1}$ (logged)	–.205	–.250	–.539	–.376
	(.195)	(.177)	(.349)	(.291)
City public order and weapons arrest rate$_{t-1}$ (logged)	.192*	.036	.289*	.069
	(.065)	(.054)	(.091)	(.078)
City serious crime arrest certainty$_{t-1}$ (logged)	–.093	–.213*	–.182	.019
	(.088)	(.091)	(.144)	(.108)
City job availability	.001	–.001	.001	–.003
	(.001)	(.001)	(.001)	(.002)
City unemployment rate	.036*	–.036*	.012	.010
	(.013)	(.015)	(.018)	(.017)
County average real wages (logged)	.214	–1.80*	–1.63*	–.983
	(.444)	(.347)	(.784)	(.651)
County firearm prevalence	.004	.001	–.006	.003
	(.002)	(.002)	(.004)	(.003)
City cocaine/heroin arrest rate (logged)	.017	.056*	.064*	.015
	(.016)	(.017)	(.026)	(.024)
County cocaine mortality rate (logged)	.016	.005	.035	.012
	(.016)	(.019)	(.030)	(.026)
City % cocaine arrests < 18	.005*	.002	.012*	–.0004
	(.002)	(.002)	(.003)	(.002)
City % crashes with a drunk driver	–.002	–.0003	–.003	–.001
	(.001)	(.002)	(.002)	(.002)
State % households with cohabiting couple	.085*	.029	.060	.079
	(.034)	(.032)	(.051)	(.042)
State % households with married couple	.005	–.008	–.024	–.009
	(.010)	(.011)	(.017)	(.014)
City % ages 15-24	.026*	.008	–.041*	.034*
	(.010)	(.008)	(.018)	(.016)
City % ages 45+	–.019*	–.009	–.009	–.026*
	(.009)	(.010)	(.017)	(.010)
City population size (logged)	.071	–.287	–.084	.394
	(.285)	(.338)	(.421)	(.412)
City % black	.030*	.037*	.011*	.047*
	(.008)	(.009)	(.014)	(.012)
R-Squared	.744	.616	.596	.589

*$p < .05$

tially. Overall, there are five noteworthy patterns revealed in the findings displayed in these two tables.

First, the coefficient on the once-lagged measure of stock incarceration is significant and negative in all but one of the crime models estimated (nongun homicide, 1984-2000). Consistent with other recent studies, the estimated elasticities for incarceration rates are higher for violence than property crimes and range from –.05 percent (burglary, Table 5-2) to –.67 (youth homicide, Table 5-3) across the crime types considered (see, e.g., Stemen, 2007). These results add to a large and growing body of evidence that reveals significant effects for incarceration during the period under consideration. Indeed, like other studies, incarceration rates emerge as particularly important here. Nevertheless, as noted earlier, there are several questions about these effects that have not received much attention in the literature, including whether stock and flow measures yield different effects and whether these patterns vary by scale or across time. To explore these issues in a preliminary way, I estimated two sets of additional models, building from the models shown in Table 5-2: (1) I substituted once-lagged indicators of rates of prison admissions and prison releases for the stock incarceration measure and (2) I assessed whether the effects of both the stock (i.e., overall incarceration rates) and flow (i.e., prison admission and release rates) measures of incarceration varied according to incarceration scale and over time by adding the relevant product terms (e.g., incarceration rate X incarceration rate; incarceration rate X year).

The supplementary analysis results (not shown in tabular form due to space constraints) indicated that despite a very strong correlation between the two flow measures ($r > .95$), increases in state prison committals per 100,000 residents tend to reduce crime in the following year, while increases in the number of persons released from state prisons per 100,000 residents tend to increase crime in the next year. The estimated coefficients were not consistently significant across crime types, but the pair of coefficients for these two indicators of prison flow (i.e., admissions and releases) is statistically significant at conventional levels for four of the eight crime types considered (overall homicide, gun homicide, robbery, and burglary) and significant using a one-tailed test for two of the others (youth homicide and adult homicide).

The supplementary analyses also revealed some significant variability in the estimated incarceration effects across time and at different levels of scale (results not shown), although the details varied across crime types. More specifically, the data examined here suggest that incarceration effects for lethal violence increased in magnitude during the 1980s and 1990s, while for the property crimes considered the evidence suggests significant diminishing returns for incarceration over time (for robbery) or no significant change (for burglary and motor vehicle theft). A parallel story emerged for the analysis of scale effects, with generally increasing elasticities for homicide as the scale of incarceration increases, declining elasticities for robbery as incarceration rates reach very high levels, and no significant scale effects for burglary and motor vehicle theft. Thus, depending on the crime type under investigation, there is evidence both for the notion that the crime reduction effects of growth in levels of incarceration have increased over time and with the scale of imprisonment, which is consistent with Spelman's (2006) research, and with "diminishing returns" arguments over time and with enhanced scale, which is consistent with recent state-level research by Liedka, Piehl, and Useem (2006). Overall, these results suggest that relying solely on the commonly used stock incarceration rate and assuming linearity and time invariance mask important information about the role of incarceration. Perhaps even the factor most often examined in crime trends research—incarceration—calls for a more systematic and comprehensive research agenda that can sort out these details (see also Spelman, 2008).

A second noteworthy finding that emerges from the regression analysis is that the policing variables yield inconsistent findings. There is no evidence in the data that cities in which the police focused more heavily on public order and weapons offenses (as measured by arrest rates) exhibited significantly lower crime rates. This finding is perhaps not surprising in light of recent evidence that such approaches had relatively small effects on crime trends in New York City, where they have evidently been implemented on a particularly grand scale (Messner et al., 2007; Rosenfeld, Fornango, and Baumer, 2005; Rosenfeld, Fornango, and Rengifo, 2007). However, the other two policing variables considered—police force size and arrest certainty for serious crimes—do yield significant effects in the expected direction, especially in the analysis restricted from 1984 to 2000 (Table 5-3). For this time frame, cities that increased their police forces experienced significantly greater declines in logged robbery, burglary, and motor vehicle theft. And areas in which the arrest certainty for serious crimes (i.e., the ratio of arrests for serious crimes to the number of serious crimes known to the police) was higher exhibited lower logged levels of homicide, robbery, and burglary.

Third, overall the results point to a relatively limited role for changes in the economy. The indicator of job availability is not significantly associated with trends in any of the crimes considered, and unemployment and wage effects appear to be limited to lethal violence. Specifically, unemployment rates during this period were positively associated with gun homicide rates, and wages were negatively associated with nongun homicide. As elaborated below, these significant effects were fairly substantial in magnitude. But none of the economic variables considered here exerted significant effects on the crimes one would most expect to see such effects influence: property crimes. Perhaps indicators better able to capture economic changes in the low-skilled sectors would fare better (e.g., Gould, Weinberg, and Mustard, 2002), but such data are not presently available over time for a large sample of cities.

Fourth, the evidence for the effects of guns, drug activity, and alcohol consumption on recent crime trends is mixed. Trends in alcohol consumption do not appear to play a significant role in shaping recent crime trends, firearm prevalence is significantly associated with overall homicide but not other crimes, and the indicators of change in crack cocaine use and market activity exert significant and meaningful effects on recent crime trends, albeit in somewhat inconsistent ways across measures and crime types. The indicator of alcohol consumption employed is insignificant in all of the estimated models. Perhaps a more direct measure of alcohol consumption, or even an age-specific version of the one used in this study, would point to a different conclusion, but as measured and modeled in this study it appears that trends in alcohol consumption did not play a significant role in recent crime trends, net of other factors. A similar story can be told for firearm prevalence. Although the indicator used here—the fraction of suicides committed with a firearm—has been used extensively in prior research and is considered by many to be the gold standard for gauging geographic variation in household gun ownership, its validity and reliability for tracking gun ownership *trends* has been critiqued (e.g., Kleck, 2004), and it is unclear how well it measures the stock of firearms available to would-be offenders. The indicators of illicit drug use and drug market conditions yield a more intuitive and substantively meaningful pattern of effects. The overall drug arrest rate for cocaine/heroin and the drug market age structure measure (as indicated by the percentage of persons arrested for possession or sale of cocaine/heroin who are under 18) yield the most consistently significant effects and are strongest for youth homicide, as expected on the basis of the underlying theoretical arguments.[4]

Finally, some of the demographic variables exert significant and interesting effects on crime trends. The indicator of the relative size of the black population exhibits a significant positive effect across all of the crime models. This reinforces a persistent finding in the literature that crime rates tend to be highest in cities with a high percentage of black residents (see, e.g., Land, McCall, and Cohen, 1990). There is much speculation about the reasons behind this association, but little convincing empirical evidence on the matter in aggregate crime studies. The age structure effects appear

[4]Additional analyses (not shown in tabular form) revealed no significant evidence of an interaction between the indicators of the legitimate economy and indicators of drug use and drug market measures. In practice, it is very difficult to assess this argument with the available aggregate-level data. But it is noteworthy that the observed effects of unemployment and wages show no evidence of being significantly conditioned by the drug indicators used in the study, or vice versa.

to be limited to homicide and in this instance are consistent with the idea that relatively larger cohorts of young persons are positively related and relatively larger cohorts of older persons are negatively related to violence. The findings for the indicators of domesticity suggest no significant effects of marriage rates but significant effects of cohabitation rates on logged robbery, burglary, and homicide. Rising levels of cohabitation yield similar patterns in the models of adult homicide, although in this instance the coefficient does not quite reach conventional levels of statistical significance. The link between cohabitation and homicide is consistent with Blumstein and Rosenfeld's (1998) domesticity argument. However, the significant association between trends in cohabitation and trends in robbery and burglary and the lack of a significant association in the models for adult homicide suggest that the cohabitation effects may reflect more general lifestyle patterns that raise the risk of victimization and offending, rather than increasing domesticity per se. It would be interesting to explore this further, especially in models of intimate partner homicide.

Levels of immigration and lagged birth cohort conditions were available only from 1984 to 2000 (Table 5-3). The results displayed in Table 5-3 show no support for the idea that increasing flows of immigration were significantly or inversely associated with aggregate-level crime rates between 1984 and 2000 (see also Butcher and Piehl, 1998). Even after trimming economic conditions from the model, which represent one of the pathways through which immigration has been posited to affect crime trends, no evidence of a significant negative immigration effect on crime trends was detected (not shown in tabular form).[5] Perhaps additional analyses that incorporate data on immigration through the early years of the 21st century (currently not available publicly) and also that adjust for the stock of foreign-born would yield different findings, but the conclusion supported here is that immigration had negligible effects on recent crime trends.

The indicators of lagged nonmartial births and the lagged prevalence of low-birth-weight babies are not associated with contemporary crime trends in the expected positive direction; in fact, these variables exhibit significant negative effects in a few cases. However, the findings do show that recent city-level homicide trends are significantly influenced by the percentage of

[5]According to these results, cities situated in metropolitan areas with greater increases in immigration actually experienced significantly elevated rates of burglary during the period. However, a supplementary analysis (not shown) on a slightly shorter time frame (1984-1997) and with a measure of city-level rates of immigration (i.e., the number of immigrants intending to live in the sampled cities—not merely the metropolitan statistical areas in which they are located—per 100,000 city residents) does not yield such a pattern and, more importantly, affirms that the most consistent pattern is that immigration flows are not significantly associated with recent crime trends.

the contemporary youthful cohort (i.e., persons ages 15-19) estimated to have been born to teenage mothers. This finding emerges as statistically significant for overall homicide and youth homicide, and it is strongest for the latter, as would be expected if the lagged teen birth prevalence indicator gauges differences in birth and childrearing conditions that yield consequences specific to the contemporary cohort defined by such conditions.[6] It is important to acknowledge, however, that this finding also could reflect more contemporary family structure effects or other types of lagged social and economic conditions that are not considered here. In general, aside from cohort size, aggregate-level crime research has paid little attention to the possible role of the conditions under which contemporary populations were born or grew up, and the results shown in Table 5-3 suggest that this could be an important oversight.

The Relative Contribution of the Factors

Overall, what do these findings tell us about which factors contributed most to contemporary crime trends? As noted above, a much more rigorous analysis should be applied to the data before one can draw precise conclusions about the bigger picture, but to address this issue in a preliminary way and make general comparisons with recent overviews of the research, I used the results shown in Table 5-3, coupled with information about observed changes in crime rates and the explanatory variables, to compute the estimated percentage of the overall change in crime rates that can be attributed to each factor considered. I used these procedures to compute the relative contributions of the factors separately for the two major crime trend eras of the past two decades, defined here as 1984-1992 and 1993-2000. Thus, I first estimated the mean change in each of the crime variables and explanatory variables across the 114 cities between 1984-1992 and 1993-2000, respectively. Using the coefficients shown in Table 5-3, which are based on models that also incorporate city and year fixed effects and city-specific time trends, I then calculated the expected or predicted change in the crime variables given the amount of observed change in each explanatory variable, and then divided it by the observed change in the crime variables to generate the fraction of the observed change that can be attributed to each factor. The end result is an estimate of the relative impact of each explanatory variable on the observed change in each of the eight crime types for the two periods under consideration. In keeping with the scope of the present

[6] The findings are very similar, and even somewhat stronger, if the youth homicide rate is defined to match more precisely the lagged birth cohort measures (i.e., homicide rates for persons ages 15-19).

investigation, I emphasize here the general conclusions that emerge from this exercise, beginning with the 1980s.

Although there has been a good deal of attention devoted to 1980s crime trends, to my knowledge there has not been a systematic assessment that breaks down given factors on the basis of their relative contributions, at least not in the same way seen in the literature on the 1990s crime decline (e.g., Levitt, 2004; Zimring, 2006). Most observers attribute the rise in youth gun violence, robbery, and some forms of auto theft during the 1980s largely to the emergence and proliferation of crack cocaine, and the results reported in Table 5-3 support that conclusion (e.g., Blumstein and Rosenfeld, 1998; Blumstein and Wallman, 2006a). Although the role of the three indicators of drug market activity and drug use vary across crime types, the results suggest that together they account for between 20 and 40 percent of the observed increases in overall homicide, gun homicide, and youth homicide and about 10 percent of the observed increase in robbery rates.

The results also point to the relevance of some factors that have not been given much weight in most discussions of crime trends during this period, however, such as the rise in cohabitation and changes in the prevalence of births to teenage mothers in an earlier period. The results suggest that the rise in cohabitation levels across the 114 cities accounts for roughly 15-25 percent of the observed increase in lethal violence between 1984 and 1992. Also, during the 1980s, the percentage of young persons estimated to have been born to teenage mothers increased slightly, and the results show that this trend accounted for about 5-10 percent of the overall increase in homicide, especially youth homicide. According to the data used in this research, there were slight declines in the availability of jobs and increases in unemployment during the 1980s, but, aside from gun homicide, for which the rise in unemployment contributed to an estimated 10 percent of the increase, the economy appears to have had relatively little direct impact on 1980s crime trends, at least based on the measures and models employed in this study. Finally, consistent with other reports (e.g., Levitt, 2004), the analysis indicates that lethal violence would have increased even more had it not been for a substantial increase in levels of incarceration and a considerable decline in the relative size of the youth population (i.e., the percentage ages 15-24). Incarceration also emerged as a primary contributor to the decline in burglary and adult homicide, accounting for more than half of the observed declines in both of these crimes (see also Rosenfeld, 1998).

What about the widespread crime decline of the 1990s? Here, there is a clearer record of claims that have been made in the extant literature with respect to what mattered and what mattered most. In particular, Levitt (2004) has boldly outlined the four factors that mattered and the six that did not, and Zimring (2006) also has drawn fairly precise conclusions about

TABLE 5-4 Conclusions About Factors Associated with the 1990s Crime Decline

Factors That Probably Mattered Quite A Bit	Factors That Probably Did Not Matter Much
A. Levitt (2004)	
Factors That Probably Mattered Quite A Bit	**Factors That Probably Did Not Matter Much**
Increases in incarceration rates	Improving economic conditions
Increases in police per capita	Changes in policing focus
Decline in crack	Smaller youth cohorts
1970s abortion legalization	
B. Zimring (2006)	
Factors That Probably Mattered Quite A Bit	**Factors That Probably Did Not Matter Much**
Increases in incarceration rates	1970s abortion legalization
Improving economic conditions	Decline in crack (except youth violence)
Smaller youth cohorts	Increases in police per capita (except NYC)
Regional cyclical factors	Changes in policing focus (except NYC)
C. The Present Study	
Factors That Probably Mattered Quite A Bit	**Factors That Probably Did Not Matter Much**
Increases in incarceration rates (10-35%)	Decline in crack
Improving economic conditions (10-30%)	Changes in policing focus
Decline in "lagged" teen births (10-35%)	Smaller youth cohorts
Larger adult cohorts (4-8%)	Changes in domesticity
Increases in police per capita (3-7%)	

NOTE: In Panel C, the percentages in parentheses represent a range across crime types of the estimated contribution of each factor to the observed crime declines.

what did and did not matter. I summarize their conclusions in Panels A and B of Table 5-4. The conclusions displayed in the upper two panels are not derived from formal meta-analyses—something that does not seem possible given the current shape of the literature—but rather in both cases the authors have culled from existing research the most pertinent evidence and provided educated overviews of what it says. I have argued in this chapter that taking a more comprehensive approach to measuring and modeling the factors thought to be associated with recent crime trends could yield different conclusions. In fact, this does appear to be the case. Panel C of Table 5-4 shows the conclusions supported by the present research, which incorporates a broader set of factors compared with previous studies.

Overall, the results concur with the conclusions drawn by others about the likely importance of incarceration for the 1990s crime decline. The models reported in Table 5-3 suggest that the continued rise in incarceration during the 1990s accounted for 10 to 35 percent of the decline in crime rates across crime types, with property crimes (i.e., robbery, burglary, and motor vehicle theft) defining the lower end of this range and lethal violence defining the higher end. The results also indicate, however, that the improving economy may have been more important during the 1990s than suggested by Levitt and Zimring. Although the effects are not uniform across crime types and, curiously, are evident only for lethal violence (and not property crime), the results indicate that the drop in unemployment during the 1990s can account for 10-15 percent of the decline in overall homicide and gun homicide. This coupled with the rise in real wages during the period explains as much as 30 percent of the observed decline in youth and nongun homicide rates. Contrary to Zimring's review, the decline in the lagged prevalence of births to teenage mothers also seems to have made a substantively important difference, accounting for about 10 percent of the decline in overall homicide and approximately one-third of the decline in youth violence during the 1990s. This is less than the estimated 50 percent attributed to the rise in abortion by Donohue and Levitt (2001), but it is still significant and also more clearly specifies one of the mechanisms that might link a rise in abortion (or other actions that control fertility) to lower subsequent crime many years later.

The findings reported here diverge somewhat from others with respect to age structure. Consistent with Levitt and contrary to Zimring, I found that changes in the relative size of youth cohorts do not appear to have made a big impact on the crime decline of the 1990s. However, the rise in the fraction of the population ages 45 and older emerges as a notable factor for the observed declines in lethal violence, accounting for between 4 and 8 percent of the observed declines in homicide subtypes considered in the study. The role of older cohorts in shaping crime trends has rarely been explored in prior work, which is somewhat surprising given the dramatic changes in the relative size of this low-offending-rate group.

Zimring (2006) does not give much weight to suggestions that increases in police force size were very consequential to the 1990s crime decline, except for perhaps New York City, where such increases were especially dramatic. Levitt (2004) also does not see enhancements to police force size as a major factor but does estimate that it probably accounted for about 5-6 percent of the decline. The results in Table 5-3 yield very similar estimates, indicating that about 3-7 percent of the observed decline in crime during the 1990s can be attributed directly to increased police forces, with property crimes defining the lower end and adult homicide and nongun homicide defining the upper end.

The other factors examined do not appear to have played a major role in the 1990s crime decline, at least as I have measured and modeled them. One of these—the prevalence of crack cocaine use and market activity—did reveal significant effects on many of the crime types considered, but the indicators used did not decline substantially during the 1990s, rendering their ability to account for the observed changes in crime to be minimal, in the neighborhood of 1-2 percent. Some of the other factors, like changes in policing focus (e.g., arrest rates for public order and weapons offenses), levels of domesticity, immigration rates, alcohol consumption, and firearm prevalence may emerge as more relevant in analyses that better attend to issues of measurement error, unit measure mismatch, stationarity, and simultaneity, but for now I would conclude that their contributions to the 1990s crime decline do not appear to be substantial.

Out-of-Sample Predictions

Thus far I have focused on attempting to explain what happened with respect to recent crime trends. Another objective of the NRC crime trends workshop was to assess the capacity for existing models to provide forecasts or predictions of subsequent crime rates beyond the period covered in the study (i.e., post-2004). Although it is unclear whether and how decent crime forecasts would be put to use, the idea of knowing what is coming is enticing. For instance, if it was known sooner in the mid-1980s what may have been on the horizon, perhaps law enforcement and other public policy agents could have responded in ways that could have reduced the dramatic rise in violence that occurred. Furthermore, in a time of tight local budgets, high levels of anxiety among the public, and claims makers who tend to sensationalize highly visible violent incidents, it might be useful to have some sense of whether crime is likely to continue the descent seen for most of the 1990s and beyond, whether it is likely to rise significantly, or whether it might maintain a steady state. Despite some courageous and sophisticated previous efforts, crime forecasting is highly undeveloped at the present time and, in part because of this, I chose to focus most of my efforts in this chapter on developing explanatory models of recent crime trends rather than forecasting crime beyond the study period. Nevertheless, part of the value in assessing the factors that contributed to recent crime trends lies in what these models say about the likely direction of crime beyond the period under study. So what do the models outlined above, which focus on trying to explain crime trends between 1980-2004, say about the path of crime in subsequent years?

To address this question, I used the coefficients from Table 5-2, which includes city and year fixed effects and city-specific time trends, to estimate crime levels (rates of homicide, robbery, burglary, and auto theft) for 2005. I first obtained, or in some cases estimated, city-specific values for each explanatory variable included in the models shown in Table 5-2. Since the focus was on estimating levels of crime in 2005, for the one-year lagged variables in the model (i.e., police force size, incarceration rates, public order and weapons arrest rates, and serious arrest certainty) the city-specific values reflect 2004 conditions, and for all other variables, which were measured contemporaneously, the city-specific values reflect 2005 conditions derived from additional data collection. I then multiplied these city-specific covariate observed values by their corresponding coefficients from the models shown in Table 5-2 to generate a predicted crime level for 2005. This process yielded predicted 2005 crime levels for each of the cities included in the study. I next obtained from the UCR the observed crime levels for the 50 largest of these cities and used the observed values to compute the percentage change between 2004 and 2005 in observed crime levels and the predicted percentage change between 2004 and 2005 using the predicted values for 2005 derived from the procedures just outlined. Table 5-5 summarizes the results of the exercise.

The UCR data reveal that the 50 largest cities included in the study experienced an average (median) increase of about 3.79 percent in logged homicide rates between 2004 (the last year of the study period) and 2005. This figure represents the observed change in homicide over the one-year period. Applying the procedures outlined above, my analysis predicted an average (median) decrease of 2.74 percent over this one-year period based on the results of the panel crime regression model displayed in Table 5-2 (including city and year fixed effects and city time trends) and the city-specific values on the explanatory variables. For robbery, the observed change was a 1 percent increase, and the prediction was for a .40 percent decline. As Table 5-5 shows, the predicted and observed change values are closer for burglary and especially motor vehicle theft; in the latter case, the model predicted a slight decline (–.27 percent) that was very close to the observed change (–.34 percent). The gaps here are not large in absolute terms, but at least for homicide, robbery, and burglary they probably are unacceptable, given the high stakes associated with crime prediction. In each of these three cases, for instance, one would have predicted decreases

TABLE 5-5 Predictions of 2005 Crime Levels for 50 Largest Cities from Regressions of Recent Crime Trends, 1980-2004

	Homicide	Robbery	Burglary	Auto Theft
% Change 2004-2005				
Predicted	–2.74	–.40	–.39	–.27
Observed	3.79	1.02	.01	–.34
% Cities predicted in right direction	44	40	46	48

NOTE: Figures for predicted and observed change represent median values for the 50 largest cities in the sample for which this information could be computed.

in crime when, in fact, there were increases. Indeed, another way to look at forecasting is to ask more simply about predictions in the *direction* of crime changes. In other words, is crime going to increase or decrease next year? The bottom row of Table 5-5 presents results relevant to this question. The procedures outlined above yielded an accurate prediction compared to the observed change in 44 percent of the cities in the case of homicide, 40 percent for robbery, 46 percent for burglary, and 48 percent for motor vehicle theft. Overall, the model based predictions that emerge from my study do not appear to be very good—one could do better in predicting the direction of changes in these crimes by flipping a coin.

It is possible that 2005 was an aberrant year. When I replicated Table 5-5 predicting changes in crime for 2003-2004, the predicted and observed robbery and burglary rates were closer and the record for predicting the direction of crime changes improved dramatically, with the right direction predicted in two-thirds to three-quarters of the cities (results not shown). However, the gap between observed and predicted homicide rates in this supplementary analyses were no better, and when I repeated the process yet again for predicting changes in crime for 2002-2003, the results were mixed (not shown), with some estimates outperforming those shown in Table 5-5 and others doing less well. Maybe 2005 was aberrant in the degree of unexplained change, maybe one or more of the other years was, maybe the types of model-based predictions summarized here are not well suited for predicting crime, or maybe crime trends are not highly predictable, save for periods of major shifts, such as the 1990s, when a predicted decline in crime would have been a good bet (as it turns out) for many years.

Overall, like crime trends research in general, the issue of forecasting crime is in the early stages of development and more work needs to be done to better understand the nuances of making future crime predictions, to outline the best approaches to take given the reality of existing data, and to define acceptable parameters of prediction performance. There are several reasons why the regression models used to predict crime in this study probably did not fare better, including measurement mismatches between the city-level outcome variables and, in some cases, state-level explanatory variables, other sources of measurement error, methodological limitations of the models used to generate the estimates (e.g., no attention to stationarity and little formal attention to endogeneity), and simpler things, like the assumption of linearity and temporal invariance in the estimated effects of the explanatory variables. With respect to the latter, as noted earlier, one of the more important factors in explaining recent crime trends—incarceration—appeared in this study to exhibit some nonlinear and temporally variable effects, and these were not captured in the prediction exercise summarized above (the pooled estimates were used instead). Other studies, too, have shown that incarceration effects could vary by location (e.g., DeFina and Arvanites, 2002), another issue not explored here that could have introduced some error into the effort of predicting crime from the models estimated. Overall, the main story that emerges from the prediction exercise is that better predictions will probably require a more comprehensive modeling strategy that attends to the fundamental methodological issues and various analytical nuances mentioned above.

CONCLUSION

In this chapter I have attempted a more comprehensive approach to the measurement and modeling of contemporary crime trends. Most of the extant literature has focused on a small number of potentially relevant factors, even though the theoretical literature highlights numerous other factors that may have been important for shaping recent crime trends. Taking a more comprehensive measurement approach required, in some cases, the use of state-, metropolitan area-, and county-level explanatory variables to explain city-level crime rates (cities were the unit of analysis chosen by the NRC). Future research should assess the implications of this type of unit mismatch by replicating the models developed here with crime rates measured at levels that match the explanatory variables.

However, given the measures and methods used in this research, one can conclude that the findings generated from a more comprehensive approach affirm some of the results reported elsewhere with respect to incarceration, drug market conditions and drug use, lagged birth cohort conditions, and the economy, but also point to some additional factors that show relevance in shaping recent crime trends, including changes in levels of cohabitation, prisoner release rates, and the drug market age structure. As summarized in Table 5-5, the overall conclusions diverge somewhat from two widely cited reviews of prior work (Levitt, 2004; Zimring, 2006), a result that underscores the importance of simultaneously considering the various factors emphasized in the theoretical literature rather than focusing on a select few factors. In essence, it seems important to take a comprehensive measurement approach to studying crime trends, especially if the goal is to assess which of the various factors hypothesized to shape recent trends actually matter (and if so, how much).

I close by reiterating that, in some respects, it is highly premature to draw definitive conclusions from this or most previous work about the factors that were mostly responsible for shaping recent crime trends. Although the public and the media are anxious to know what happened and why with respect to contemporary crime trends, the reality is that empirical literature on crime trends is in the early stages of development. Much more research is needed to develop answers in which there can be a high degree of confidence. I have argued that increasing the breadth of empirical studies to incorporate measures of each of the major factors emphasized in theoretical discussion and policy debates is important, but there are other fundamental issues that require more attention as well before strong inference can be drawn. For one, the magnitude of the effects of criminal justice factors and other variables may be misestimated in most studies, including the present research, because of possible simultaneous relationships between these indicators and crime rates. One of the trade-offs of doing a comprehensive study is that it is very difficult to deal with these issues adequately, but doing so is an important next step.

A second, perhaps even more fundamental issue, which needs to be addressed more systematically in research on contemporary crime trends before definitive conclusions can be drawn, concerns the time-series properties of crime rates and the factors thought to be important for shaping crime trends. As noted at the outset, most of the extant research on contemporary crime trends and the present study assume stationarity in the variables and proceed by estimating panel regression models in levels. Although this may be an appropriate approach, if crime rates or the explanatory variables (or both) are nonstationary, the results that emerge could be spurious, which obviously has important implications about the most important factors in shaping recent crime trends. A variety of methodological issues need to be sorted out to satisfactorily address the time-series properties of variables considered, many of which currently are or have been explored (Baumer and Rapach, 2007; Moody, 2007; Spelman, 2008) but are not yet resolved. Pursuing such research more vigorously should better clarify the methods most appropriate for drawing valid inferences from panel studies of crime trends.

In conclusion, this work takes some small but necessary steps toward addressing the two questions around which the NRC crime trends workshop has been organized: (1) Which factors were most important for explaining city-level crime trends observed between 1980-2004? (2) What might one reasonably expect for city crime levels in the years following this period? Tentative answers to these questions have been generated from a database supplied by the NRC, to which I added several measures. A more definitive resolution to these issues would be valuable, but achieving that goal will require a much larger and elaborated effort that retains the comprehensive approach to measurement and modeling outlined here, but also attends to fundamental methodological issues with respect to time-series estimation, simultaneity, model selection, spatial dependence, forecasting, and other issues. Although the NRC workshop on crime trends is a good start, much more research is needed to gain a full understanding of the past and future path of crime in the United States.

ACKNOWLEDGMENTS

Thanks to Richard Rosenfeld for his insights on many of the issues discussed in this paper and to David Rapach for advice on many of the econometric issues that arise in a study of recent crime trends. Thanks also to Robert Fornango, Kim Martin, Michele Stacey, and Jessica Johnston for research assistance. Direct correspondence to Eric Baumer, College of Criminology and Criminal Justice, Florida State University, Tallahassee, FL 32306.

REFERENCES

Amato, Paul R., Alan Booth, David R. Johnson, and Stacy J. Rogers. (2007). *Alone together: How marriage in America is changing*. Cambridge, MA: Harvard University Press.

Baumer, Eric P., and David Rapach. (2007). *Spurious relationships in panel crime regressions*. Unpublished manuscript. University of Missouri-St. Louis.

Baumer, Eric P., Janet L. Lauritsen, Richard Rosenfeld, and Richard Wright. (1998). The influence of crack cocaine on robbery, burglary, and homicide rates: A cross-city, longitudinal analysis. *Journal of Research in Crime and Delinquency, 35*, 316-340.

Beck, Nathaniel, and Jonathan N. Katz. (1995). What to do (and not to do) with time-series cross-section data. *American Political Science Review, 89*, 634-647.

Berk, Richard, Susan Sorenson, Douglas Wiebe, and Dawn Upchurch. (2003). The legalization of abortion and subsequent youth homicide: A time series analysis. *Analyses of Social Issues and Public Policy, 3*, 45-64.

Blumstein, Alfred. (1995). Youth violence, guns, and the illicit-drug industry. *Journal of Criminal Law and Criminology, 86*, 10-36.

Blumstein, Alfred, and Richard Rosenfeld. (1998). Explaining recent trends in U.S. homicide rates. *Journal of Criminal Law and Criminology, 88*, 1175-1216.

Blumstein, Alfred, and Joel Wallman. (2006a). *The crime drop in America* (revised ed.). New York: Cambridge University Press.

Blumstein, Alfred, and Joel Wallman. (2006b). The crime drop and beyond. *Annual Review of Law and Social Science, 2*, 125-146.

Braga, Anthony, David M. Kennedy, Elin J. Waring, and Anne M. Piehl. (2001). Problem-oriented policing, youth violence, and deterrence: An evaluation of Boston's Operation Ceasefire. *Journal of Research in Crime and Delinquency, 38*, 195-225.

Brownridge, Douglas A. (2004). Understanding women's heightened risk of violence in common-law unions. *Violence Against Women, 10*, 626-651.

Bushway, Shawn D., and David McDowall. (2006). Here we go again—Can we learn anything from aggregate-level studies of policy interventions? *Criminology & Public Policy, 5*, 461-470.

Butcher, Kristin F., and Anne M. Piehl. (1998). Cross-city evidence on the relationship between immigration and crime. *Journal of Policy Analysis and Management, 17*, 457-493.

Casper, Lynne M., and Phillip N. Cohen. (2000). How does POSSLQ measure up? New historical estimates of cohabitation. *Demography, 37*, 237-245.

Conklin, John E. (2003). *Why crime rates fell*. Boston: Allyn and Bacon.

Cook, Philip J., and John H. Laub. (1998). The unprecedented epidemic in youth violence. *Crime and Justice, 24*, 27-64.

Cook, Philip J., and Gary A. Zarkin. (1985). Crime and the business cycle. *Journal of Legal Studies, 14*, 115-128.

Cork, Daniel. (1999). Examining space-time interaction in city-level homicide data: Crack markets and the diffusion of guns among youth. *Journal of Quantitative Criminology, 15*, 379-406.

Corman, Hope, and H. Naci Mocan. (2000). A time-series analysis of crime, deterrence, and drug abuse in New York City. *American Economic Review, 90*, 584-604.

Donohue, John, and Steven Levitt. (2001). The impact of legalized abortion on crime. *Quarterly Journal of Economics, 116*, 379-420.

Donohue, John, and Steven Levitt. (2006). *Measurement error, legalized abortion, and the decline in crime: A response to Foote and Goetz.* Unpublished manuscript, Yale University Law School.

Dugan, Laura, Daniel Nagin, and Richard Rosenfeld. (1999). Explaining the decline in intimate partner homicide: The effects of changing domesticity, women's status, and domestic violence resources. *Homicide Studies, 3*, 187-214.

Eck, John E., and Edward R. Maguire. (2006). Have changes in policing reduced violent crime? An assessment of the evidence. In Alfred Blumstein and Joel Wallman (Eds.), *The crime drop in America* (revised ed.). New York: Cambridge University Press.

Fagan, Jeffrey. (1990). Intoxication and aggression. *Crime and Justice, 13*, 241-320.

Fagan, Jeffrey, and Richard B. Freeman. (1999). Crime and work. *Crime and Justice, 25*, 225-290.

Foote, Christopher, and Christopher Goetz. (2005). *Testing economic hypotheses with state-level data: A comment on Donohue and Levitt.* Federal Reserve Bank of Boston Working Paper No. 05-15, 1-18.

Fox, James Allen. (2006). Demographics and U.S. homicide. In Alfred Blumstein and Joel Wallman (Eds.), *The crime drop in America* (revised ed.). New York: Cambridge University Press.

Fryer, Roland, Paul Heaton, Steven Levitt, and Kevin Murphy. (2006). *Measuring the impact of crack cocaine.* (NBER Working Paper #11318.) Cambridge, MA: National Bureau of Economic Research.

Gallup-Black, Adria. (2005). Twenty years of rural and urban trends in family and intimate partner homicide: Does place matter? *Homicide Studies, 9*, 149-173.

Gould, Eric D., Bruce. A. Weinberg, and David B. Mustard. (2002). Crime rates and local labor market opportunities in the United States, 1979-1997. *Review of Economics and Statistics, 84*, 45-61.

Greenberg, David. (2001). Time series analysis of crime rates. *Journal of Quantitative Criminology, 17*, 291-327.

Greenberg, David F., Ronald C. Kessler, and Charles H. Logan. (1979). A panel model of crime rates and arrest rates. *American Sociological Review, 44*, 843-850.

Grogger, Jeffrey. (1998). Market wages and youth crime. *Journal of Labor Economics, 16*, 756-792.

Grogger, Jeffrey. (2006). An economic model of recent trends in violence. In Alfred Blumstein and Joel Wallman (Eds.), *The crime drop in America* (revised ed.). New York: Cambridge University Press.

Grogger, Jeffrey, and Michael Willis. (2000). The emergence of crack cocaine and the rise in urban crime rates. *Review of Economics and Statistics, 82*, 519-529.

Hagan, John, and Alberto Palloni. (1998). Immigration and crime in the United States. In National Research Council, *The immigration debate.* James P. Smith and Barry Edmonston (Eds.). Panel on the Demographic and Economic Impacts of Immigration. Committee on Population and Committee on National Statistics, Commission on Behavioral and Social Sciences and Education. Washington, DC: National Academy Press.

Johnson, Bruce D., Andrew Golub, and Eloise Dunlap. (2006). The rise and decline of hard drugs, drug markets, and violence in inner-city New York. In Alfred Blumstein and Joel Wallman (Eds.), *The crime drop in America* (revised ed.). New York: Cambridge University Press.

Joyce, Ted. (2004). *Further tests of abortion and crime.* (NBER Working Paper #10564.) Cambridge, MA: National Bureau of Economic Research.

Kennedy, David M., Anthony A. Braga, Anne M. Piehl, and Elin J. Waring. (2001). *Reducing gun violence: The Boston Gun Project's Operation Ceasefire.* National Institute of Justice Research Report. Washington, DC: U.S. Department of Justice.

Kleck, Gary. (2004). Measures of gun ownership levels for macro-level crime and violence research. *Journal of Research in Crime and Delinquency, 41*, 3-36.

Kleck, Gary, Tomislav Kovandzic, and Mark E. Schaffer. (2005). *Gun prevalence, homicide rates and causality: A GMM approach to endogeneity bias.* (CEPR Discussion Paper #5357.) London: Center for Economic Policy Research. Available: http://www.cepr.org/pubs/new-dps/dplist.asp?dpno=5357 [accessed August 2008].

Kovandzic, Tomislav V., Thomas B. Marvell, Lynn M. Vieraitis, and Carlisle E. Moody. (2004). When prisoners get out: The impact of prison releases on homicide rates, 1975-1999. *Criminal Justice Policy Review, 15*, 212-228.

Kubrin, Charis E., and Jerald Herting. (2003). Neighborhood correlates of homicide trends: An analysis using growth-curve modeling. *Sociological Quarterly, 44*, 329-350.

LaFree, Gary. (1998). *Losing legitimacy: Street crime and the decline of institutions in America.* Boulder, CO: Westview.

Land, Kenneth C., Patricia L. McCall, and Lawrence E. Cohen. (1990). Structural covariates of homicide rates: Are there any invariances across time and social space? *American Journal of Sociology, 95*, 922-963.

Lattimore, Pamela K., K. Jack Riley, James Trudeau, Jordan Leiter, and Steven Edwards. (1997). *A study of homicide in eight U.S. cities: An NIJ intramural research project.* (National Institute of Justice Research in Brief, November.) Washington, DC: U.S. Department of Justice.

Levitt, Steven D. (1996). The effect of prison population size on crime rates: Evidence from prison overcrowding litigation. *Quarterly Journal of Economics, 111*, 319-352.

Levitt, Steven D. (1997). Using electoral cycles in police hiring to estimate the effect of police on crime. *American Economic Review, 8*, 280-290.

Levitt, Steven D. (2001). Alternative strategies for identifying the link between unemployment and crime. *Journal of Quantitative Criminology, 17*, 377-390.

Levitt, Steven D. (2002). Using electoral cycles in police hiring to estimate the effects of police on crime: Reply. *American Economic Review, 92*, 1244-1250.

Levitt, Steven D. (2004). Understanding why crime fell in the 1990s: Four factors that explain the decline and six that do not. *Journal of Economic Perspectives, 18*, 163-190.

Liedka, Raymond V., Anne Morrison Piehl, and Bert Useem. (2006). The crime control effect of incarceration: Does scale matter? *Criminology and Public Policy, 5*, 245-276.

Lott, John. (1998). *More guns, less crime: Understanding crime and gun-control laws.* Chicago: University of Chicago Press.

MacDonald, John M. (2002). The effectiveness of community policing in reducing urban violence. *Crime and Delinquency, 48*, 592-618.

Martinez, Ramiro, and Matthew T. Lee. (2000). On immigration and crime. In Gary LaFree (Ed.), *The nature of crime: Continuity and change* (vol. 1, pp. 485-524). Washington, DC: National Institute of Justice. Available: http://www.nicic.org/Library/016702 [accessed August 2008].

Marvell, Thomas B., and Carlisle E. Moody. (1994). Prison population growth and crime reduction. *Journal of Quantitative Criminology, 10*, 109-140.

Marvell, Thomas B., and Carlisle E. Moody. (1996). Specification problems, police levels, and crime rates. *Criminology, 34*, 609-646.

Marvell, Thomas B., and Carlisle E. Moody. (1997). The impact of prison growth on homicide. *Homicide Studies, 1*, 215-233.

McDowall, David, Colin Loftin, and Brian Wiersema. (2000). The impact of youth curfew laws on juvenile crime rates. *Crime and Delinquency, 46*, 76-91.

Messner, Steven F., Glenn D. Deane, Luc Anselin, and Benjamin Pearson-Nelson. (2005). Locating the vanguard in rising and falling homicide rates across U.S. cities. *Criminology, 43*, 661-696.

Messner, Steven F., Sandro Galea, Kenneth J. Tardiff, Melissa Tracy, Angela Bucciarelli, Tinka Markham Piper, Victoria Frye, and David Vlahov. (2007). Policing, drugs, and the homicide decline in the 1990s. *Criminology, 45*, 385-414.

Moody, Carlisle E. (2007). *Is crime a random walk?* Unpublished manuscript, College of William and Mary.

Moody, Carlisle E., and Thomas B. Marvell. (2005). Guns and crime. *Southern Economic Journal, 71*, 720-736.

O'Brien, Robert M., and Jean Stockard. (2005). Variations in age-specific homicide death rates: A cohort explanation for changes in the age distribution of homicide deaths. *Social Science Research, 31*, 124-150.

O'Brien, Robert M., Jean Stockard, and Lynne Isaacson. (1999). The enduring effects of cohort characteristics on age-specific homicide rates, 1960-1995. *American Journal of Sociology, 104*, 1061-1095.

Ousey, Graham C., and Matthew R. Lee. (2002). Examining the conditional nature of the illicit drug market-homicide relationship: A partial test of the theory of contingent causation. *Criminology, 40*, 73-102.

Ousey, Graham C., and Matthew R. Lee. (2004). Investigating the connections between race, illicit drug markets, and lethal violence, 1984-1997. *Journal of Research in Crime and Delinquency, 41*, 352-383.

Parker, Robert Nash, and Randi S. Cartmill. (1998). Alcohol and homicide in the United States 1934-1995: Or one reason why U.S. rates of violence may be going down. *Journal of Criminal Law and Criminology, 88*, 1369-1398.

Parker, Robert Nash, and Linda-Anne Rebhun. (1995). *Alcohol and homicide: A deadly combination of two American traditions.* Albany: State University of New York Press.

Phillips, Julie A. (2006). The relationship between age structure and homicide rates in the United States, 1970-1999. *Journal of Research in Crime and Delinquency, 43*, 230-260.

Phillips, Julie A., and David F. Greenberg. (2008). A comparison of methods for analyzing criminological panel data. *Journal of Quantitative Criminology, 24*, 51-72.

Piehl, Anne M., Suzanne J. Cooper, Anthony A. Braga, and David M. Kennedy. (2003). Testing for structural breaks in the evaluation of programs. *Review of Economics and Statistics, 85*, 550-558.

Police Executive Research Forum. (2006). *Chief concerns: A gathering storm—violent crime in America.* Washington, DC: Police Executive Research Forum.

Press, Eyal. (2006, December 3). Do immigrants make us safer? *The New York Times.*

Raphael, Stephen, and Rudolf Winter-Ebmer. (2001). Identifying the effect of unemployment on crime. *Journal of Law and Economics, 44*, 259-283.

Reid, Lesley W., Harald E. Weiss, Robert M. Adelman, and Charles Jaret. (2005). The immigration-crime relationship: Evidence across U.S. metropolitan areas. *Social Science Research, 34*, 757-780.

Rosenfeld, Richard. (1997). Changing relationships between men and women: A note on the decline in intimate partner homicide. *Homicide Studies, 1*, 72-83.

Rosenfeld, Richard. (2004, February). The case of the unsolved crime decline. *Scientific American,* 82-89.

Rosenfeld, Richard. (2006). Patterns in adult homicide: 1980-1995. In Alfred Blumstein and Joel Wallman (Eds.), *The crime drop in America* (revised ed.). New York: Cambridge University Press.

Rosenfeld, Richard, and Robert Fornango. (2007). The impact of economic conditions on robbery and property crime: The role of consumer sentiment. *Criminology, 45*(4), 735-769.

Rosenfeld, Richard, Robert Fornango, and Eric Baumer. (2005). Did Ceasefire, Compstat, and Exile reduce homicide? *Criminology and Public Policy, 4*, 419-450.

Rosenfeld, Richard, Joel Wallman, and Robert Fornango. (2005). The contribution of ex-prisoners to crime rates. In Jeremy Travis and Christy Visher (Eds.), *Prisoner reentry and crime in America* (pp. 80-104). New York: Cambridge University Press.

Rosenfeld, Richard, Eric Baumer, and Steven F. Messner. (2007). Social trust, firearm prevalence, and homicide. *Annals of Epidemiology, 17*, 119-125.

Rosenfeld, Richard, Robert Fornango, and Andres Rengifo. (2007). The impact of order-maintenance policing on New York City robbery and homicide rates: 1988-2001. *Criminology, 45*, 355-383.

Sampson, Robert J. (2006, March 11). Open doors don't invite criminals. *The New York Times.*

Sampson, Robert J. (2008). Rethinking crime and immigration. *Contexts,* (Winter), 28-33.

Sampson, Robert J., and Jacqueline Cohen. (1988). Deterrent effects of the police on crime: A replication and theoretical extension. *Law and Society Review, 22*, 163-189.

Sampson, Robert J., and John H. Laub. (1993). *Crime in the making: Pathways and turning points through life.* Cambridge, MA: Harvard University Press.

Sampson, Robert J., and William Julius Wilson. (1995). Toward a theory of race, crime and urban inequality. In John Hagan and Ruth D. Peterson (Eds.), *Crime and inequality* (pp. 37-54). Stanford, CA: Stanford University Press.

Sampson, Robert J., Jeffrey D. Morenoff, and Stephen Raudenbush. (2005). Social anatomy of racial and ethnic disparities in violence. *American Journal of Public Health, 95*, 224-232.

Shackelford, Todd K. (2005). Partner killing by men in cohabiting and marital relationships. *Journal of Interpersonal Violence, 20*, 1310-1324.

Simanski, John. (2005). *Mapping trends in U.S. legal immigration: 1980-2003.* Working paper, Homeland Security, Office of Immigration Statistics.

Sorenson, Susan, Douglas Wiebe, and Richard Berk. (2002). Legalized abortion and the homicide of young children: An empirical investigation. *Analyses of Social Issues and Public Policy, 2*, 239-256.

Spelman, W. (2000). The limited importance of prison expansion. In Alfred Blumstein and Joel Wallman (Eds.), *The crime drop in America.* Cambridge: Cambridge University Press.

Spelman, William. (2005). Jobs or jails? The crime drop in Texas. *Journal of Policy Analysis and Management, 24*, 133-165.

Spelman, William. (2006). The limited importance of prison expansion. In Alfred Blumstein and Joel Wallman (Eds.), *The crime drop in America* (revised ed.). New York: Cambridge University Press.

Spelman, William. (2008). Specifying the relationship between crime and prisons. *Journal of Quantitative Criminology, 24*, 149-178.

Stemen, Donald. (2007). *Reconsidering incarceration: New directions for reducing crime.* New York: Vera Institute.

Sykes, Bryan L., Dominik Hangartner, and Earl Hathaway. (2007). *Fertility and the abortion-crime debate*. Unpublished manuscript, Department of Sociology, University of California, Berkeley.

Tierney, John. (2007). The crime mystery. *The New York Times*, February 16.

Travis, Jeremy. (1998). Symposium: Why is crime decreasing? Foreword. *The Journal of Criminal Law and Criminology, 88*(4), 1173-1174.

Travis, Jeremy, and Christy Visher. (2005). *Prisoner reentry and crime in America*. New York: Cambridge University Press.

Travis, Jeremy, and Michelle Waul. (2002). *Reflections on the crime decline: Lessons for the future?* Washington, DC: Urban Institute Justice Policy Center.

Wilson, Sven E., and Daniel M. Butler. (2007). A lot more to do: The sensitivity of time-series cross-section analyses to simple alternative specifications. *Political Analysis, 15*, 101-123.

Wolfers, Justin. (2006). Did unilateral divorce laws raise divorce rates? A reconciliation and new results. *American Economic Review, 96*, 1802-1820.

Worrall, John, and Travis Pratt. (2004). Estimation issues associated with time-series-cross-section analysis in criminology. *Western Criminology Review, 5*, 35-49.

Zimring, Franklin E. (2006). *The great American crime decline*. New York: Oxford University Press.

Zimring, Franklin E., and Gordon Hawkins. (1973). *Deterrence: The legal threat in crime control*. Chicago: University of Chicago Press.

Zimring, Franklin, and Gordon Hawkins. (1997). *Crime is not the problem: Lethal violence in America*. New York: Oxford University Press.

6

Forecasting Crime: A City-Level Analysis

John V. Pepper

It's tough to make predictions, especially about the future.
Yogi Berra

INTRODUCTION

Over the past three decades, a handful of criminologists have tried unsuccessfully to forecast aggregate crime rates. Long-run forecasts have been notoriously poor. Crime rates have risen when forecasted to fall (e.g., the mid-1980s) and have fallen when predicted to rise (e.g., the 1990s).[1] Despite the need these difficulties suggest, there is little relevant research to guide future forecasting efforts. Without a developed body of methodological and applied research in forecasting crime rates, errors of the past are likely to be repeated.

In this light, I explore some of the practical issues involved in forecasting city-level crime rates using a common panel dataset. In particular, I focus on the problem of predicting future crime rates from observed data, not the problem of predicting how different policy levers impact crime. Although clearly important, causal questions are distinct from the forecasting question considered in this chapter. Research on cause and effect must address the fundamental identification problem that arises when trying to predict outcomes under some hypothetical regime, say new sentencing or policing practices. My more modest objective is to examine whether historical time-series data can be used to provide accurate forecasts of future crime rates.

To do this, I analyze forecasts from a number of basic and parsimoniously specified mean regression models. While the problem of effectively

[1] Land and McCall (2001) and Levitt (2004) review and critique the crime forecasting literature.

forecasting crime may ultimately require more complex models, there is ample precedent for applying simple alternatives (Baltagi, 2006; Diebold, 1998).[2] I thus focus on basic linear models that do not allow for structural breaks in the time-series process, do not incorporate cross-state or cross-crime interactions, and include only a small number of observed covariates. Finally, I focus on point rather than interval forecasts. Sampling variability plays a key role in forecasting, but a natural starting point is to examine the sensitivity of point forecasts to different modeling assumptions. Thus, my focus is on forecasting variability across different models. Adding confidence intervals will only increase the uncertainty associated with these forecasts.

I begin by considering the problem of forecasting the national homicide rate. This homicide series lies at the center of much of the controversy surrounding the few earlier forecasting exercises that have proven so futile. Using annual data on homicide rates, I estimate a basic autoregressive model that captures some important features of the time-series variation in homicide rates and does reasonably well at shorter run forecasts. As for the longer run forecasts, the statistical models clearly predict a sharp drop in crime during the 1990s, but they fail to forecast the steep rise in crime during the late 1980s.

After illustrating the basic approach using the national homicide series, I then focus on the problem of forecasting city-level crime rates. Using panel data on annual city-level crime rates for the period 1980-2000, I again estimate a series of autoregressive lag models for four different crimes: homicide, robbery, burglary, and motor vehicle theft (MVT). Data for 2001-2004 are used for out-of-sample analyses.

The key objective is to compare the performance of various city-level forecasting models. First, I examine basic panel data models with and without covariates and with and without autoregressive lags. Most importantly, I contrast the homogeneous panel data model with heterogeneous models in which the process can vary arbitrarily across cities. I also consider two naïve models, one in which the forecast simply equals the city-level mean or fixed effect—*the best constant forecast*—and the other in which the forecast equals the last observed rate—*a random walk forecast.* In addition to considering the basic plausibility of the various model estimates, I examine differences in prediction accuracy and bias over 1-, 2-, 4-, and 10-year forecast horizons.

---

[2]Diebold refers to this idea as the *parsimony principle;* all else equal, simple models are preferable to complex models. Certainly, imposing *correct* restrictions on a model should improve the forecasting performance, but even incorrect restrictions may be useful in finite samples. Simple models can be more precisely estimated and may lessen the likelihood of overfitting the observed data at the expense of effective forecasting of unrealized outcomes. Finally, empirical evidence from other settings reveals that simpler models can do at least as well and possibly better at forecasting than more complex alternatives.

I found considerable variability in the parameters and forecasting performance across models, cities, crimes, and horizons. While there is evidence of heterogeneity across cities, heterogeneous models do not perform notably better than the homogeneous alternatives. A naïve random walk forecasting model performs quite well for shorter run forecast horizons, but the regression models are superior for longer horizon forecasts.

Finally, I use the basic homogeneous panel data models to provide point forecasts for city-level crime rates in 2005, 2006, and 2009. This out-of-sample forecasting exercise reveals predictions that are sensitive to the covariate specification. All models generally indicate modest changes in city-level crime rates over the next several years. However, forecasts found using one model imply that city-level crime rates will tend to increase over the remainder of the decade, whereas forecasts from another model imply that crime rates will fall.

In closing, I draw conclusions about the limitations of forecasting in general and the specific problems associated with forecasting crime. Forecasting city-level crime rates appears to be a volatile exercise, with few generalizable lessons for how best to proceed.

NATIONAL HOMICIDE RATE TRENDS

While my primary interest is to forecast city-level crime rates, I begin by considering the national time series in homicide rates. Some of the basic issues involved in forecasting crime can be illustrated effectively by considering this single national time series. Attempts to forecast this series in the 1980s and 1990s have been notoriously inaccurate.

Using data on annual homicide rates per 100,000 persons from the National Center for Health Statistics, I display the annual time series in the log rate for 1935-2002 in Figure 6-1.[3] The series appears to be quite persistent over time, with some periods of fluctuation and notable turns. From 1935 until around 1960, the homicide rate tended downward and then began sharply rising, reaching a peak of just over 10 homicides per 100,000 (log rate of 2.31) in 1974. Over the next 15 years, homicide rates fluctuated between 8 and 10 per 100,000 (log rates between 2.13 and 2.33) and then unexpectedly began to sharply and steadily fall in the 1990s. By the end of the century, the homicide rate hit a 34-year low of 6.1 per 100,000 (log rate of 1.81).

[3]Data come from the National Center for Health Statistics and were downloaded in January 2007 from the Bureau of Justice Statistics Historical Crime Data Series at http://www.ojp.usdoj.gov/bjs/glance/tables/hmrttab.htm. The victims of the terrorist attacks of September 11, 2001, are not included in this analysis. Some concerns have been raised about the reliability of the annual time-series data on crime prior to 1960, but the effect on homicide trends is thought to be minimal. For further discussion of these issues, see Zahn and McCall (1999).

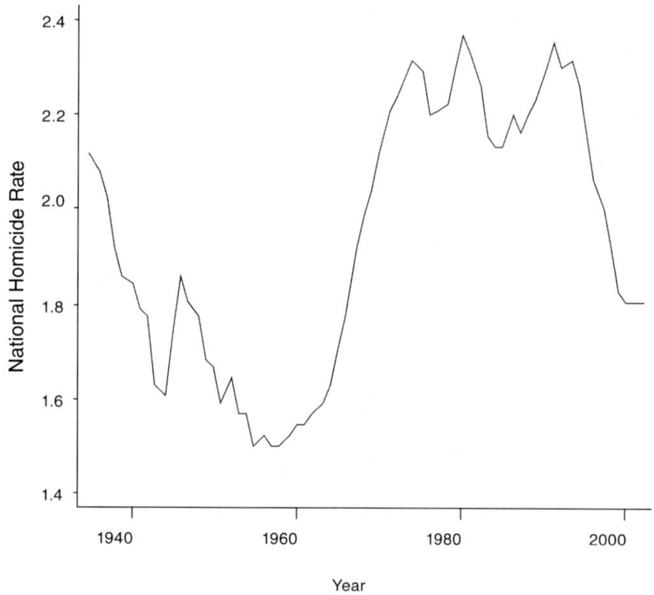

FIGURE 6-1 National annual homicide rate, 1935-2002.

A variety of demographic, economic, and criminal justice factors are known to be correlated with this series and have been used to predict aggregate crime rates. Demographic characteristics of the population—namely, gender, age, and race distributions—have all played a primary role in crime forecasting models (see Land and McCall, 2001). Criminal justice policies, including the number of police and the incarceration rates, are also thought to be important factors in explaining aggregate crime rates and trends. Macroeconomic variables appear to play only a modest role in explaining aggregate crime rates, especially for violent crimes such as homicide (Levitt, 2004).

For this study, I use two primary covariates, the percentage of the population who are 18-year-old men and the fraction of the population (per 100,000) that is incarcerated.[4] Figure 6-2 displays the time series for these two random variables along with the homicide rate series. All three series are normalized to be relative to a 1935 base. This figure reveals that

[4]Data on the population size and demographics comes from the U.S. Census Bureau, and year-end incarceration counts for prisoners sentenced to more than one year were obtained from the Bureau of Justice Statistics. The national incarceration series can be found at http://www.census.gov/statab/hist/HS-24.pdf.

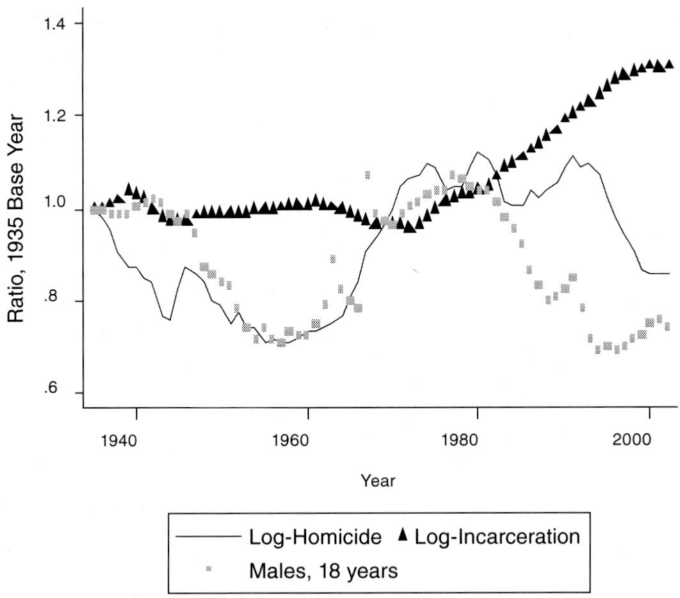

FIGURE 6-2 Homicide, incarceration, and demographics, 1935-2002.

the fraction of young men (18-year-olds) is closely related to the homicide rate. In contrast, the variation in incarceration rates does not mirror the analogous variation in crime rates. Rather, incarceration rates tended to increase over the entire century, with the sharpest increases beginning in the mid-1970s. The notable exceptions are during peak draft years during World War II and the Vietnam War.

I follow the convention in the literature by taking the natural logarithm of the crime and incarceration rates. I estimate the regression models using the annual data for 1935-2000, leaving out pre-1935 data because accurate homicide rate and covariate information is not readily available, and the post-2000 data to assess forecasting performance.

The means and standard deviations of the variables used in the analysis are displayed in Table 6-1. Figures for 2001-2002 are separated out, as these data are not used to estimate the model. Notice the difference between the historical series for 1935-2000, in which mean log-homicide rate equals 7.26 per 100,000 persons, and the 2001-2002 rate, which is over one point less.

TABLE 6-1 Means and Standard Deviations by Selected Years for the National Homicide Rate Series Data

	1935-2000		2001-2002
Variable	Mean	SD	Mean
Homicide rate	7.26	2.00	6.10
Log-homicide rate	1.94	0.28	1.81
Log-incarceration rate	4.98	0.48	6.16
Fraction male, 18	0.008	0.001	0.007
N	66		2

The Best Linear Predictor

To forecast the homicide series in Figure 6-1, I fit the following autoregressive regression model:

$$y_t = \gamma_1 y_{t-1} + \gamma_2 y_{t-2} + x_t \beta + \varepsilon_t , \qquad (1)$$

where y_t is the log-homicide rate in year t, x_t is a 1xK vector of observed covariates, and ε_t is an iid unobserved random variable assumed to be uncorrelated with x_t.[5] Finally, $\{\gamma, \beta\}$ are unobserved covariates that are consistently estimated using least squares.

Table 6-2 displays estimates and standard errors from two variations on this specification: Model A includes the AR(2) lags and Model C presents estimates from the full unrestricted specification. Consistent with Figure 6-1, there is a strong autoregressive component to the series, with the period t homicide rate being strongly associated with the lagged rates. In the unrestricted Model C, the regression coefficients associated with the incarceration rate are positive, small, and statistically insignificant. Likewise, the coefficient on the demographic variable is statistically insignificant and relatively small in magnitude.

In-Sample Forecasts

How well does this model do at forecasting crime in the 1980s and 1990s? Figure 6-3 presents the predicted series under different starting dates

[5]Several statistical tests were used to aid in the selection of the specification in Equation (1). Based on a visual inspection of the correlogram and on an augmented Dickey-Fuller test, I found no evidence of a unit root in the homicide series. Thus, there appears to be no need to difference this series. The AR(2) model was then selected using the AIC and BIC criteria, among the class of ARIMA(3,0,3) models. Finally, McDowall (2002) provides evidence favoring a linear specification over a number of nonlinear alternatives.

TABLE 6-2 National Homicide Rate Regression Model Estimates and Standard Errors

	Model A	Model C
y_{t-1}	1.46	1.42
	(0.12)	(0.12)
y_{t-2}	–0.50	–0.48
	(0.12)	(0.13)
Ln(inc)		0.01
		(0.03)
Fraction male, 18		11.38
		(11.25)
RMSE	0.06	0.06
R^2	0.96	0.96
N	64	64

NOTE: Ln(inc) = log-incarceration rate; y_t = log-homicide rate in year t.

for the forecast. In Panel A, the forecasted series begins in 1981 (i.e., 1980 is assumed to be the last observed year), in Panel B the forecasts begin in 1986, in Panel C the forecasts begin in 1991, and finally, in Panel D, the series begins in 1996. In each case, the forecasts are dynamic in y_{t-1} and y_{t-2}; the forecasted lagged homicide rates, not the actual rates, are used. Importantly, these forecasts are not dynamic in the covariates; for Model C, actual covariate data are used for all forecasts.

The forecasts beginning in 1981 (Panel A) and 1986 (Panel B) have the same qualitative errors found in the predictions made nearly three decades ago. In particular, the model forecasts a steady drop in homicide rates throughout the 1980s, yet the actual rates rose in the late 1980s.

Ultimately, the ability of this model to effectively forecast crime depends on observed relationships continuing into future periods. The model cannot effectively capture new phenomena, such as the rise or fall of new drug markets. What, then, should forecasters have predicted at the start of the 1990s? Is one to believe that the mid-1980s were just a deviation from the norm, or that there had been a regime shift? Normal deviations and turns in a series are notoriously difficult to predict, and the 1980s might be nothing more. If so, then the historical time series might have been used to accurately forecast crime in the 1990s, even if it mischaracterized crime trends in the late 1980s. Instead, however, the forecasting errors in the 1980s might have reflected a structural change in the time-series process that cannot be identified by the historical data.

With hindsight, one can see that the forecasts made for the 1990s based on the historical series are relatively accurate. Crime is forecasted to fall

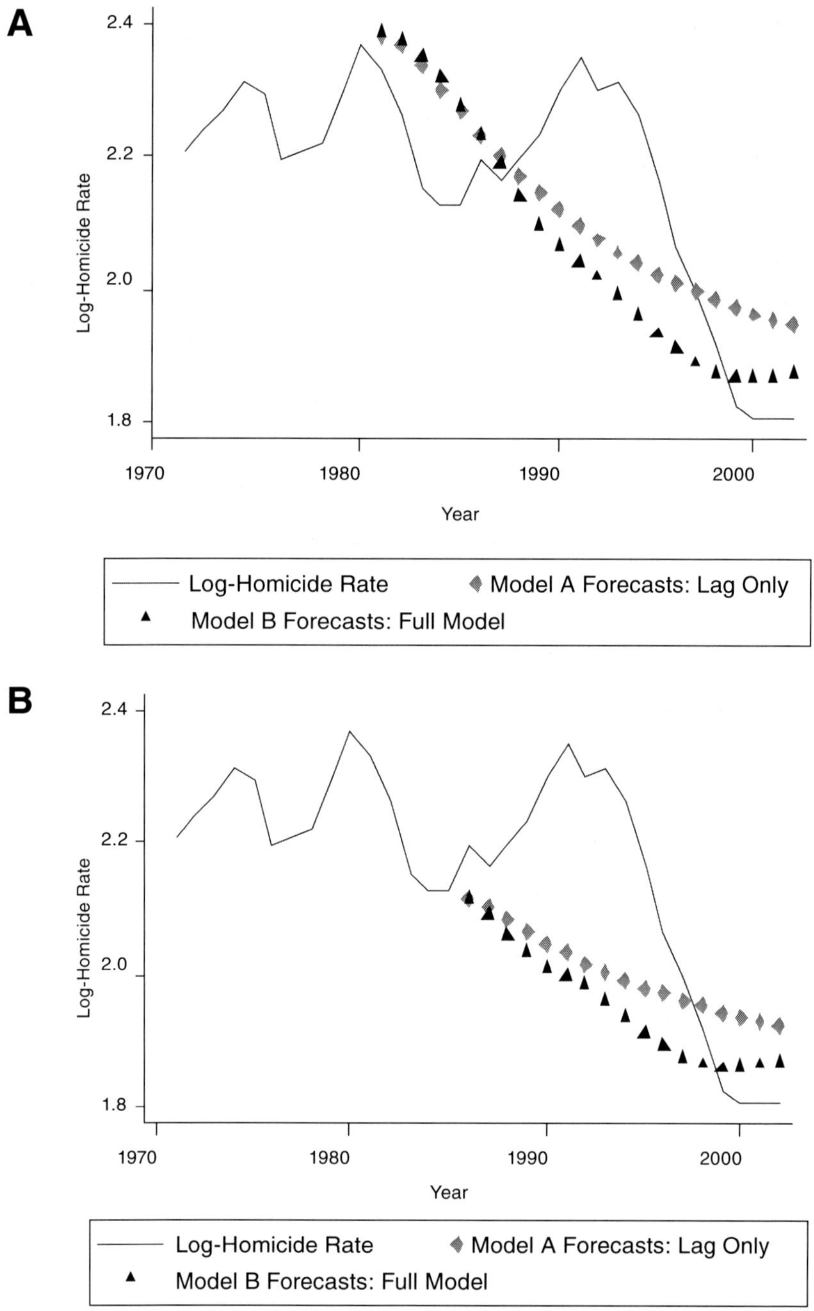

FIGURE 6-3 Realized and forecasted homicide rates.

C

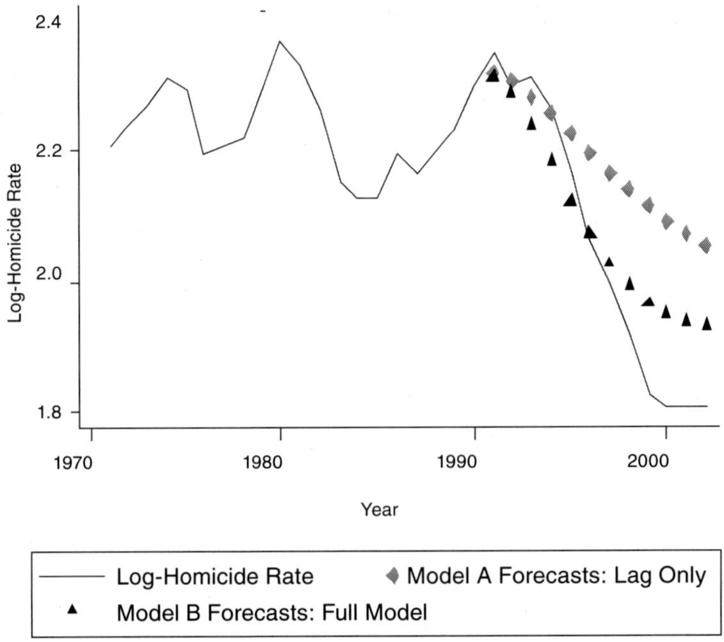

D

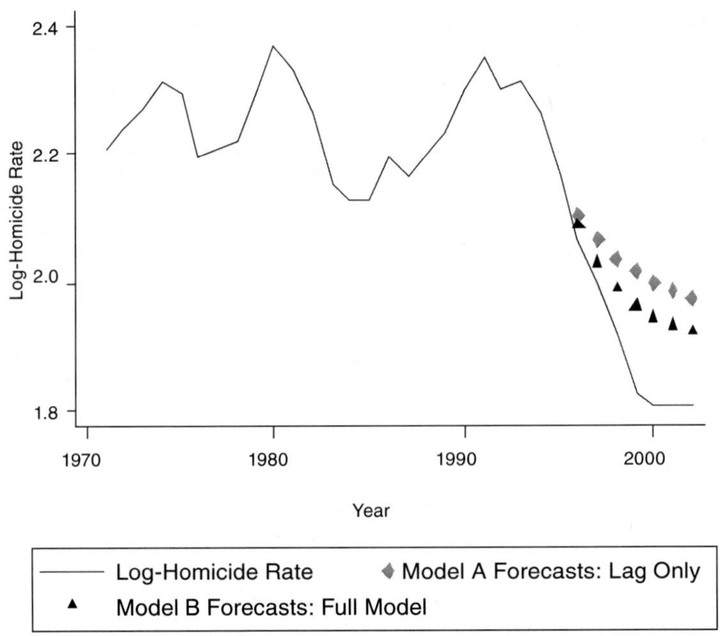

FIGURE 6-3 Continued

(see Figure 6-3c), although the regression models miss the steepness of the realized decline. Thus, the historical time series, as modeled in Equation (1), are sufficient to predict the direction if not the full magnitude of the drop in homicide rates during the 1990s. These general patterns are consistent with the hypothesized notion of a short "bubble" in the homicide rate that was induced by violence associated with the crack cocaine epidemic in the 1980s (Land and McCall, 2001).

A more systematic evaluation is found by measuring the errors associated with different fixed forecast horizons. In particular, I compute the two- and five-year-ahead forecasts for each year from 1980 to 2002. Given these predictions, I then report measures of forecast bias and accuracy. I compute mean error (ME) as an indicator of the statistical bias of the forecasts and the root mean squared error (RMSE) and mean absolute error (MAE) as measures of the accuracy of the forecasts (Congressional Budget Office, 2005). The MAE and RMSE show the size of the error without regard to sign, with RMSE giving more weight to larger errors. If small errors are less important, the RMSE error will give the best indication of accuracy. Also, as a different indictor of systematic one-sided error or forecasting bias, I compute the fraction of positive errors (FPE).

Table 6-3 displays the realized log-homicide rates and the two- and five-year-ahead forecasts for each year from 1980 to 2002. I also include forecasts derived from a naïve random walk model that uses the last observed rate to predict future outcomes. So, in the two-period-ahead analysis, the naïve forecast would be the rate observed two periods prior, and likewise the five-period-ahead forecast is the rate in period t–5. The bottom rows of Table 6-3 display the four summary measures of bias and accuracy of the forecasts.

Several general conclusions emerge from the results displayed in this table. First, as expected, the two-period-ahead forecasts are more accurate than the five-period-ahead counterparts. The RMSE for the two-period-ahead forecasts is about 0.10 and the MAE is around 0.09, whereas for the five-period-ahead forecasts these measures are around 0.18 and 0.15, respectively. For comparison, the RMSE for the in-sample predictions is about 0.06 (see Table 6-2). Second, in general, the forecasting models outperform the naïve random walk model, especially for the longer run forecasts. For the shorter two-period-ahead forecast, the naïve model performs nearly as well as the AR(2) model in Equation (1). For the shorter horizons, the differences in forecasting performance across these three models appear small and, to a large degree, may reflect sampling variability. Finally, during this 23-year period, the forecasting models consistently underpredict during the period from 1989 to 1994 and overpredict homicide rates after 1995.

Out-of-Sample Forecasts

In Figure 6-4, I display the actual log-homicide series and the one-step-ahead predictions for each year from 1970 to 2000. These in-sample predictions nearly match the realized crime rates; the regression model closely fits the observed data.

I also display dynamic forecasts of the homicide rate for 2001-2010. For these forecasts, I assume that last observed year is 2000.[6] In this setting, forecasts of the homicide series are sensitive to variations in the choice of explanatory variables included in the regression model. Both models predict relatively modest changes to the homicide rate over the period, yet they have different qualitative implications. The Model A forecasts imply that homicide rates will continue to fall during the period, whereas the Model C forecasts suggest that homicide rates will increase.

FORECASTING CITY-LEVEL CRIME RATES

To forecast city-level crime rates, the Committee on Law and Justice provided a panel dataset of annual crime rates in the 101 largest U.S. cities (approximately all cities with greater than 200,000 persons) over the period 1980-2004.[7] The data consist of rates of homicide, robbery, burglary, and motor vehicle theft as measured by the Federal Bureau of Investigations Uniform Crime Reports. The data also include annual measures of drug-related arrest, state-level incarceration rates, and the number of police per 100,000 population. I supplemented these data with annual county-level demographic information on the fraction of the population who are men ages 20-29 and ages 30-39 and the natural logarithm of the total county population. As with the national series, I follow the convention in the literature by taking the natural logarithm of the crime, incarceration, and policing rates.

Using these data, I provide out-of-sample city-level forecasts for 2005 and 2006. When providing out-of-sample forecasts, one must either predict contemporaneous covariates or use lagged covariates in the forecasting model. I use lagged covariates. That is, to address the practical problem that arises when forecasting using covariates, I lag all covariates by two periods.

Given this lag structure, I estimate the models using data for 1982-2000, leaving out pre-1982 data to incorporate the lagged covariates and the post-2000 data to assess forecasting performance. Thus, for each of the

[6]For the Model C forecasts, observed covariate data from 2001 and 2002 are used in the corresponding forecasts. Unobserved covariate data for 2003-2010 are assumed to be unchanged from the 2002 realizations.

[7]Most of the crime data from Kansas City are missing. Thus, while there are 101 cities in this sample, Kansas City is dropped from most of the analysis.

TABLE 6-3 Two- and Five-Year-Ahead Forecasts of National Log-Homicide Rates, 1980-2002

		Two-Year-Ahead Forecasts						Five-Year-Ahead Forecasts					
		Model A		Model C		Naïve Model		Model A		Model C		Naïve Model	
Year	Log	Forecast	Error	Forecast	Error	Forecast	Error	Forecast	Error	Forecast	Error	Forecast	Error
1980	2.37	2.17	–0.20	2.23	–0.14	2.22	–0.15	2.10	–0.27	2.28	–0.09	2.29	–0.08
1981	2.33	2.28	–0.06	2.31	–0.02	2.30	–0.03	2.02	–0.31	2.21	–0.12	2.20	–0.13
1982	2.26	2.32	0.06	2.36	0.10	2.37	0.11	2.08	–0.19	2.23	–0.03	2.21	–0.05
1983	2.15	2.23	0.08	2.30	0.15	2.33	0.18	2.08	–0.07	2.22	0.07	2.22	0.07
1984	2.13	2.16	0.03	2.23	0.10	2.26	0.13	2.15	0.03	2.28	0.15	2.30	0.17
1985	2.13	2.05	–0.08	2.12	–0.01	2.15	0.02	2.18	0.05	2.30	0.17	2.37	0.24
1986	2.20	2.08	–0.12	2.01	–0.10	2.13	–0.07	2.11	–0.08	2.23	0.03	2.33	0.13
1987	2.16	2.09	–0.07	2.09	–0.08	2.13	–0.04	2.06	–0.10	2.15	–0.01	2.26	0.10
1988	2.20	2.18	–0.01	2.15	–0.05	2.20	0.00	1.99	–0.20	2.05	–0.15	2.15	–0.05
1989	2.23	2.10	–0.13	2.01	–0.13	2.16	–0.07	2.02	–0.21	2.02	–0.21	2.13	–0.10
1990	2.30	2.16	–0.14	2.14	–0.16	2.20	–0.11	2.03	–0.27	2.01	–0.29	2.13	–0.17
1991	2.35	2.19	–0.16	2.18	–0.17	2.23	–0.12	2.01	–0.26	2.07	–0.28	2.20	–0.15
1992	2.30	2.27	–0.03	2.24	–0.06	2.30	0.00	2.03	–0.27	2.03	–0.27	2.16	–0.14
1993	2.31	2.30	–0.02	2.26	–0.05	2.35	0.04	2.08	–0.23	2.05	–0.26	2.20	–0.12
1994	2.26	2.20	–0.06	2.18	–0.08	2.30	0.04	2.01	–0.17	2.05	–0.21	2.23	–0.03
1995	2.16	2.24	0.08	2.20	0.04	2.31	0.15	2.15	–0.01	2.09	–0.08	2.30	0.14
1996	2.07	2.17	0.10	2.15	0.08	2.26	0.19	2.16	0.01	2.09	0.02	2.35	0.28
1997	2.00	2.07	0.06	2.06	0.06	2.16	0.16	2.09	0.09	2.04	0.04	2.30	0.30
1998	1.92	1.99	0.07	1.98	0.06	2.07	0.15	2.13	0.21	2.06	0.14	2.31	0.40
1999	1.82	1.95	0.13	1.94	0.11	2.00	0.18	2.07	0.25	2.02	0.20	2.26	0.44
2000	1.81	1.87	0.07	1.87	0.06	1.92	0.11	2.00	0.20	1.96	0.16	2.16	0.36
2001	1.96	1.80	–0.16	1.79	–0.17	1.82	–0.14	1.96	–0.00	1.92	–0.04	2.07	0.11
2002	1.81	1.82	0.02	1.79	–0.01	1.81	0.00	1.94	0.13	1.89	0.08	2.00	0.19
Mean	2.14	2.12		2.12		2.17		2.07		2.10		2.22	

Mean error	–0.02	–0.02	0.03	–0.07	–0.04	0.08
Fraction positive	43%	39%	52%	35%	43%	57%
RMSE	0.01	0.10	0.11	0.18	0.16	0.20
NAE	0.08	0.09	0.09	0.16	0.13	0.17

NOTES: Model A includes the AR(2) parameters, and Model C includes both the AR(2) terms and the covariates. The naïve model simply forecasts crime as the last observed crime rate, a random walk forecast.

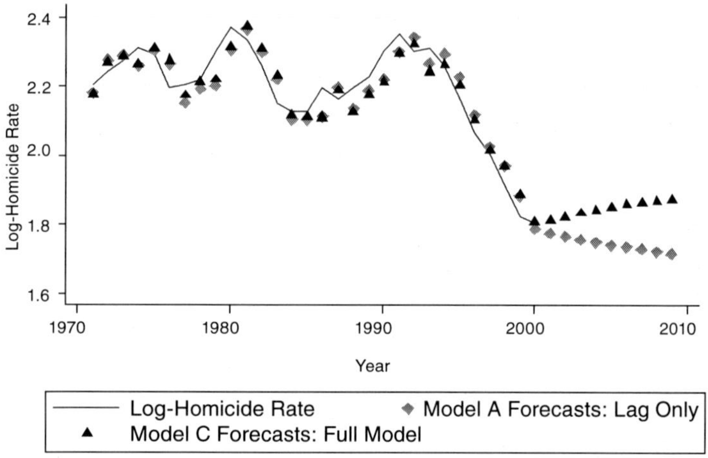

FIGURE 6-4 Realized and forecasted national homicide rates, 1970-2010.

101 cities, there are 19 years of data used to estimate the parameters and 4 years of data to evaluate forecasting performance.

Summary statistics for these variables are provided in Table 6-4. As in the national homicide series, the pre-2000 average crime rates are notably different than the analogous rates for 2001-2004. The average log-homicide rate, for example, is 2.55 in the 1982-2000 period and 2.31 for 2001-2004. Likewise, the mean log-incarceration rate for 1982-2000 is 5.50, much less than the average rate of 6.04 for 2001-2004.

By using a common dataset and specification, I provide insights into how different regression models perform in forecasting city-level crime rates. I examine the suitability of these models in several ways. First, I describe the basic model and examine the estimated parameters. I find considerable variability in the parameter estimates even among the models that are restricted to be the same across all cities. I then assess forecast performance of these models to 1-, 2-, 4-, and 10-year-ahead forecasts of city-level crime rates. I compare the performance of a basic homogeneous panel data regression model with a flexible heterogeneous alternative. These results show much variability in the forecast performance of various models across cities, crimes, and forecast horizons. The heterogeneous models are not always superior. For short-run forecasts, a naïve random walk fore-

TABLE 6-4 Means and Standard Deviations by Selected Years for City-Level Crime Panel

	1982-2000		2001-2004	
Variable	Mean	SD	Mean	SD
Log-homicide	2.55	0.77	2.31	0.77
Log-robbery	5.96	0.72	5.71	0.62
Log-burglary	7.45	0.45	7.00	0.46
Log-MVT	6.78	0.63	6.69	0.56
Log-drug_*t*–2	4.83	1.65	5.46	1.08
Log-prison_*t*–2	5.50	5.30	6.04	0.38
Log-police_*t*–2	5.35	0.35	5.45	0.36
pp2029_*t*–2	17.71	2.83	14.95	2.12
pp3039_*t*–2	16.56	1.67	15.80	1.27
Log-pop_*t*–2	13.46	0.78	13.56	0.81

casting model appears to perform well, whereas the homogeneous models seems to perform relatively well for longer run forecasts.

Next, I provide out-of-sample forecasts of the city-level crime rates using the homogeneous dynamic panel data model. As with the forecasted national homicide rate series, I find the qualitative predictions are sensitive to the underlying model.

Best Linear Predictor

To forecast city-level crime rates, I begin by considering the following dynamic panel data model:

$$y_{it} = \gamma_i y_{i,t-1} + x_{i,t-2}\beta + v_i + \varepsilon_{it}, \tag{2}$$

where y_{it} is the log-crime rate in state i for year t, x_{it} is the set of observed covariates, v_i reflects unobserved city-level fixed effects, and ε_{it} is an iid unobserved random variable, independent of x and v. The unknown parameters, $\{\gamma, \beta\}$ are estimated by ordinary least-squares (OLS).[8]

Table 6-5 displays estimates and standard errors from three variations on the specification in Equation (2): Model A includes the autoregressive lag, $\beta = 0$; Model B includes the covariates, $\gamma = 0$; and Model C is the full unrestricted specification. All three specifications include the city-level fixed effects, v_i.

[8]The OLS estimator will generally be inconsistent for fixed-T. Alternative instrumental variable estimators are, under certain assumptions, consistent in this situation. I did not evaluate the forecasts found under alternative estimators.

TABLE 6-5 City-Level Crime Rate Regressions, 1982-2000

	Homicide			Robbery			Burglary			Motor Vehicle Theft		
	A	B	C	A	B	C	A	B	C	A	B	C
y_{t-1}	0.452		0.343	0.759		0.672	0.923		0.623	0.851		0.765
	(0.022)		(0.024)	(0.016)		(0.020)	(0.012)		(0.021)	(0.012)		(0.017)
$Ldrug_{t-2}$		0.051	0.036		0.052	0.018		0.032	0.012		0.069	0.016
		(0.010)	(0.009)		(0.007)	(0.005)		(0.006)	(0.004)		(0.009)	(0.006)
$Linc_{t-2}$		–0.246	–0.148		–0.323	–0.054		–0.362	–0.068		–0.271	–0.055
		(0.050)	(0.047)		(0.037)	(0.029)		(0.030)	(0.026)		(0.045)	(0.030)
$Lpolice_{t-2}$		–0.362	–0.272		–0.195	–0.099		–0.174	–0.122		–0.181	–0.060
		(0.077)	(0.073)		(0.058)	(0.043)		(0.046)	(0.037)		(0.070)	(0.045)
$pp2029_{t-2}$		0.016	0.020		0.008	0.023		0.063	0.039		0.002	0.022
		(0.009)	(0.009)		(0.007)	(0.005)		(0.005)	(0.004)		(0.008)	(0.005)
$pp3039_{t-2}$		0.094	0.070		0.097	0.044		0.051	0.020		0.159	0.052
		(0.010)	(0.009)		(0.007)	(0.006)		(0.006)	(0.005)		(0.009)	(0.006)
$Lpop_{t-2}$		0.080	1.130		8.789	4.829		6.494	3.449		9.111	5.052
		2.130	(2.003)		(1.596)	(1.194)		(1.261)	(1.007)		(1.922)	(1.248)
$Lpop^2_{t-2}$		–0.015	–0.051		–0.309	–0.175		–0.258	–0.137		–0.302	–0.178
		(0.078)	(0.073)		(0.058)	(0.044)		(0.046)	(0.037)		(0.070)	(0.046)
RMSE	0.306	0.315	0.296	0.181	0.238	0.177	0.158	0.188	0.149	0.188	0.287	0.186
R^2	0.846	0.833	0.852	0.940	0.892	0.940	0.884	0.844	0.902	0.916	0.797	0.915
N	1963	1586	1572	1980	1594	1585	1980	1594	1585	1980	1594	1585

NOTE: All regressions include city-level fixed effects.

The estimates from Model A reveal a notable autoregressive component in the four crime rate series, such that the period t crime rate is strongly associated with the lagged rate. There is, however, much variation in this autoregressive coefficient across the four crimes, varying from 0.452 for homicide to 0.923 for burglary. The autoregressive coefficient estimate uniformly falls but still remains substantial and statistically significant when covariates are added to the model.

The association between crime and covariates seems to generally conform to expectations. Log-crime rates increase with the natural logarithm of drug arrests and the fraction of young men, and they decrease with the log-incarceration rates and the log-number of police. Again, there is much variability across crimes and specifications. For example, in Model B, the absolute elasticity of the crime rate with respect to the per-capita number of police ranges from a high of 0.362 for homicide to a low of 0.174 for burglary.

In panel data, the forecast precision depends both on the stability of the process over time and across cross-sectional units. Variation in the slope parameters across the cross-sectional units may compromise the ability of the homogeneous dynamic panel data model in Equation (2) to accurately forecast crime rates. There is, in fact, some evidence suggesting heterogeneity in mean crime regression functions across geographic units. DeFina and Arvanties (2002), for example, conclude that a regression coefficient measuring the association between crime and incarceration rates differs widely across states, with the estimated coefficient being negative for some states and positive for others.

To assess whether and how this heterogeneity plays a role in forecasting city-level crime rates, I estimate city-specific regression models. For this illustration, I focus on the Model A regression with a lag dependent variable but without covariates. That is,

$$y_{it} = \gamma_i y_{i,t-1} + \nu_i + \varepsilon_{it}, \tag{3}$$

where γ_i is the unobserved city i coefficient on the lagged dependent variable. I estimate this coefficient for all cities in the sample using ordinary least squares. As before, ε_{it} is assumed to be a mean zero iid unobserved random variable.

Summary information on the city-level coefficient estimates are presented in Table 6-6. In particular, I present the mean, median, maximum, minimum, and interquartile range (IQR) of the coefficient estimates. While the means and medians are close to the estimated value from the homogeneous panel data model in Equation (2), there is much variability in the coefficient estimates, particularly for violent crimes. The IQR for homicide has a width of over 0.5 and for robbery a width of over 0.25. In contrast,

TABLE 6-6 Summary of 100 City-Specific AR(1) Coefficients

	Homicide	Robbery	Burglary	MVT
Heterogeneous model				
IQR	[0.220,0.751]	[0.634, 0.894]	[0.832, 1.012]	[0.805, 0.919]
Median	0.567	0.798	0.963	0.861
Mean	0.486	0.752	0.902	0.822
Minimum	–0.585	0.023	0.029	–0.021
Maximum	1.059	1.129	1.371	1.117
Homogeneous model	0.452	0.759	0.923	0.851

TABLE 6-7 Heterogeneous Model Coefficient Estimates for Selected Cities

	Homicide	Robbery	Burglary	MVT
Denver	0.63	0.94	1.02	0.68
Knoxville	–0.03	0.76	1.01	0.73
Madison	0.25	0.65	0.95	0.93
New York	1.06	1.13	1.07	1.12
Richmond	0.76	0.73	0.90	0.67
San Francisco	0.73	0.94	0.94	0.95

the IQR has a width of 0.18 for burglary and a width of 0.11 for motor vehicle theft.

To gain insight on the variation in the estimates across specific cities, Table 6-7 displays the coefficient estimates for six cities: Denver, Knoxville, Madison, New York, Richmond, and San Francisco. These cities were selected to provide diversity in size and location.[9] In some cases, the city-specific coefficient estimates are similar to those found from the homogeneous panel data model in Equation (2), but in others the estimates are notably different. Consider, for example, the coefficient estimates found using the robbery rate series. The autoregressive coefficient estimate found using the homogeneous model is 0.759, similar to the city-specific estimates found for Knoxville (0.76), Richmond (0.73), and Madison (0.65). In contrast, the two sets of estimates are notably different for Denver (0.94), New York (1.13), and San Francisco (0.94).

This heterogeneity in the lagged coefficient would seem to have important implications for the ability to accurately forecast city-level crime rates. The heterogeneous estimators have the desirable property of allowing for

[9]Results for other cities in the sample are available from the author.

differences across cities. Yet one might fit the observed data quite well at the expense of forecasting the future very poorly. In particular, estimates from the city-specific models will be less precise and may be highly influenced by short-run bubbles and other departures from a "stationary" trend. In this application, in which the time series includes 19 observations per city, this trade-off seems especially important. Ultimately, whether and how the heterogeneity in crime rate regression models impacts the forecasting performance of these models is unknown. I take up that issue in the next section.

In-Sample Forecasts

How well does the homogeneous panel data model do at forecasting crime rates? Given my focus on two-period-ahead forecasts, I begin by using this model to predict the 2003 and 2004 crimes rates for each city. Recall that the models are estimated using data through 2000, so forecasts of the 2003 and 2004 rates constitute an out-of-sample forecast for which one observes the realized crime rate. For this exercise, I treat 2002 as the last observed year, so that predictions for 2003 are one-period-ahead forecasts and predictions for 2004 are two steps ahead. For each city crime pair, I compute forecasts using the restricted Model A and the unrestricted Model C.

Forecasts for the six selected cities are presented in Table 6-8. The results vary across crimes, cities, time, and model. The forecast errors are generally smaller in 2003 than 2004 and generally larger for homicide than other crimes. However, models that do relatively well at predicting a particular crime in a particular city need not provide accurate predictions about other crimes, in other time periods or cities. For example, both models do poorly at forecasting the 2003 homicide rate in Madison yet are relatively accurate at forecasting the 2004 homicide rate, as well as the robbery rate in 2003 and 2004. Likewise, the models do well at predicting the 2003 homicide and motor vehicle theft rates in Denver but do poorly at predicting robbery and burglary. There is also variation across forecasting models. In general, Model A appears to provide more accurate forecasts, but there are many notable exceptions (e.g., the 2003 homicide rate in Knoxville).

To provide a more systematic assessment of the capabilities of these models, I compute basic summary measures of the errors in forecasting crime in every city in the sample. Table 6-9 displays the mean error, the fraction of positive errors, the RMSE, and the MAE for forecasts from Model A, Model C, and a naïve random walk forecasting model in which the 2002 rate is used as the prediction for 2003 and 2004.

In examining these results, it is useful to first compare the summary measures across different crimes. The models do relatively poorly at forecasting homicide. The RMSE and MAE for the 2003 homicide forecasts are

TABLE 6-8 Homogeneous Model Forecasts for Selected Cities, 2003-2004

		2003					2004				
			Model A		Model C			Model A		Model C	
		y	Forecast	Error	Forecast	Error	y	Forecast	Error	Forecast	Error
Homicide	Denver	2.41	2.40	–0.01	2.35	–0.06	2.73	2.50	–0.23	2.42	–0.32
	Knoxville	2.33	2.54	0.21	2.27	–0.06	2.43	2.56	0.12	2.21	–0.23
	Madison	1.31	0.51	–0.80	0.27	–1.04	0.34	0.59	0.25	0.23	–0.10
	New York	2.00	2.49	0.48	2.46	0.46	1.95	2.71	0.77	2.60	0.66
	Richmond	3.83	3.76	–0.07	3.62	–0.21	3.86	3.78	–0.08	3.60	–0.26
	San Francisco	2.19	2.30	0.12	2.31	0.12	2.45	2.38	–0.07	2.37	–0.08
Robbery	Denver	5.53	5.39	–0.14	5.43	–0.10	5.54	5.44	–0.11	5.50	–0.05
	Knoxville	5.54	5.74	0.20	5.63	0.09	5.69	5.74	0.04	5.56	–0.13
	Madison	4.86	4.84	–0.01	4.69	–0.16	4.89	4.85	–0.04	4.59	–0.30
	New York	5.77	6.03	0.26	6.04	0.27	5.71	6.19	0.48	6.18	0.48
	Richmond	6.38	6.45	0.07	6.30	–0.08	6.53	6.45	–0.08	6.20	–0.32
	San Francisco	5.98	6.11	0.13	6.19	0.20	5.99	6.20	0.21	6.33	0.33
Burglary	Denver	7.13	6.94	–0.19	7.01	–0.04	7.17	6.92	–0.25	7.19	0.02
	Knoxville	7.20	7.08	–0.12	6.99	–0.21	7.27	7.07	–0.20	6.93	–0.34
	Madison	6.61	6.58	–0.03	6.49	–0.12	6.49	6.55	0.06	6.42	–0.07
	New York	5.86	5.93	0.08	6.17	0.31	5.78	5.95	0.17	6.32	0.54
	Richmond	7.25	7.30	0.04	7.25	0.00	7.24	7.30	0.06	7.23	–0.01
	San Francisco	6.62	6.60	–0.02	6.71	0.09	6.69	6.59	–0.10	6.78	0.01
MVT	Denver	7.14	7.13	–0.01	7.14	0.01	7.20	7.11	–0.09	7.14	–0.06
	Knoxville	6.69	6.57	–0.12	6.51	–0.19	6.67	6.61	–0.06	6.49	–0.18
	Madison	5.67	5.71	0.04	5.57	–0.10	5.54	5.73	0.19	5.47	–0.07
	New York	5.68	5.95	0.28	6.02	0.34	5.56	6.07	0.51	6.16	0.60
	Richmond	7.21	7.11	–0.11	6.91	–0.30	7.01	7.01	–0.00	6.75	–0.35
	San Francisco	6.81	6.67	–0.13	6.76	–0.05	6.97	6.70	–0.27	6.85	–0.11

TABLE 6-9 Homogeneous Model Forecast Error Summary, All Cities, 2003-2004

	2003			2004		
	Model A	Model C	Naïve _02	Model A	Model C	Naïve _02
Homicide						
Mean	2.32	2.32	2.32	2.29	2.29	2.29
Mean forecast	2.44	2.16	2.31	2.49	2.16	2.31
Mean error	0.12	–0.09	–0.01	0.20	–0.08	0.02
Fraction positive	0.67	0.36	0.46	0.71	0.36	0.52
RMSE	0.37	0.41	0.40	0.37	0.35	0.34
MAE	0.25	0.28	0.25	0.30	0.28	0.25
Robbery						
Mean	5.68	5.68	5.68	5.67	5.67	5.67
Mean forecast	5.78	5.59	5.73	5.82	5.58	5.73
Mean error	0.10	–0.00	0.05	0.14	–0.04	0.05
Fraction positive	0.75	0.38	0.59	0.77	0.42	0.59
RMSE	0.24	0.25	0.22	0.23	0.22	0.17
MAE	0.14	0.14	0.11	0.19	0.18	0.13
Burglary						
Mean	6.99	6.99	6.99	6.99	6.99	6.99
Mean forecast	7.01	6.90	7.01	7.01	6.87	7.01
Mean error	0.01	–0.04	0.01	0.01	–0.08	0.02
Fraction positive	0.52	0.35	0.50	0.59	0.29	0.59
RMSE	0.18	0.23	0.18	0.13	0.23	0.13
MAE	0.09	0.13	0.08	0.10	0.16	0.10
MVT						
Mean	6.69	6.69	6.69	6.66	6.66	6.69
Mean forecast	6.72	6.59	6.71	6.73	6.55	6.71
Mean error	0.03	–0.06	0.02	0.07	–0.10	0.05
Fraction positive	0.58	0.43	0.54	0.59	0.29	0.59
RMSE	0.24	0.28	0.23	0.22	0.29	0.20
MAE	0.13	0.18	0.12	0.17	0.24	0.16

NOTE: Naïve (02) is a random walk forecast where 2002 is treated as the last observed year.

around 0.40 and 0.25, substantially larger than analogous measures found for the other three crime rates. These relatively large errors seem to reflect the wide variation in the city-specific coefficient estimates found above (see Tables 6-6 and 6-7).

Comparing the results across the different models is also instructive. For these one- and two-year-ahead predictions, the naïve random walk forecasts seem to be at least as accurate as the regression model forecasts. In other words, for shorter run forecasts, the basic panel data models do no better, on average, than simply guessing that next year's crime rate will be the same as this year's. In terms of the two regression models, Model A does at least as well if not better than the unconstrained Model C. Moreover, these models seem to lead to qualitatively different prediction errors. The fraction of positive errors for Model A is greater than one-half, implying that the model tends to predict crime rates in excess of the realized outcomes. For Model C, the fraction positive is always less than 0.50, suggesting that predictions tend to fall short of the realized crimes rates.

Finally, notice that errors are slightly larger for the one-step-ahead 2003 prediction than the 2004 two-step-ahead predictions. This paradoxical result can be explained by the forecasting error from a single city, Louisville. The 2003 realizations for Louisville were outliers that were not repeated again in 2004. As a result, the 2003 forecast errors were substantially inflated. For example, the log-MVT forecast is 6.70, whereas the realized rate is 4.76, for a forecast error of nearly 2.0. No other absolute forecast error for log-MVT in 2003 exceeded 0.36. If we remove Louisville, the RMSE for the 2003 forecasts made from Model A falls to 0.31 for log-homicide, to 0.15 for log-robbery, to 0.09 for log-burglary, and to 0.14 for log-MVT. The analogous figures for the 2004 forecasts errors barely change. Thus, except for Louisville, these summary measures imply that the forecast errors are smaller in 2003 than 2004.

An important objective of this chapter is to assess how the dynamic panel data model in Equation (2) performs relative to alternative models, most notably the heterogeneous model in Equation (3). The two models can produce very different predictions.

Insights into the primary issues are found by comparing forecasts for a particular crime across different cities. Figures 6-5a–f display the log-robbery time series and forecasts for the six cities analyzed above (see Tables 6-7 and 6-8). For each city, I display dynamic forecasts that start in 2001 and end in 2004 using both the homogeneous and the heterogeneous models. The one-step-ahead predictions from the heterogeneous model for each year from 1982 to 2000 are also displayed. These in-sample predictions nearly match the realized crime rates; the heterogeneous model closely fits the observed data.

For the three cities in which the coefficient estimates from the two models are similar—Knoxville, Madison, and Richmond—the two forecasts are nearly identical and seem to provide accurate four-period-ahead predictions of general trends and, to some extent, the levels in log-robbery rates. The most striking results are found in the three cities in which the autoregressive coefficient estimates are notably different across the two models, Denver (0.94), New York (1.13), and San Francisco (0.94). Forecasts of robbery rates for these cities are sensitive to the underlying model. In particular, for these three cities the homogeneous model suggests an increase in

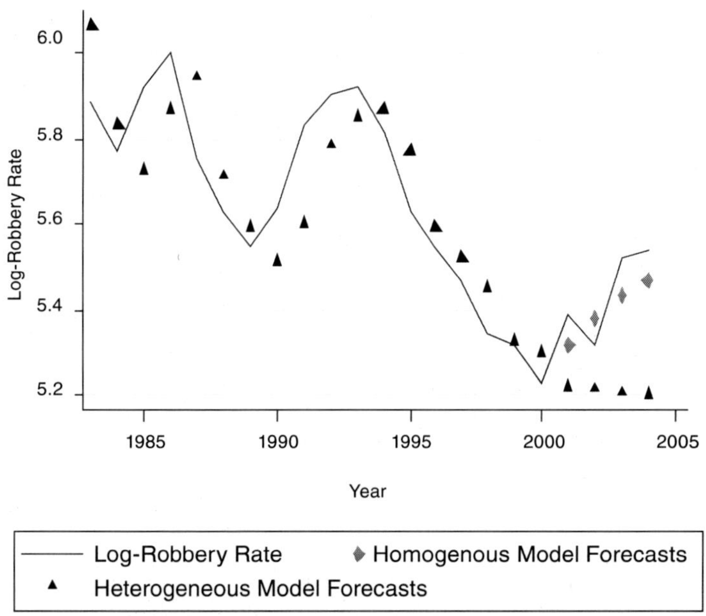

FIGURE 6-5a Realized and forecasted log-robbery rates, Denver.

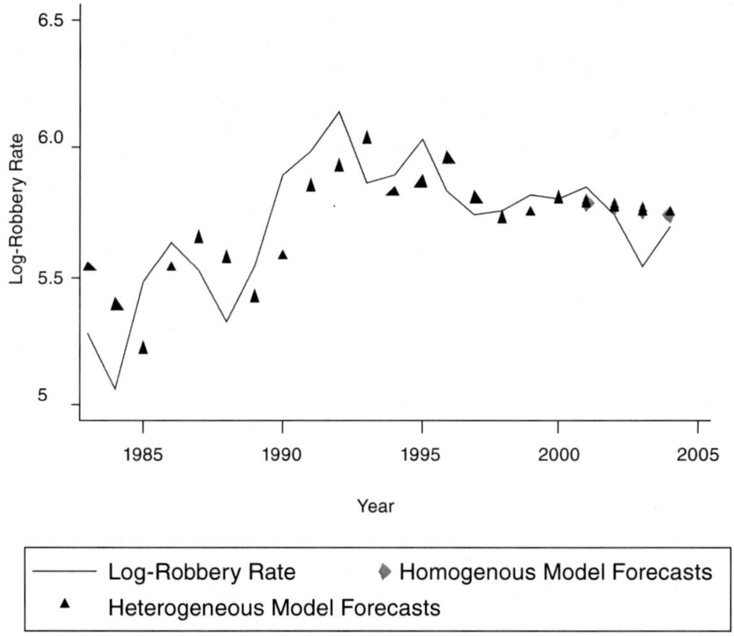

FIGURE 6-5b Realized and forecasted log-robbery rates, Knoxville.

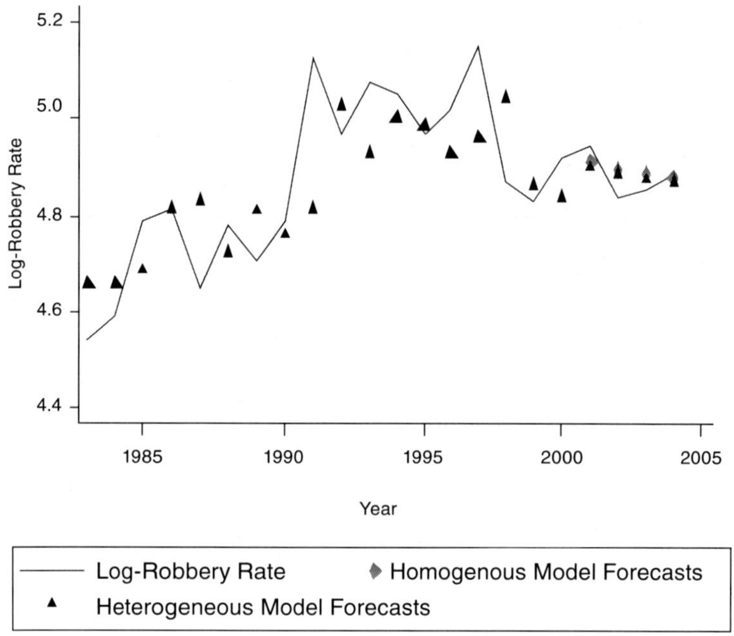

FIGURE 6-5c Realized and forecasted log-robbery rates, Madison.

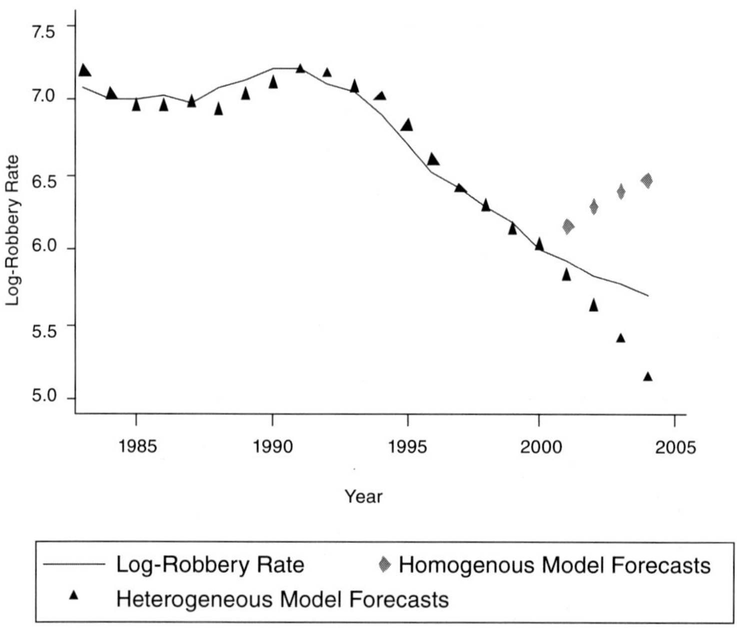

FIGURE 6-5d Realized and forecasted log-robbery rates, New York.

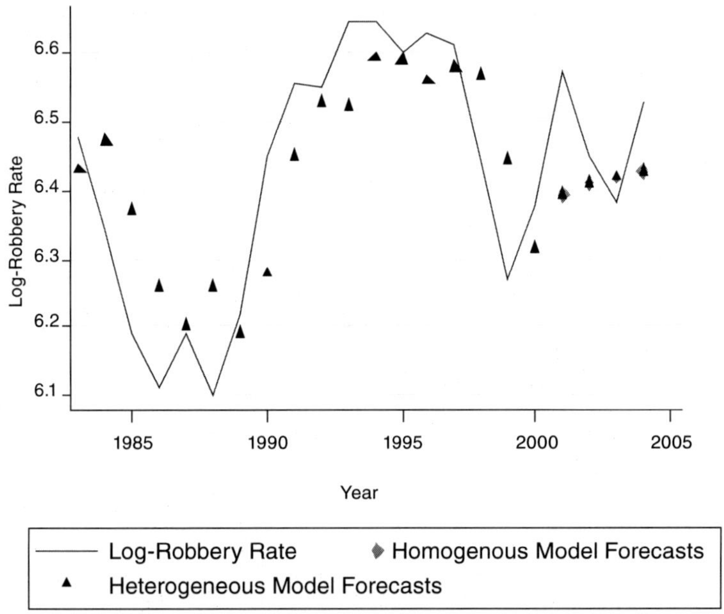

FIGURE 6-5e Realized and forecasted log-robbery rates, Richmond.

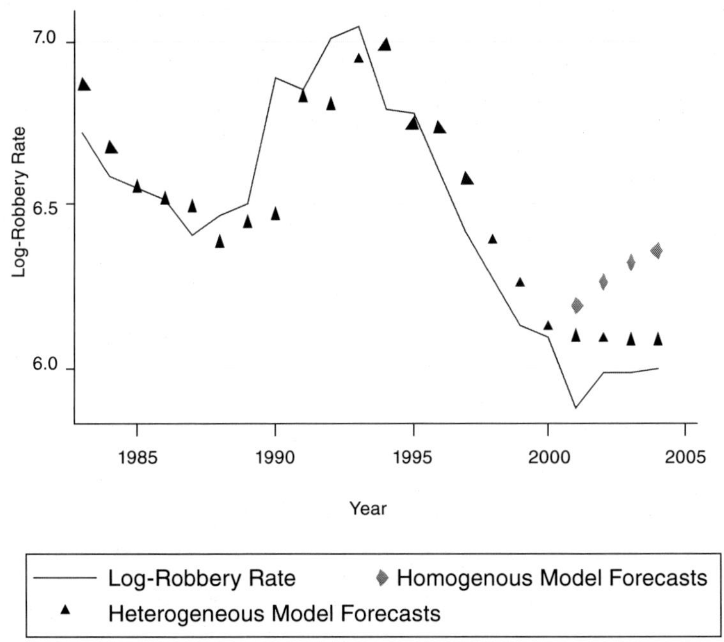

FIGURE 6-5f Realized and forecasted log-robbery rates, San Francisco.

robbery rates over the four-year period, whereas the heterogeneous model leads to the opposite conclusion. Realized robbery rates over this four-year period closely track the forecasts from the homogeneous model in Denver and from the heterogeneous model in San Francisco, and they lie between the two forecasts for New York.

Clearly, the heterogeneous model does not provide uniformly superior out-of-sample forecasts. Table 6-10 displays the RMSE across all cities for these different models and different forecast horizons. In addition to analyzing the forecasting performance of the models in Equations (2) and (3), I also consider two naïve models, one in which the forecast equals the city-level mean or fixed effect—the best constant forecast—and the other in which the forecast equals the last observed rate—the random walk forecast. Finally, I display the RMSE from the one-step-ahead forecasts that, in practice, is only feasible if the period t-1 realization is known (or perfectly forecasted).

Each model is used to provide forecasts of annual crime rates for three different overlapping horizons, 2003-2004, 2001-2004, and 1995-2004, and three different starting points, 2002, 2000, and 1994. Thus, dynamic forecasts starting in 1994 are used to make 10-year-ahead predictions for the 2004 crime rate. Importantly, these forecasts are not dynamic in the covariates; for Model C, actual covariate data are used for all forecasts, even those that go beyond two-year-ahead predictions.

Many of the findings reported in this table confirm the earlier results. In particular, for shorter run forecasts, the restricted Model A seems to do at least as well as the unrestricted Model C, and both of these homogeneous models provide slightly less accurate forecasts than the naïve random walk model. As before, these differences are modest and may simply reflect sampling variability rather than true differences in forecasting performance.

In both cases, however, these patterns are not consistent across forecast horizons; models that work relatively well for the shorter run do not necessarily provide accurate forecasts for longer horizons. Long-horizon random walk forecasts, for example, perform poorly. The RMSE for the random walk forecasts of homicide rates for 1995-2004, for instance, is 0.52, much greater than the RMSE of 0.41 found using the sample average (i.e., the best constant predictor) and Model A, in which the RMSE is 0.39.

Likewise, for longer run forecasting problems, the unrestricted Model C provides more accurate forecasts than the restricted alternative. For example, the RMSE for the 1995-2004 forecasts of the homicide rate using the unrestricted Model C is 0.33, 0.06 less than the analogous RMSE of the forecasts made from the restricted Model A. This finding, however, may reflect the fact that the long-run (over two years forward) Model C forecasts utilize realized covariate data. In practice, the necessary covariate data will not be observed.

TABLE 6-10 Root Mean Squared Forecast Error for Different Prediction Horizons and Models, All Cities

	Homicide			Robbery			Burglary			MVT		
Model	2003-04	2001-04	1995-04	2003-04	2001-04	1995-04	2003-04	2001-04	1995-04	2003-04	2001-04	1995-04
Homogeneous models												
Lag, No Cov, 2002	0.37			0.24			0.16			0.23		
Lag, No Cov, 2000	0.43	0.39		0.32	0.26		0.22	0.19		0.32	0.26	
Lag, No Cov, 1995	0.44	0.43	0.39	0.41	0.38	0.31	0.31	0.29	0.25	0.42	0.38	0.32
Lag, No Cov, *t*–1	0.35	0.34	0.32	0.21	0.18	0.16	0.17	0.15	0.14	0.21	0.19	0.17
No Lag, Cov	0.42	0.39	0.35	0.36	0.34	0.27	0.33	0.32	0.24	0.48	0.46	0.37
Lag, Cov, 2002	0.38			0.24			0.23			0.28		
Lag, Cov, 2000	0.42	0.38		0.33	0.28		0.33	0.28		0.43	0.36	
Lag, Cov, 1995	0.40	0.36	0.33	0.37	0.33	0.25	0.30	0.27	0.21	0.49	0.43	0.32
Lag, Cov, *t*–1	0.37	0.35	0.31	0.21	0.20	0.16	0.21	0.19	0.16	0.25	0.23	0.19
Naïve, 2002	0.37			0.20			0.16			0.22		
Naïve, 2000	0.42	0.40		0.26	0.21		0.22	0.19		0.30	0.24	
Naïve, 1995	0.61	0.60	0.52	0.57	0.54	0.45	0.50	0.48	0.39	0.55	0.51	0.42
Average	0.46	0.45	0.41	0.45	0.42	0.34	0.58	0.57	0.48	0.45	0.42	0.37
Heterogeneous models												
Lag, No Cov, 2002	0.19			0.19			0.16			0.19		
Lag, No Cov, 2000	0.23	0.20		0.21	0.17		0.20	0.16		0.23	0.20	
Lag, No Cov, 1995	0.36	0.33	0.30	0.36	0.33	0.29	0.24	0.24	0.22	0.36	0.33	0.30
Lag, No Cov, *t*–1	0.18	0.16	0.16	0.17	0.15	0.14	0.15	0.13	0.13	0.18	0.16	0.16

NOTES:

Lag:	Autoregressive lag inluded in the regression.
No Cov/Cov	Indicates if covariates are included.
1995, 2000, 2002	Last observed year for dynamic forecasts.
t–1	Year *t*–1 is assumed to be observed. This is the one step-ahead forecast.
Naïve	Forecast equals the crime rate in the "last observed" year, namely 2002, 2000, and 1995.
Average	Forecast is the city-specific average crime rate from 1980-2000.

Finally, the added flexibility of the heterogeneous forecasting model in Equation (3) leads to some improvements in forecasting accuracy. As might be expected, the results are especially striking for homicide, in which there is evidence of much heterogeneity in the parameter estimates. Assuming the 2002 log-homicide rate is the last observed data point, the RMSE for the 2003-2004 forecasts is 0.37 using the homogeneous Model A and 0.19 using the heterogeneous alternative.

For the other crimes, however, the forecasting gains from the heterogeneous model are less pronounced. For example, the RMSE for forecasts of burglary rates in 2003-2004 is 0.16 for both models, and the analogous RMSE for motor vehicle theft is 0.23 for the homogeneous model and 0.19 for the heterogeneous alternative. Except for the homicide series, the efficiency gains from the homogeneous model appear to nearly offset any biases due to heterogeneities.

Out-of-Sample Forecasts

As noted above, I forecasted city-level crime rates using the observations through 2004. For this illustration, I use the panel data models from Equation (2) to provide forecasts of city-level crime rates for 2005 and 2006. I also use Model A to forecasts crime rates in 2009. Without covariate data over this period, long-run Model C forecasts are not feasible.

In Table 6-11, I present these out-of-sample forecasts for the six selected cities analyzed throughout this chapter. Except for New York City, the forecasted changes across these six cities are generally modest. For example, the log-robbery rates in Denver, Knoxville, and Madison are all predicted to change by less than 0.03 points over the five-year period from 2004 to 2009. During the preceding five years, 1999-2004, log-robbery rates increased by 0.23 in Denver and 0.04 in Madison and decreased by 0.14 in Knoxville.

The specific changes vary by city and by crime. To see this, notice the five-year-ahead forecasts. In San Francisco, log-robbery rates are forecasted to increase by 0.38 points, whereas forecasts for the other three crime rates are slightly less than the 2004 levels. In Madison, log-homicide rates are forecasted to increase by 0.31 and log-MVT rates by 0.15, whereas the log-crime rates for both robbery and burglary are forecasted to drop over the same period.

Finally, there are notable differences in the predictions made from the two models. In several cases, Model A implies an increase in crime, whereas Model C predicts a slight drop, and in nearly every case the Model A forecasts exceed the Model C counterparts.

Overall patterns regarding these forecasts can be found by examining Table 6-12, which displays summary measures for the forecasts in every

TABLE 6-11 Homogeneous Model Forecasts for Selected Cities, 2005-2009

		2005		2006		2009	
		Model		Model		Model	2009-
	2004	A	C	A	C	A	2004
Homicide							
Denver	2.73	2.65	2.55	2.61	2.47	2.59	–0.15
Knoxville	2.43	2.51	2.25	2.54	2.20	2.56	0.13
Madison	0.34	0.51	0.25	0.59	0.22	0.64	0.31
New York	1.95	2.47		2.70		2.88	0.93
Richmond	3.86	3.82	3.66	3.81	3.58	3.79	–0.06
San Francisco	2.45	2.45	2.41	2.45	2.40	2.45	–0.01
Robbery							
Denver	5.54	5.55	5.58	5.56	5.59	5.58	0.03
Knoxville	5.69	5.70	5.60	5.71	5.54	5.72	0.02
Madison	4.89	4.88	4.72	4.88	4.60	4.87	–0.02
New York	5.71	5.94		6.12		6.44	0.73
Richmond	6.53	6.51	6.35	6.49	6.22	6.47	–0.06
San Francisco	5.99	6.11	6.19	6.20	6.32	6.37	0.38
Burglary							
Denver	7.17	7.14	7.23	7.11	7.27	7.03	–0.14
Knoxville	7.27	7.24	7.01	7.21	6.99	7.14	–0.12
Madison	6.49	6.47	6.41	6.45	6.36	6.41	–0.08
New York	5.78	5.80		5.82		5.88	0.11
Richmond	7.24	7.24	7.21	7.25	7.19	7.26	0.02
San Francisco	6.69	6.67	6.76	6.66	6.81	6.62	–0.07
MVT							
Denver	7.20	7.17	7.18	7.14	7.15	7.09	–0.11
Knoxville	6.67	6.69	6.61	6.71	6.57	6.75	0.08
Madison	5.54	5.58	5.44	5.61	5.37	5.69	0.15
New York	5.56	5.74		5.89		6.22	0.66
Richmond	7.01	7.09	6.89	7.08	6.73	7.06	–0.03
San Francisco	6.97	6.95	7.01	6.93	7.03	6.90	–0.07

city. In particular, for each crime and each forecast period, I report the mean forecast, the mean predicted change, the fraction of positive predicted changes, the IQR of the predicted change, and the mean absolute predicted change.

The results in this table confirm that Models A and C provide different pictures about what to expect for crime in large cities over this period. Forecasts made using Model A generally imply modest increases (e.g., homicide)

TABLE 6-12 Homogeneous Model Forecasts Summary, All Cities, 2005-2009

		2005		2006		2009
	2004	Model A	Model C	Model A	Model C	Model A
Homicide						
Mean forecast	2.29	2.42	2.17	2.49	2.14	2.53
Mean change from 2004		0.14	−0.07	0.20	−0.10	0.24
Fraction positive change		0.75	0.35	0.75	0.34	0.75
IQR		[0.01, 0.26]	[−0.23, 0.07]	[0.01, 0.37]	[−0.30, 0.10]	[0.01, 0.46]
Mean absolute change		0.19	0.20	0.27	0.27	0.33
Robbery						
Mean forecast	5.67	5.73	5.57	5.78	5.54	5.87
Mean change from 2004		0.06	−0.04	0.11	−0.07	0.20
Fraction positive change		0.82	0.35	0.82	0.36	0.82
IQR		[0.01, 0.12]	[−0.12, 0.01]	[0.02, 0.21]	[−0.20, 0.02]	[0.04, 0.37]
Mean absolute change		0.08	0.09	0.13	0.15	0.23
Burglary						
Mean forecast	6.99	6.99	6.91	6.99	6.88	6.99
Mean change from 2004		0.00	−0.06	0.00	−0.09	0.00
Fraction positive change		0.54	0.28	0.54	0.28	0.54
IQR		[−0.01, 0.01]	[−0.10, 0.01]	[−.0.02, 0.02]	[−0.18, 0.01]	[−.0.04, 0.05]
Mean absolute change		0.01	0.09	0.03	0.15	0.06
MVT						
Mean forecast	6.66	6.68	6.59	6.70	6.52	6.74
Mean change from 2004		0.02	−0.08	0.03	−0.14	0.07
Fraction positive change		0.68	0.19	0.68	0.17	0.68
IQR		[−0.02, 0.05]	[−0.14, −0.03]	[−0.04, 0.10]	[−0.25, −0.05]	[−0.08, 0.20]
Mean absolute change		0.05	0.11	0.09	0.20	0.18

or little overall change (e.g., burglary) in city-level crime rates throughout the reminder of this decade. Forecasts made using Model C paint a different picture, with crime rates continuing to fall, in general, over the period. For example, the IQR in the forecasted change in log-robbery rates from 2004 to 2006 is [0.02, 0.21] when using Model A but is [–0.20, 0.02] when using Model C. Likewise, the fraction of cities forecasted to see increases in the robbery rate is 82 percent under Model A but only 36 percent in Model C. Finally, Model C generally predicts slightly larger absolute changes in the crime rates, and both predict much larger absolute changes in the homicide rates than the other three crimes.

Forecasts of the log-crime rate series are sensitive to variation in the choice of explanatory variables in the regression model. That is, whether one concludes that city-level crime rates will increase or decrease based on models of this type depends on which control variables are included.

This variability in the forecasts is difficult to reconcile given the current state of the literature. As far as I can tell, there is almost no research on how best to forecast crime, and there is much disagreement about the proper set of covariates to include. The limited results presented here suggest that Model A provides somewhat more accurate forecasts for one- and two-year horizons. If true, this would imply that city-level crime rates will tend to increase over the period. Yet these results also reveal that, for short-run forecasts, the naïve random walk model provides slightly more accurate forecasts than either panel data model. That is, for these short-run forecasts, one might not be able to do better than the predicting that tomorrow will look like today.

CONCLUSION

In this chapter, I compare the forecasting performance of a basic homogeneous model to the heterogeneous counterpart using the city-level panel data provided by the Committee on Law and Justice. The results reveal the fragility of the forecasting exercise. Seemingly minor changes to a model can produce qualitatively different forecasts, and models that appear to provide sound forecasts in some scenarios do poorly in others. In the end, the naïve random walk forecasts that tomorrow will be like today do well relative to the linear time-series models, especially for shorter run forecast horizons.

Two factors contribute to the variability and uncertainty illustrated here. First, forecasting is an inherently difficult undertaking. Social phenomena such as crime can sometimes evolve in subtle but substantial ways that are very difficult to identify using historical data and can take a long time to understand. Forecasts are invariably error ridden around turning points, especially when these movements are largely the result of external events that are themselves unpredictable.

Second, little serious attention has been devoted to crime rate forecasting, and there is no well-developed research program on the problem. Effective forecasts of social processes that evolve over time would seem to require a scientific process that evolves as well. Certainly, periodic efforts to forecast crime or analyze forecasting models cannot hope to provide meaningful guidance.

For further headway to be made, a focused and sustained research effort is needed. This research would necessarily include an applied component, providing and assessing crime rate forecasts at regularly scheduled intervals. To make notable advances, there would also need to be a sustained methodological research program aimed at developing and assessing the performance of different forecasting approaches. In this chapter, I consider a very limited set of models and estimators. There are many other forecasting approaches that could be considered. Baltagi (2006) for example, assesses a variety of forecasting models and estimators using the same structure as those considered in this chapter. More sophisticated models that incorporate, for example, structural breaks, cross-state or cross-crime interactions, and a larger set of observed covariates might also be evaluated. Model-averaging techniques similar to those described by Durlauf, Navarro, and Rivers (Chapter 7 in this volume) have been shown to be effective at reducing forecasting errors in other settings. Finally, one might consider using entirely different approaches, such as the prediction market forecasting techniques described by Gürkaynak and Wolfers (2006).

ACKNOWLEDGMENTS

I have benefited from the comments of Phil Cook, Richard Rosenfeld, Jose Fernandez, Elizabeth Wittner, several anonymous referees, the University of Virginia Public Economics Lunch Group, and participants at the Committee on Law and Justice Workshop on Understanding Crime Trends. I thank Rosemary Liu for assistance in formatting and organizing the data file. The data used in this chapter were assembled by Rob Fornango and made available by the Committee on Law and Justice. The author remains solely responsible for how the data have been used and interpreted.

REFERENCES

Baltagi, Badi H. (2006). *Forecasting with panel data.* Center for Policy Research Working Paper No. 91, Syracuse University.

Congressional Budget Office. (2005). *CBO's economic forecasting record: An evaluation of the economic forecasts CBO made from January 1976 through January 2003.* Available: http://www.cbo.gov/ftpdocs/68xx/doc6812/10-25-EconomicForecastingRecord.pdf [accessed August 2008].

DeFina, Robert H., and Thomas M. Arvanites. (2002). The weak effect of imprisonment on crime: 1971-1998. *Social Science Quarterly, 83*(3), 635-653.

Diebold, Francis X. (1998). *Elements of forecasting.* Cincinnati: South-Western College.

Gürkaynak, Refet, and Justin Wolfers. (2006). *Macroeconomic derivatives: An initial analysis of market-based macro forecasts, uncertainty, and risks.* (NBER Working Paper # 11929.) Cambridge, MA: National Bureau of Economic Research.

Land, Kenneth C., and Patricia L. McCall. (2001). The indeterminacy of forecasts of crime rates and juvenile offenses. In National Research Council and Institute of Medicine, *Juvenile crime, juvenile justice*, Panel on Juvenile Crime: Prevention, Treatment, and Control, Joan McCord, Cathy Spatz Widom, and Nancy A. Crowell (Eds.). Committee on Law and Justice and Board on Children, Youth, and Families. Washington, DC: National Academy Press.

Levitt, Steven D. (2004). Understanding why crime fell in the 1990s: Four factors that explain the decline and six that do not. *Journal of Economic Perspective*, *18*(1), 163-190.

McDowall, D. (2002). Tests of nonlinear dynamics in the U.S. homicide time series, and their implications. *Criminology, 40*(3), 722-736.

Zahn, Margaret A., and Patricia L. McCall. (1999). Trends and patterns of homicide in the 20th-century United States. In M. Dwayne Smith and Margaret Zahn (Eds.), *Homicide: A sourcebook of social research* (pp. 9-26). Thousand Oaks, CA: Sage.

7

On the Use of Aggregate Crime Regressions in Policy Evaluation

Steven N. Durlauf, Salvador Navarro, and David A. Rivers

Despite recent efforts to employ microeconomic data and natural experiments, aggregate crime regressions continue to play a significant role in criminological analyses. One use of these regressions is predictive, as illustrated by the papers in this volume that employ aggregate crime trends regressions—Baumer (Chapter 5) and Pepper (Chapter 6). A second use involves policy evaluation: Prominent and controversial cases include the deterrent effect of shall-issue concealed weapons legislation (e.g., Ayres and Donohue, 2003; Black and Nagin, 1998; Lott, 1998; Lott and Mustard, 1997; Plassmann and Whitley, 2003) and the deterrent effect of capital punishment (e.g., Dezhbakhsh, Rubin, and Shepherd, 2003; Donohue and Wolfers, 2005). These uses are interrelated, as is evident from the effort to evaluate how changes in criminal justice policies explain the great reduction of crime in the 1990s.

The goal of this chapter is to examine the construction and interpretation of aggregate crime regressions. Specifically, we employ contemporary economic and econometric reasoning to understand how aggregate crime regressions may be appropriately used to inform positive and normative questions. While by no means comprehensive, we hope our discussion will prove useful in highlighting some of the limitations of the use of these regressions and in particular will indicate how empirical findings may be misinterpreted when careful attention is not given to the link between the aggregate data and individual behavior.[1]

[1]The interpretation of aggregate data continues to be one of the most difficult questions in social science; Stoker (1993) and Blundell and Stoker (2005) provide valuable overviews.

The chapter is organized as follows. We begin by describing a standard choice-based model of crime. We then discuss how this individual-level model can be aggregated to produce crime regressions of the type found in the literature. In the next three sections we discuss the analysis of counterfactuals, issues of model uncertainty in crime regressions, and the relationship between statistical models and policy evaluation. We then apply our general arguments to areas in the empirical criminology literature: the convergence of crime rates, capital punishment, and shall-issue concealed weapons laws. The next section discusses whether the limitations that exist in using crime regressions mean that they should be replaced by quasi-experimental methods, and a final section concludes the chapter. Our discussion is conceptual; Durlauf, Navarro, and Rivers (2008) provide a more systematic treatment of many of the issues we raise as well as an empirical application.

CRIME AS A CHOICE

From the vantage point of economics, the fundamental idea underlying the analysis of crime is that each criminal act constitutes a purposeful choice on the part of the criminal. In turn, this means that the development of a theory of the aggregate crime rate should be explicitly understood as deriving from the aggregation of individual decisions. The basic logic of the economic approach to crime was originally developed by Gary Becker (1968) and extended by Isaac Ehrlich (1972, 1973). This logic underlies the renaissance of crime research in economics, exemplified in the work of, for example, Levitt (1996) and Donohue and Levitt (2001).

In constructing a formal model, the idea that crime is purposeful means that an observed criminal act is understood as the outcome of a decision problem in which a criminal maximizes an expected utility function subject to whatever constraints he faces. The utility function is not a primitive assumption about behavior (i.e., no economist thinks that agents carry explicit representations of utility functions in their heads); rather, it is a mathematical representation of an individual's preferences, one that constitutes a rank ordering across the potential actions the individual may take.

The choice-theoretic conception does not, by itself, have any implications for the process by which agents make these decisions, although certain behavioral restrictions are standard for economists. For example, to say that the commission of a crime is a purposeful act says nothing about how an individual assesses the various probabilities that are relevant to the choice, such as the conditional probability of being caught given that the crime is committed. That said, the economic analyses typically assume that an individual's subjective beliefs—that is, the probabilities that inform his decision—are rational in the sense that they correspond to the probabilities generated by the optimal use of the individual's available information. While the relaxation of this notion of rationality has been a major theme in recent economic research (behavioral economics is now an established field of the discipline), it has not generally been a central focus in crime research, at least as conducted by economists. But we emphasize that the choice-based approach does not require rationality as conventionally understood. As Becker (1993, p. 386) has written: "The analysis assumes that individuals maximize welfare as they conceive it, whether they be selfish, altruistic, loyal, spiteful, or masochistic. Their behavior is forward looking, and it is also assumed to be consistent over time. In particular they try as best they can to anticipate the consequences of their actions."

To see how crime choice may be formally described, we follow the standard binary choice model of economics. We consider the decision problem of individuals indexed by i each of whom decides at each period t whether or not to commit a crime. Individuals live in locations l, and it is assumed that a person commits crimes only within the location in which he lives. Individual behaviors are coded as $\omega_{i,t} = 1$ if a crime is committed, 0 otherwise. A common form for the expected utility associated with the choice $u_{i,t}(\omega_{i,t})$ is

$$u_{i,t}(\omega_{i,t}) = Z_{l,t}\beta\omega_{i,t} + X_{i,t}\gamma\omega_{i,t} + \xi_{l,t}(\omega_{i,t}) + \varepsilon_{i,t}(\omega_{i,t}). \quad (1)$$

In this expression, $Z_{l,t}$ denotes a set of observable (to the modeler) location-specific characteristics, and $X_{i,t}$ denotes a vector of observable individual-specific characteristics. The multiplication of the terms $Z_{l,t}\,\beta$ and $X_{i,t}\,\gamma$ by $\omega_{i,t}$ capture the idea that the utility effect of these variables depends on whether the crime is committed. For example, the effect of a particular set of punishments on an individual's utility will differ according to whether or not he commits a crime. The terms $\xi_{l,t}(\omega_{i,t})$ and $\varepsilon_{i,t}(\omega_{i,t})$ denote unobservable (to the modeler) location-specific and individual-specific utility terms. These are functions of $\omega_{i,t}$ because these effects also depend on whether a crime was committed. From the perspective of a modeler, an individual's sense of guilt is unobservable, and may be thought of as a utility consequence that occurs if he commits a crime. Similarly, the quality of the police force in a location is not observable (even if empirical proxies exist) and will affect utility only if a crime is committed, in this case via the effect on the likelihood of apprehension and punishment.

The assumption of linearity of the utility function, while common in binary choice analysis, represents a statistical simplification and does not derive from choice-based reasoning per se. It is possible to consider nonparametric forms of the utility function (see Matzkin, 1992). We focus on the linear case both because it is the empirical standard in much of social science and because it is not clear that more general forms will be particularly informative for the issues we wish to address. Some forms of nonlinearity may be trivially introduced, such as including the products of elements of any initial choice of $X_{i,t}$ as additional observables.

The distinction between observable and unobservable variables is fundamental to the relationship between choice-based theories of crime and their embodiment in a statistical framework. We assume that the individual and location-specific unobservables are independent of each other both contemporaneously and across time. We further assume that the individual-specific errors are independent of both the individual-specific and location-specific observables. We do *not* assume that the location-specific unobservables are independent of the location-specific observables; there is no good theoretical reason why they should be so and, unlike the other independence assumptions, whether it holds or not is important in the interpretation of aggregate regressions.

Under our specification, the net expected utility from committing a crime is

$$v_{i,t} = Z_{l,t}\beta + X_{i,t}\gamma + \xi_{l,t}(1) - \xi_{l,t}(0) + \varepsilon_{i,t}(1) - \varepsilon_{i,t}(0), \tag{2}$$

and the choice-based perspective amounts to saying that a person chooses to commit a crime if the net utility is positive, that is, $\omega_{i,t} = 1$, if and only if

$$Z_{l,t}\beta + X_{i,t}\gamma + \xi_{l,t}(1) - \xi_{l,t}(0) > \varepsilon_{i,t}(0) - \varepsilon_{i,t}(1). \tag{3}$$

Inequality (3) is useful as it provides a way of assigning probabilities to crime choices. Conditional on $X_{i,t}$, $Z_{l,t}$, and $\xi_{l,t}(1) - \xi_{l,t}(0)$, the individual choices are stochastic; the distribution function of $\varepsilon_{i,t}(0) - \varepsilon_{i,t}(1)$, which we denote by $G_{i,t}$, determines the probability that a crime is committed. Formally,

$$\Pr\left(\omega_{i,t} = 1 \middle| Z_{l,t}, X_{i,t}, \xi_{l,t}(1) - \xi_{l,t}(0)\right) = G_{i,t}\left(Z_{l,t}\beta + X_{i,t}\gamma + \xi_{l,t}(1) - \xi_{l,t}(0)\right). \tag{4}$$

This conditional probability structure captures the microfoundations of the economic model we wish to study. This formulation is in fact a relatively simple behavioral model, in that we ignore issues such as (1) selection into and out of the population generated by the dynamics of incarceration and (2) those aspects of a crime decision at t in which a choice is a single component in a sequence of decisions that collectively determine an individual's utility; that is, a more general preference specification is one in which agents make decisions to maximize a weighted average of current and future utility, accounting for the intertemporal effects of their decisions in each period. While the introduction of dynamic considerations into the choice problem raises numerous issues, such as state dependence, heterogeneity, and dynamic selection, these can in principle be dealt with using the analysis of Heckman and Navarro (2007), albeit at the expense of considerable complication of the analysis.

AGGREGATION

How do the conditional crime probabilities for individuals described by (4) aggregate within a location? Let $\rho_{l,t}$ denote the realized crime rate in locality l at time t. Notice that we define the crime rate as the percentage of individuals committing crimes, not the number of crimes per se, so we are ignoring multiple acts by a single criminal. Given our assumptions, for the location-specific choice model (4), if individuals are constrained to commit crimes in the location of residence, then the aggregate crime rate in a locality is determined by integrating over the observable individual-specific heterogeneity in the location's population. Let $F_{X_{l,t}}$ denote the empirical distribution function of $X_{i,t}$ within l. The expected crime rate in a location at a given time is

$$E\left(\rho_{l,t}\middle|Z_{l,t},F_{X_{l,t}},\xi_{l,t}(1)-\xi_{l,t}(0)\right)=\int G_{i,t}\left(Z_{l,t}\beta+X\gamma+\xi_{l,t}(1)-\xi_{l,t}(0)\right)dF_{X_{l,t}} \quad (5)$$

In order to convert this aggregate relationship into a linear regression form, it is necessary to further restrict the distribution function $G_{i,t}$. Suppose that the associated probability densities $dG_{i,t}$ are uniform; a uniform density produces what is known as a linear probability model for the individual choices. In this case, the crime rate in locality l at time t obeys

$$\rho_{l,t}=Z_{l,t}\beta+\overline{X}_{l,t}\gamma+\xi_{l,t}(1)-\xi_{l,t}(0)+\theta_{l,t}, \quad (6)$$

where $\overline{X}_{l,t}$ is the empirical mean of $X_{i,t}$ within l and $\theta_{l,t}=\rho_{l,t}-E\left(\rho_{l,t}\middle|Z_{l,t},F_{X_{l,t}},\xi_{l,t}(1)-\xi_{l,t}(0)\right)$ captures the difference between the realized and expected crime rate in a locality. This is the model typically employed in aggregate crime regressions.

Our construction of equation (6) from choice-based foundations illustrates how standard aggregate crime regressions require a number of statistical assumptions if they are to be interpreted as aggregations of individual behavior. The assumption of a uniform density for the individual specific heterogeneity is of concern; in order to ensure that the probabilities of each choice are bounded between 0 and 1, the support of the uniform density may need to be agent-specific.[2] Unfortunately, other random utility speci-

[2]See Aldrich and Nelson (1984, Chapter 1) for an accessible discussion of the problems of the linear probability model.

fications do not aggregate in a straightforward manner. To illustrate the problem, note that if one assumes that $\varepsilon_{i,t}(\omega_{i,t})$ has a type-I extreme value distribution, which is the implicit assumption in the logit binary choice model, then $\log\left(\frac{\Pr_{i,t}\left(\omega_{i,t}=1 \middle| Z_{l,t}, X_{i,t}, \xi_{l,t}(1)-\xi_{l,t}(0)\right)}{1-\Pr_{i,t}\left(\omega_{i,t}=1 \middle| Z_{l,t}, X_{i,t}, \xi_{l,t}(1)-\xi_{l,t}(0)\right)}\right)$ will be linear in the various payoff components but will not produce a closed form solution for the aggregate crime rate. Methods are available to allow for analysis of aggregate data under logit type assumptions (see Berry, Levinsohn, and Pakes, 1995) but have not been applied, as far as we know, to the crime context.

On its own terms, our development of a linear crime regression indicates how aggregation affects the consistency of particular estimators. While we have assumed that the individual-specific unobserved and observed determinants of crime choices are independent, we have not made an analogous assumption on the location-specific unobservables $\xi_{l,t}(\omega_{i,t})$. In the aggregate regression, these may be correlated with either the aggregate observables that appear in the utility function $Z_{l,t}$ or those variables that appear as a consequence of aggregation $\overline{X}_{l,t}$. From the perspective of theorizing about individual behavior, there is no reason why the regression residual $\xi_{l,t}(1)-\xi_{l,t}(0)+\theta_{l,t}$ should be orthogonal to any of the regressors in equation (6). By implication, this means that all the variables in equation (6) should be instrumented. Hence in our judgment the focus on instrumenting endogenous regressors that one finds in empirical crime analyses is often insufficient, in that, while this strategy addresses endogeneity, it does not address unobserved location-specific heterogeneity. Notice that if individual-level data were available, this problem would not arise, since one would normally allow for location-specific, time-specific, and location-time-specific fixed effects for a panel.

COUNTERFACTUAL ANALYSIS

How can an aggregate crime regression be used to evaluate counterfactuals such as a change in policy? Given our choice-theoretic framework, a counterfactual analysis may be understood as a comparison of choices under alternative policy regimes A and B. The net utility to the commission of a crime will depend on the regime, so that

$$v_{i,t}^{A} = Z_{l,t}^{A}\beta^{A} + X_{i,t}^{A}\gamma^{A} + \xi_{l,t}^{A}(1) - \xi_{l,t}^{A}(0) + \varepsilon_{i,t}^{A}(1) - \varepsilon_{i,t}^{A}(0) \qquad (7)$$

and

$$v_{i,t}^{B} = Z_{l,t}^{B}\beta^{B} + X_{i,t}^{B}\gamma^{B} + \xi_{l,t}^{B}(1) - \xi_{l,t}^{B}(0) + \varepsilon_{i,t}^{B}(1) - \varepsilon_{i,t}^{B}(0) \tag{8}$$

respectively. The net utility to individual i of committing a crime equals

$$\begin{aligned} v_{i,t} = \\ Z_{l,t}^{A}\beta^{A} + X_{i,t}^{A}\gamma^{A} + \xi_{l,t}^{A}(1) - \xi_{l,t}^{A}(0) + \varepsilon_{i,t}^{A}(1) - \varepsilon_{i,t}^{A}(0) + \\ D_{l,t}\left(Z_{l,t}^{B}\beta^{B} - Z_{l,t}^{A}\beta^{A}\right) + D_{l,t}\left(X_{i,t}^{B}\gamma^{B} - X_{i,t}^{A}\gamma^{A}\right) + \\ D_{l,t}\left(\xi_{l,t}^{B}(1) - \xi_{l,t}^{B}(0) - \left(\xi_{l,t}^{A}(1) - \xi_{l,t}^{A}(0)\right)\right) + \\ D_{l,t}\left(\varepsilon_{i,t}^{B}(1) - \varepsilon_{i,t}^{B}(0) - \left(\varepsilon_{i,t}^{A}(1) - \varepsilon_{i,t}^{A}(0)\right)\right). \end{aligned} \tag{9}$$

where $D_{l,t} = 1$ if regime B applies to locality l at t; 0 otherwise. The analogous linear aggregate crime rate regression is

$$\begin{aligned} \rho_{l,t} = \\ Z_{l,t}^{A}\beta^{A} + \overline{X}_{l,t}^{A}\gamma^{A} + D_{l,t}\left(Z_{l,t}^{B}\beta^{B} - Z_{l,t}^{A}\beta^{A}\right) + D_{l,t}\left(\overline{X}_{l,t}^{B}\gamma^{B} - \overline{X}_{l,t}^{A}\gamma^{A}\right) + \\ \xi_{l,t}^{A}(1) - \xi_{l,t}^{A}(0) + \theta_{l,t}^{A} + D_{l,t}\left(\xi_{l,t}^{B}(1) - \xi_{l,t}^{B}(0) - \left(\xi_{l,t}^{A}(1) - \xi_{l,t}^{A}(0)\right) + \theta_{l,t}^{B} - \theta_{l,t}^{A}\right). \end{aligned} \tag{10}$$

The standard approach measuring how different policies affect the crime rate, in this case regimes A versus B, is to embody the policy change in $Z_{l,t}^{A}$ versus $Z_{l,t}^{B}$ and to assume that all model parameters are constant across regimes. This allows the policy effect to be measured by $\left(Z_{l,t}^{B} - Z_{l,t}^{A}\right)\beta$. Equation (10) indicates how a number of assumptions are embedded in the standard approach, in particular the requirement that $\xi_{l,t}^{B}(1) - \xi_{l,t}^{B}(0) - \left(\xi_{l,t}^{A}(1) - \xi_{l,t}^{A}(0)\right) = 0$, that is, that the change of regime does not change the location-specific unobserved utility differential between committing a crime and not doing so. This requirement seems problematic, as it means that the researcher must be willing to assume that the regime change is fully measured by the changes in $\overline{X}_{l,t}$ and $Z_{l,t}$. Changes in the detection probabilities and penalties for crimes typically come in bundles, and we argue below that there are cases, specifically capital punishment, in which this does not receive adequate attention in the relevant empirical formulations.

MODEL UNCERTAINTY

Our derivation of aggregate crime rates from microfoundations assumed that the researcher had strong prior information about the individual decision process. Put differently, our derivation of an aggregate crime regression was based on certainty about the underlying model of criminal behavior. In this section, we discuss ways to relax this assumption, that is, we consider the case of model uncertainty. In raising this, we emphasize that the problem of inadequate attention to model uncertainty is in no way unique to criminology. Nor do we mean to suggest that criminological studies are unique in the extent to which authors fail to investigate how modifications in baseline models affect inferences.

Characterizing Model Uncertainty

Our reading of the criminology literature suggests several general sources of model uncertainty. The categories we describe have previously been proposed by Brock, Durlauf, and West (2003) for economic growth models and Brock, Durlauf, and West (2007) for business cycle models. These categories are meant to identify general types of model uncertainty that are common in social science analyses. At the same time, our decomposition of model uncertainty is not unique; one can well imagine alternative divisions.

Theory Uncertainty

Social science theories for a given phenomenon are often open-ended (Brock and Durlauf, 2001), which means that one theory does not logically exclude another as having additional explanatory power. Hence there is often no justification for focusing on a subset of plausible explanations in empirical work. Some evidence of why this matters is suggested by Levitt's (2004) evaluation of sources of the crime decline of the 1990s. Levitt identifies 10 alternative theories of the crime decline, all of which are mutually consistent. Without questioning any of his substantive conclusions, we do note that Levitt is to a large extent forced to evaluate the roles of the different theories based on studies that, typically, do not account for the full range of the competing explanations when measuring the empirical salience of a particular one.

Statistical Instantiation

Models may differ with respect to details of statistical specification that have nothing to do with the underlying social science theories that motivate them, but rather are employed in order to translate these theories into representations that are amenable to data analysis. This is typically so even when the social science theories are themselves expressed mathematically. Differences in these assumptions can lead to different findings.

A good example of how differences in statistical assumptions can affect substantive conclusions is specification of time trends. In the context of the deterrence effects of shall-issue concealed weapons carry laws, different time trend choices have proven to be important. Specifically, Black and Nagin (1998) found that the use of quadratic time trends in place of state-specific linear time trends eliminates the evidence of a link between liberalization of concealed weapons laws and crime rates found in Lott and Mustard (1997). Lott's rejoinder (1998) argues that it is hard to identify the effects of a policy change (in this case, concealed weapons legality) because a quadratic trend will mask it; intuitively, if crime is rising before a law is passed and decreases thereafter, this will be approximated by the quadratic trend.[3] Lott's intuition may be reasonable, but his argument is question begging, as it applies in both directions. If crime follows an exogenously determined quadratic trend over some time interval and rising crime levels lead to a change in legislation, then Lott's approach will spuriously identify a causal effect from the legislation. This is true even if state-specific trends are employed.

From the perspective of model uncertainty, Black and Nagin and Lott are working with different statistical instantiations of unexplained temporal heterogeneity. Under the Black and Nagin specification, there may be, as Lott argues, substantial collinearity between the variable used to measure temporal heterogeneity and the variables used to measure the effects of shall-issue concealed weapons legislation. This multicollinearity does not invalidate the Black and Nagin model on logical grounds. In our judgment, the differences between Black and Nagin and Lott on this issue reflect the absence of good explanations for much of the temporal evolution of crime rates. Neither a linear specification nor a quadratic specification (or for that matter, more flexible splines or alternative semiparametric methods) instantiate substantive ideas about the crime process. Rather, they constitute efforts to purge the data so that the residual components may be analyzed.

Trend specification also matters in the analysis of unemployment rates and crime. Greenberg (2001) criticizes Cantor and Land (1985) for modeling trends using deterministic rather than unit root methods. Again, social science theory does not dictate a preference for one type of trend over another. While both Greenberg and Cantor suggest justifications in favor of their trend specifications that derive from individual behavioral determinants, neither of them demonstrates a one-to-one or even precise mapping from these determinants to their statistical modeling assumptions.

Other examples of this type of model uncertainty include assumptions about additivity, linearity, and the use of logarithms versus levels.

---

[3]This argument is further developed in Plassmann and Whitley (2003).

Parameter Heterogeneity

A third type of model uncertainty concerns parameter heterogeneity. Researchers often disagree on whether or not observations are simply draws from a common data-generating process, so that any heterogeneity in the observations derives from differences in values of some set of observable control variables and different realizations of the model errors. Social science theory typically does not impose that parameters are constant across observations. For example, the argument that there is a deterrent effect from a given penalty does not imply that the effect is independent of the geographical unit in which the penalty is present. Parameter heterogeneity may be linked to deep questions about the interpretation of statistical models; see Brock and Durlauf (2001) for a discussion of parameter heterogeneity and the concept of exchangeability of observations. Exchangeability, roughly speaking, captures the idea that observations, such as state-specific crime rates, may be treated as draws from a common statistical process.

One example of sensitivity of empirical claims to assumptions about parameter heterogeneity is again found in the controversy between Black and Nagin and Mustard and Lott. Black and Nagin found that evidence of crime reductions associated with shall-issue laws are sensitive to the presence of Florida in the dataset. They found that eliminating data from Florida eliminated the evidentiary support for a handgun-crime link from some of the Lott and Mustard specifications.

Another example appears in the capital punishment literature. Donohue and Wolfers (2005) challenge findings of Dezhbakhsh, Rubin, and Shepherd (2003) on the grounds that the findings are not robust to the exclusion of California and Texas. As argued by Cohen-Cole et al. (2008), this disagreement may be understood as a disagreement about parameter homogeneity.

Model Averaging

How can the dependence of empirical claims on model specification be constructively addressed? We describe a strategy based on model averaging; ideas associated with model averaging appear to originate in Leamer (1978). They have become prominent in the past decade in statistics; a valuable conceptual argument is made in Draper (1995), and the development of formal methods has been greatly advanced by Raftery (e.g., Raftery, Madigan, and Hoeting, 1997). We proceed using Bayesian language for expositional convenience, although the analysis can be done using frequentist estimators.

For a given exercise, suppose that the objective of the researcher is to construct a conditional density of crime rates $\rho_{l,t+1}$ based on data D_t and model m, that is, $\Pr\left(\rho_{l,t+1}|D_t,m\right)$. Many disagreements about substantive empirical questions, such as forecasts or the effects of alternative policies, derive from disagreements about the choice of model m. This is, of course, why model selection plays such a significant role in empirical work. From the perspective of some empirical questions, it is not obvious that this is the appropriate role for model choice. If the goal of an exercise is to compare policies, the model choice is a nuisance parameter. Similarly, if one wants to construct a forecast, then the model itself is not intrinsically interesting.

In order to avoid dependence on a particular model specification, an alternative strategy is to develop conclusions based on a space of candidate models; denote this space as M. Probability statements about a future outcome such as $\rho_{l,t+1}$ can then be constructed conditioning on the entire model space rather than on one of its elements. In other words, one computes the probability density $\Pr\left(\rho_{l,t+1}|D_t,M\right)$, which is the conditional density of the crime rate given the data and a model space. From this perspective, the true model is an unknown that needs to be integrated out of the probability density. Formally,

$$\Pr\left(\rho_{l,t+1}|D_t,M\right)=\sum_{m\in M}\Pr\left(\rho_{l,t+1}|D_t,m\right)\Pr\left(m|D_t\right). \tag{11}$$

Here $\Pr\left(m|D_t\right)$ denotes the posterior probability that m is the correct model given the data. Conditioning on M means that the analyst knows which models comprise M. Intuitively, one constructs probability statements about an outcome, such as a crime rate, based on aggregating the information available across each of the models under consideration. This aggregation places greater weight on models that are more likely, as measured by $\Pr\left(m|D_t\right)$. The linear structure in equation (11) derives from the law of conditional probability, hence the term averaging.

Model averaging is emerging as a common methodology in economics; its increasing popularity reflects a combination of improved computational capacity and theoretical advances. The approach has been used to study economic growth (Brock, Durlauf, and West, 2003; Doppelhofer, Miller, and Sala-i-Martin, 2004; Fernandez, Ley, and Steel, 2001), finance (Avramov, 2002), forecasting (Garratt et al., 2003), and monetary policy (Brock, Durlauf, and West, 2003). An application to a crime context, the deterrent effect of capital punishment, is Cohen-Cole et al. (2008). While we regard model-averaging methods as very promising, we also emphasize that the methodology is still being developed and a number of outstanding theoretical questions still exist.[4] And of course, model averaging still

[4]One issue concerning model priors that is worth noting concerns the assignment of priors to similar models. Most of the model-averaging literature has employed diffuse priors, that is, all models are assigned equal prior weights. However, it can be the case that some models in

requires specification of the model space, which itself can be subjected to questioning.

From Model Estimation to Policy Evaluation

This discussion of model uncertainty contains an important limitation, in that it does not account for the objectives of a given empirical exercise. Focusing on the use of a single model, it seems intuitive that this model must be correctly specified in order for it to yield usable findings, so that no distinct considerations arise when one considers the reason why the model is employed. But even in this case, such intuition needs to be qualified.

For example, Horowitz argues that in order to use cross-county data to evaluate the average effect of shall-issue laws, if there are differences between the states,[5] so that the crime rate in a county is determined by some set of factors X, then in order to identify the effect of the laws "one must use a set that consists of just the right variables and, in general, no extra ones." But as shown in Heckman and Navarro (2004), this is true only for a particular set of empirical strategies known as matching,[6] of which linear regression is a special case. Heckman and Navarro demonstrate that there are other strategies that are designed to deal with the problem of missing information, in particular the use of control functions (see Navarro, 2007, for an overview). The control function approach is based on the idea that the presence of unobservable variables matters only to the extent that their relationship to the observables cannot be determined; for many cases, this relationship can be determined. And if so, then other information contained in the omitted variables is irrelevant. The standard example is the Heckman selection correction method, in which one adds a "Mills ratio" term to the

---

a model space are quite similar, that is, differ only with respect to a single included variable, whereas others are much more different from the perspective of theoretical or statistical assumptions. In this case, the diffuse prior can be very misleading. Brock, Durlauf, and West (2003) propose ways to construct model priors that mirror the nested structure of modern discrete choice theory, but much more needs to be done. The issue of model similarity is usually ignored in ad hoc analyses of the robustness of findings. Lott (1998) defends his findings on concealed weapons permits by stating "my article with David Mustard and my forthcoming book report nearly 1,000 regressions that implied a very consistent effect . . ." (p. 242). This claim is of little intrinsic interest without knowing what classes of models these regressions cover; put most simply, the different regression results are not independent, so the number 1,000 is not informative.

[5]Relative to equation (13), if $\xi_{l,t}^{B}(1)-\xi_{l,t}^{B}(0)-\left(\xi_{l,t}^{A}(1)-\xi_{l,t}^{A}(0)\right)\neq 0$, then the observables $Z_{l,t}$ and $\overline{X}_{l,t}$ do not constitute the correct set to use when estimating the model, since one needs to also control for the effect of the location-time unobservables.

[6]Under matching, endogeneity is solved by assuming that there exists a set of variables such that, conditional on these variables, endogeneity is eliminated. That is, the endogenous variables are not independent of the errors, rather it is assumed they are conditionally independent when the correct set of observable variables (to the econometrician) is conditioned on.

regression under the assumption of normality, but one can be much more general and use semiparametric methods to estimate the control function term (see Navarro, 2007).

More generally, one cannot decouple the assessment of a model's specification from the objective for which the model is employed. Similarly, any assessment of fragility (or the lack thereof) of empirical claims can be fully understood only with reference to a decision problem.

POLICY-RELEVANT CALCULATIONS

Basic Ideas

In this section, we explicitly consider the relationship between statistical models and policy evaluation from a decision-theoretic perspective. The fact that statistical significance levels do not equate to policy statements is well known (see Goldberger, 1991, for a nice discussion), our goal here is to suggest some ways of reporting and interpreting results for policy contexts. In making this argument, we are drawing both on classic ideas in statistics, notably Savage (1951) and Wald (1950, sections 1.4.2, 1.6.2, and elsewhere), as well as recent work in econometrics (e.g., Brock, Durlauf, and West, 2003, 2007; Brock et al., 2007; Heckman, 2005; Manski, 2005, 2006) to implement some of these ideas. Again, our remarks apply with equal force to work in social sciences other than criminology.

Suppose that the policy maker has a payoff function

$$V\left(\rho_{l,t+1} \middle| D_t, p\right) \tag{12}$$

where $p \in \{A, B\}$ denotes the policy regime and, as before, D_t represents the information available to the policy maker at time t. The conditioning of the utility function on D_t allows for the possibility that the policy maker's preferences depend on aspects of the particular locality since location-specific data $D_{l,t}$ are a subset of D_t. For an expected payoff maximizer, the optimal policy problem is

$$\max_{p\in\{A,B\}} \int V\left(\rho_{l,t+1} \middle| D_t, p\right) \Pr\left(\rho_{l,t+1} \middle| D_t, p, m\right) \tag{13}$$

Expression (13) implies that the sufficient objects for policy analysis are $\Pr\left(\rho_{l,t+1} \middle| D_t, A, m\right)$ and $\Pr\left(\rho_{l,t+1} \middle| D_t, B, m\right)$; these are the posterior distributions of the crime rate given the data, model, and policy. These probabilities fully capture the aspects of the data that are relevant to policy evaluation calculation. Notice that these calculations may not require all aspects of a model to be correctly specified. This was seen in our discussion of the use of matching versus control functions. Heckman (2005) provides a deep analysis of the relationship between models and policy calculations, emphasizing what he denotes as "Marschak's maxim" given ideas found in Marschak (1953): "For many policy questions it is unnecessary to identify full structural models. . . . All that is needed are combinations of subsets of the structural parameters, corresponding to the parameters required to forecast particular policy modifications, which are much easier to identify (i.e., require fewer and weaker assumptions)" (p. 49).

One advantage of explicit calculations of posterior densities for policy effects is that they naturally allow one to assess the effects of portfolios of policies. Evidence on the effects of individual policies may be imprecise, whereas evidence on the effects of combinations of policies may not be. We do not know whether there are cases of this type in criminology.

Another advantage is that such calculations avoid confusion between the lack of statistical significance of a coefficient for a policy variable and the claim that a policy has no effect; while this is a banal observation, the mistake is often seen. An example of this is found in Lott (1998), who, in evaluating Black and Nagin's (1998) critique of his work, asserts "on the basis of Black and Nagin's comment and our original article, the choice is between concealed handguns producing a deterrent effect or having no effect (one way or the other) on murders and violent crime generally" (p. 242). Lott's exclusion of the possibility of any crime-enhancing effect of concealed weapons ignores the uncertainty associated with point estimates of the effects. That is, concluding that one cannot reject that the effect is equal to zero does not mean that the effect is indeed zero. One may not be able to reject that it is 0.1 (or –0.1), either. The point estimate is only the most likely (in a particular sense) value of the parameter given the data, not the only possible one. The policy-relevant calculation requires assessing the probabilities for different magnitudes of positive and negative effects, which cannot be ascertained from the numbers he (and other participants in this literature) report.

Model Averaging and Policy Evaluation

When model uncertainty is present, the optimal policy calculation equation (13) may be generalized in a straightforward fashion, as the policy maker simply conditions on M rather than m. The relevant calculation in this case is

$$\max_{p\in\{A,B\}} \sum_{m\in M} \left(\int V\left(\rho_{l,t+1}|D_t,p\right)\Pr\left(\rho_{l,t+1}|D_t,p,m\right)\right)\Pr\left(m|D_t\right) = \max_{p\in\{A,B\}} \int V\left(\rho_{l,t+1}|D_t,p\right)\Pr\left(\rho_{l,t+1}|D_t,p,M\right). \quad (14)$$

For the model uncertainty case, the empirical objects that are required for policy evaluation are $\Pr\left(\rho_{l,t+1} \middle| D_t, A, m\right)$ and $R(p,d,m)$, which represent the posterior distributions of crime rates conditional on the data, the policy, and the model space.

Equation (14) indicates an important feature of policy evaluation, namely, that unless the payoff function is model-specific, the identity of the true model does not directly affect policy evaluation. For the purposes of policy evaluation, what matters is the distribution of outcomes under alternative policies. Unlike the case of the social scientist, the model has no intrinsic interest to a policy maker; it is simply an additional source of uncertainty in the effects of a policy.

Beyond Model Averaging

Once model uncertainty is involved in policy evaluation, new considerations can arise. One reason for this is that a policy maker may be unwilling to condition decisions on model priors; without these, one cannot assign posterior model probabilities and engage in model averaging. The absence of a basis for constructing priors is one reason for recent theoretical work on decision making under ambiguity, which focuses on how agents should make decisions in environments in which certain probabilities cannot be defined. For our purposes, what matters is that, in such cases, there exist ways to engage in policy evaluation that do not require that one is able to calculate model probabilities. The minimax approach, advocated by Wald (1950) and recently explored in macroeconomic contexts by Hansen and Sargent (2007), evaluates policies by the criterion

$$\max_{p \in \{A,B\}} \min_{m \in M} \int V\left(\rho_{l,t+1} \middle| D_t, p\right) \Pr\left(\rho_{l,t+1} \middle| D_t, p, m\right). \tag{15}$$

Minimax selects the policy that does best for the least favorable model in the model space. Metaphorically, the policy maker plays a game against nature in which nature is assumed to choose the model that minimizes the policy maker's payoff. This sets a lower bound on the payoff from the policy.

An alternative approach is known as minimax regret, due to Savage (1951) and recently explored in microeconomic contexts by Manski (2005, 2006), which evaluates policies by the criterion

$$\min_{p \in \{A,B\}} \max_{m \in M} R\left(p, D_t, m\right) \tag{16}$$

where regret, $R(p,d,m)$, is defined by

$$R(p,d,m) = \max_{p \in P}\left(\int V\left(\rho_{l,t+1} \middle| D_t, p\right)\Pr\left(\rho_{l,t+1} \middle| D_t, p, m\right)\right) - \int V\left(\rho_{l,t+1} \middle| D_t, p\right)\Pr\left(\rho_{l,t+1} \middle| D_t, p, m\right). \quad (17)$$

Minimax regret selects the policy with the property that the gap between the model-specific optimal policy and its performance is smallest when comparisons are made across the model space. The criterion is generally regarded as a less conservative criterion for policy evaluation than minimax. Brock et al. (2007) employ minimax regret in monetary policy evaluation. Manski (2006) applies minimax regret in the context of treatment assignment. An important finding is that optimal treatment rules can be fractional as agents with identical observables receiving different treatments. This may be of particular interest in crime policy contexts, as it suggests a trade-off between the fairness and deterrence objectives of punishment that policy makers ought to address.

APPLICATIONS TO CRIMINOLOGY ISSUES

In this section, we apply some of our general arguments to current controversies in criminology.

Convergence in Crime Rates

A first example in which more careful attention is needed to the determinants of aggregate crime regressions involves efforts to evaluate convergence among aggregate crime rates. Two examples of studies of this type are O'Brien (1999), which focuses on male-female differences in arrest rates, and LaFree (2005), which considers cross-country homicide rates. Both papers interpret convergence in terms of the time-series properties of the differences between the series of interest.

Both papers lack formal attention to the determinants of individual behavior and their associated aggregate implications. The substantive social science notion of convergence involves the question of whether contemporaneous disparities between two time series may be expected to disappear over time. As formulated in Bernard and Durlauf (1995), convergence between $\rho_{1,t}$ and $\rho_{2,t}$ means that

$$\lim_{k \Rightarrow \infty} E\left(\rho_{1,t+k} - \rho_{2,t+k} \middle| F_t\right) = 0 \quad (18)$$

where F_t denotes the information available at time t. Hence the focus of O'Brien and LaFree on the presence of time trends or unit roots in the difference in crime rates would seem to be sensible. The problem, identified in Bernard and Durlauf (1996), is that, without a theory of how individual crime choices are determined, there is no basis for regarding either of these tests as appropriate. The reason is that the unit root and time trend analyses presuppose that the series $\Delta\rho_{1,t}$ and $\Delta\rho_{2,t}$ are second-order stationary processes.

The statistical assumption of second-order stationarity has substantive behavioral implications. Specifically, it means that the series are generated by social processes that are local to their long-run behaviors and rules out the case in which social processes are in transition to a long-run type of behavior. When societies are in transition, the stochastic process characterizing a socioeconomic outcome will not have time-invariant moments, which is what is assumed in time-series analyses of the type conducted by O'Brien and LaFree. These issues have been long understood in the economic growth literature, in which convergence has been studied primarily with respect to per capita output (and in which the relationship among trends, unit roots, and convergence were precisely characterized long before the papers we are discussing).

In the crime context, it is easy to develop intuition as to why time-series analysis of convergence may be invalid. Consider O'Brien's analysis of gender differences. The period 1960-1995 is one of changing gender roles and family structure, among other things. If one considers the determinants of female crime rates, there is no reason to believe that the changes between 1960 and 1975 are simply another draw from the same process generating the changes between 1975 and 1990. Similarly, LaFree's evaluation of convergence between industrializing poor nations and industrialized rich ones assumes that intracountry homicide rate changes are generated by a second-order stationary process. However, LaFree's invocation of the modernization process as explaining national crime dynamics is inconsistent with his statistical methodology. Countries experiencing crime that "results when modern values and norms come into contact with and disrupt older, established systems of role allocation" (LaFree, 2005, p. 192) are in transition; their associated stochastic processes of crime rate changes will not fulfill the invariance requirements needed to apply the time-series methods we employ.

These convergence analyses may be criticized from a second vantage point, namely, the absence of any distinction between conditional and unconditional convergence. Conditional convergence means that there exists a set of initial conditions such that convergence between two units (gender, country) occurs only if these initial conditions are identical. Denoting these conditions as X_t, conditional convergence means that

$$\lim_{k\Rightarrow\infty} E\left(\rho_{1,t+k} - \rho_{2,t+k} \middle| F_t, X_{1,t} = X_{2,t}\right) = 0. \tag{19}$$

In the economic growth literature, it is well understood that conditional rather than unconditional convergence is the natural object of interest. Two countries with different savings rates are not expected to unconditionally converge, and there is no substantive theoretical implication when unconditional convergence fails; see Mankiw, Romer, and Weil (1992) for the classic analysis. In the crime context, it is unclear what is learned from unconditional convergence exercises. O'Brien is relatively circumspect in interpreting his results, but even his speculations on how to explain the finding of no convergence in homicide with convergence in other crimes are not justifiable, since without a theory as to why unconditional convergence is to be expected, there are so many ways to differentiate the experiences of men and women that it is not clear whether there is a fact to be explained. As for LaFree, if there are factors outside the modernization process that determine crime rates—and obvious candidates include socioeconomic factors, such as levels of unemployment and inequality, demography, and differences in national criminal justice systems—then the absence of unconditional convergence does not speak to the empirical relevance of modernization or any other theory considered in isolation.

Deterrence Effect of Capital Punishment

Our second example concerns recent arguments about the deterrence effects of capital punishment. We focus on two papers, the empirical study of deterrent effects by Dezhbakhsh, Rubin, and Shepherd (2003) and the normative study by Sunstein and Vermeule (2005). We choose the first paper because it has been quite influential in resurrecting claims in favor of a deterrent effect and because it has recently come under criticism by Donohue and Wolfers (2005). Dezhbakhsh, Rubin, and Shepherd do not make general policy claims about the desirability of capital punishment given their findings. Sunstein and Vermeule (2005), however, do make this connection. They argue that evidence in favor of a capital punishment deterrence effect can render the punishment morally obligatory. Hence our interest in this second paper.

The behavioral foundations of Dezhbakhsh, Rubin, and Shepherd recognize that the consequences for the commission of a murder involve three separate stages: apprehension, sentencing, and carrying out of the sentence. Defining the variables C = caught, S = sentenced to be executed, and E = executed, Dezhbakhsh, Rubin, and Shepherd estimate the murder rate regression

$$\rho_{l,t} = \alpha + Z_{l,t}\beta + P_{l,t}(C)\beta_C + P_{l,t}(S|C)\beta_S + P_{l,t}(E|S)\beta_E + \kappa_{l,t}, \qquad (20)$$

where

$P_{l,t}(C)$ = probability of being caught conditional on committing a murder,
$P_{l,t}(S|C)$ = probability of being sentenced to be executed conditional on being caught,
$P_{l,t}(E|S)$ = probability of being executed conditional on receiving a death sentence,

and other variables follow the definitions associated with equation (6). Dezhbakhsh, Rubin, and Shepherd argue in favor of a deterrence effect based on the negative point estimates and statistical significance of the coefficients on the various conditional probabilities.

Microfoundations

From the perspective of our first argument, that aggregate models should flow from aggregation of individual behavioral equations, the Dezhbakhsh, Rubin, and Shepherd specification can be shown to be flawed. Specifically, the way in which probabilities are used does not correspond to the probabilities that arise in the appropriate decision problem. For Dezhbakhsh, Rubin, and Shepherd, the potential outcomes are

NC = not caught,
CNS = caught and not sentenced to death,
$CSNE$ = caught, sentenced to death, and not executed,
CSE = caught, sentenced to death, and executed.

The expected utility of a person who commits a murder is therefore

$$\begin{aligned}&\Pr_{l,t}(NC)u_{i,t}(NC)+\Pr_{l,t}(CNS)u_{i,t}(CNS)+\\&\Pr_{l,t}(CSNE)u_{i,t}(CSNE)+\Pr_{l,t}(CSE)u_{i,t}(CSE).\end{aligned} \tag{21}$$

The unconditional probabilities of the four possible outcomes are, of course, related to the conditional probabilities. In terms of conditional probabilities, expected utility may be written as

$$\begin{aligned}&\left(1-\Pr_{l,t}(C)\right)u_{i,t}(NC)+\\&\left(1-\Pr_{l,t}(S|C)\right)\Pr_{l,t}(C)u_{i,t}(CNS)+\\&\left(1-\Pr_{l,t}(E|S)\right)\Pr_{l,t}(S|C)\Pr_{l,t}(C)u_{i,t}(CNSE)+\\&\Pr_{l,t}(E|S)\Pr_{l,t}(S|C)\Pr_{l,t}(C)u_{i,t}(CSE).\end{aligned} \tag{22}$$

A comparison of expressions (22) and (20) reveals that the Dezhbakhsh, Rubin, and Shepherd specification does not derive naturally from individual choices, since the conditional probabilities in (20) interact with each other in the calculation of expected utility as in (22). If one substitutes in a linear representation of the utility functions for the different outcomes, it is evident that (22) cannot be rearranged to produce an aggregate crime equation in which the conditional probabilities appear additively, as in (20); a full analysis appears in Durlauf, Navarro, and Rivers (2008). Put differently, the effect on behavior of the conditional probability of execution given a death sentence cannot be understood separately from the effects of the conditional probability of being caught and being sentenced to death if caught.

We therefore conclude that the Dezhbakhsh, Rubin, and Shepherd specification fails to properly model the implicit decision problem involved in homicides. Their analysis is based on a misspecification of the implications of their assumed behavioral model.

Aggregation

Our aggregation discussion suggests how correlations can arise between regressors and model errors because of unobserved location characteristics. Dezhbakhsh, Rubin, and Shepherd instrument only the conditional crime probabilities in (20), doing so on the basis that these probabilities are collective choice variables by the localities. However, in the presence of unobserved location characteristics, it is necessary to instrument the regressors contained in $Z_{l,t}$ as well. Since instrumenting a subset of the variables in a regression that correlate with the regression errors does not ensure consistency of the associated subset of parameters, the estimates in Dezhbakhsh, Rubin, and Shepherd would appear to be inconsistent (in the statistical sense).

Dezhbakhsh, Rubin, and Shepherd might respond to this objection by noting that they use location-specific fixed effects. However, these will not be sufficient to solve the problem, since the location-specific unobservables $\xi_{l,t}(\omega_{i,t})$ can vary over time.

Policy Effect Estimation

Our discussion of policy effect evaluation also calls into question the Dezhbakhsh, Rubin, and Shepherd analysis, as it assumes that the fluctuations in their arrest, sentencing, and execution probabilities constitute the full set of changes in policies across time periods. This seems problematic. The decision to commit a homicide, under the economic model of crime, depends on the entire range of penalties and their associated probabilities. Changes in the rates at which murderers are sentenced to life imprisonment without parole, for example, are not accounted for by Dezhbakhsh, Rubin, and Shepherd or, as far as we know, any other capital punishment deterrence studies. Hence these studies suffer from an obvious omitted variables problem.

This argument can be pushed farther. As shown in Gelman et al. (2004), the probability that a given death sentence will be overturned by a state or federal appeals court is at least 2/3. These authors also find that only 5 percent of the death sentences between 1975 and 1993 led to the eventual execution of those sentenced. Relative to our choice model, the Gelman et al. findings mean that the reintroduction of capital punishment in a state, on average, substantially increases the probability that the commission of murder leads to the outcome *CSNE*—that is, arrested, sentenced to death, and not executed. Since exonerations are rare, it is reasonable to conjecture that murderers with outcome *CSNE* experience longer prison sentences than they would have had they not been sentenced to death. This suggests that periods in which criminals face higher probabilities of capital sentencing and actual execution are also associated with longer prison sentences. Yet this increase is not reflected in the Dezhbakhsh, Rubin, and Shepherd regression. Put differently, if an increase in the conditional probability of a death sentence given arrest, $\Pr_{l,t}\left(S|C\right)$, is associated with an increase in $\Pr_{l,t}\left(CSNE\right)$, then it is no longer clear what it means to say that a Dezhbakhsh, Rubin, and Shepherd-type regression provides evidence on the effects of capital punishment. Does an increase in long prison sentences because of death sentences followed by reversals correspond to what is understood to be the deterrent effect of capital punishment?

Model Uncertainty

Donohue and Wolfers (2005) have argued that the Dezhbakhsh, Rubin, and Shepherd findings of strong deterrence effects are fragile, as small changes in their baseline specification can lead to an absence of a statistically significant effect or even evidence that a larger number of executions is associated with a larger number of murders. Specifically, Donohue and Wolfers show that the Dezhbakhsh, Rubin, and Shepherd findings change when one alters the lag structure for the instrumental variables used for the punishment probabilities, as well as when one drops California and Texas from the sample. The latter may be interpreted as a change in the assumption that all states are exchangeable with respect to the model employed by Dezhbakhsh, Rubin, and Shepherd.

Cohen-Cole et al. (2008) attempt to adjudicate the differences between Dezhbakhsh, Rubin, and Shepherd and Donohue and Wolfers by treating the problem as one of model uncertainty. To do this, a space of potential models was generated using different combinations of the assumptions found in the two papers. Cohen-Cole et al. conclude that the evidence for deterrence in the sample studied by Dezhbakhsh, Rubin, and Shepherd is weak.

Policy-Relevant Calculations

Following our general discussion, the statistical significance of the capital punishment variables in a murder regression does not produce the appropriate information needed to make policy comparisons. This has implications for the way such evidence is employed in death penalty debates. Sunstein and Vermeule (2005) argue that evidence of a deterrent effect can produce a moral case for capital punishment, in that the decision of a government to fail to implement a life-saving policy is equivalent to the decision to implement a policy that costs lives.

Sunstein and Vermeule (2005) develop their argument conditioning on evidence of a deterrence effect. Leaving aside the insouciance with which they treat the empirical literature,[7] their argument lacks attention to the appropriate nature of the policy maker's loss function and the nature of the uncertainty of the empirical evidence.

The Sunstein and Vermeule analysis treats the expected number of lives saved as the variable of interest to the policy maker; in Dezhbakhsh, Rubin, and Shepherd, this value is a function of the estimated parameter β_E in (20). The expected number of lives saved is not necessarily sufficient in describing a policy maker's utility function, even if this function is a monotonically increasing function of the number of lives saved. As such, their attention to this figure is analogous to making a utilitarian as opposed to a welfarist calculation (see Sen, 1979). While Sunstein and Vermeule would presumably respond that they are assuming that the precision associated with estimates of the expected number of lives saved is high, precision needs to be defined with respect to the policy maker's utility function. It is not an independent object.

The sensitivity of deterrence evidence to model choice, as demonstrated by Donohue and Wolfers and extended in Cohen-Cole et al. (2008), raises the issues we have discussed with respect to decision making under ambiguity and the evaluation of policies when one does not wish to base them on a choice of model priors. Without a justification of the choice of priors, there is no expected deterrence effect on which Sunstein and Vermeule can even rely. Our impression of the philosophy literature is that

---

[7] At the same time they also state that

> "The foundation of our argument is a large and growing body of evidence that capital punishment may well have a deterrent effect, possibly a quite powerful one. . . . The particular numbers do not much matter" (p. 706).

the issue of policy evaluation under ambiguity has generally not been discussed, although Gaus (2006) makes an interesting argument in favor of following principles rather than expected-effect calculations when assessing policies, the effects of which are associated with substantial uncertainty.

To be clear, none of this means that Sunstein and Vermeule (2005) are incorrect in their conclusions about the ethical implications of a certain deterrent effect for a policy maker or that the death penalty is either moral or immoral per se. Rather, our claim is that the policy implications of the uncertainty associated with deterrence effects cannot be assessed outside of the policy maker's preferences.

Right-to-Carry Laws and Crime: *Firearms and Violence* Revisited

Our third example is the controversy over the effects of shall-issue concealed weapons laws in the National Academies report *Firearms and Violence* (National Research Council, 2005). This report concluded (pp. 150-151):

> with the current evidence it is not possible to determine that there is a causal link between the right-to-carry laws and crime rates. It is also the committee's view that additional analysis along the lines of the current literature is unlikely to yield results that will persuasively demonstrate a causal link between right-to-carry laws and crime rates (unless substantial numbers of states were to adopt or repeal right-to-carry laws), because of the sensitivity of the results to model specification.

Committee member James Q. Wilson dissented from this part of the study, on the grounds that the sensitivity to specification found in the report did not account for the sensibility of different models; in particular, he questioned whether the failure of models that excluded socioeconomic control variables to find deterrent effects was of importance in assessing the deterrent effect. Wilson observes (National Research Council, 2005, p. 270):

> Suppose Professor Jones wrote a paper saying that increasing the number of police in a city reduced the crime rate and Professor Smith wrote a rival paper saying that cities with few police officers have low crime rates. Suppose that neither Smith nor Jones used any control variables, such as income, unemployment, population density, or the frequency with which offenders are sent to prison in reaching their conclusions. *If* such papers were published, they would be rejected out of hand by the committee for the obvious reason that they failed to supply a complete account of the factors that affect the crime rate.

The committee's rejoinder to Wilson argued (National Research Council, 2005, pp. 273-274):

> Everyone (including Wilson and the rest of the committee) agrees that control variables matter, but there is disagreement on the correct set. Thus, the facts that there is no way to statistically test for the correct specification and that researchers using reasonable specifications find different answers are highly relevant. Given the existing data and methods, the rest of the committee sees little hope of resolving this fundamental statistical problem.

We believe that this conclusion is too pessimistic. The disagreement between Wilson and the rest of the National Academies committee reflects the absence in the report of an explicit evaluation of how model uncertainty interacts with evidence of shall-issue laws. While the assertion that it is impossible to statistically identify the correct specification of a statistical model is true at some level of generality (although the report is frankly unclear on what is meant by this), this argument is hardly novel; it is known in the philosophy literature as the Duhem-Quine hypothesis (Quine, 1951, is the classic statement) and refers to the idea that all theories are undetermined by available data.

At this level of generality the National Academies committee claim is an uninteresting observation with respect to social science research, since it begs the question of the relative plausibility of assumptions.[8] For the dispute at hand, we believe that Wilson is correct in his argument that a model whose specification includes controls suggested by social science theory should receive greater weight than one that does not. Furthermore, these two models are statistically distinguishable. To conclude that one should regard evidence of a deterrent effect as persuasive only if both models produce the same findings makes little sense. The report implicitly suggests that the models without control variables are intrinsically interesting: "No link between right-to-carry laws and changes in crime is apparent in the raw data . . . ; it is only once numerous covariates are included that the . . . effects . . . emerge" (p. 150). This remark ignores the classic Simpson's paradox, in which a bivariate relationship has one direction, whereas a multivariate relationship does not. The standard example of Simpson's paradox is the positive relationship between admission to the hospital and the probability of death.

---

[8]The report's suggestion that randomized experiments represent the gold standard for research ignores the assumptions required for their conduct—integrity of the researcher, accuracy of data collection, etc. An advocate of randomized experiments would presumably dismiss concerns about such factors as implausible—but this is precisely our point.

Model averaging provides a natural way of integrating the information across the alternative specifications considered in the National Academies report. As we see it, the committee could have addressed the sensitivity of shall-issue deterrence effects by constructing a set of specifications that included those found in the literature as well as others that are formed by combining the assumptions underlying these models. Intuitively, one thinks of the assumptions that differentiate models as the axes of the model space, and one fills the model space out with those combinations of assumptions that are coherent with one another. Averaging over this space would have integrated the information in the different models and indicated whether evidence of a shall-issue deterrent effect is present when one conditions on a model space rather than a particular model.

One answer to our advocacy of model averaging as a tool to address model uncertainty of the type facing the National Academies committee is that a given body of empirical studies captures only a small fraction of the universe of potential models (and indeed might represent a measure 0 set). This is certainly a tenable position. But if this position is taken, then it would be irrelevant whether a given body of studies produced similar or conflicting results. If it is then claimed that the degree of consistency in results across models contained in a subspace is informative about the results that would be ascertained were the model space expanded, then it is difficult to see why the relative prior plausibility and relative evidentiary support within an initial model space are not informative as well.

A second answer to the use of model averaging might rely on the absence of a principled basis for assigning prior model probabilities. We are certainly sympathetic to this view. But if this position is taken, then the implications of the body of model-specific findings of an effect of shall-issue laws to policy need to be explicitly considered. It is not obvious, for example, that the fragility that the National Academies report claims to be present in concealed weapons regressions is even an argument against the laws. Suppose that a policy maker possesses minimax preferences with respect to model uncertainty. Fragility of deterrence evidence does not logically lead to rejection of the policy; one needs to know the payoffs under the different models under consideration. The National Academies report seems to take the position that, in absence of strong evidence that the laws reduce crime, they should not be implemented. But minimax preferences do not, by themselves, generate this conclusion, which really is based on the presumption that the law should not be implemented unless there is compelling evidence of crime reduction. This line of reasoning can be justified (e.g., Brock, Durlauf, and West, 2003), but it requires context-specific argumentation.

Therefore, a recommendation we make for policy evaluation studies such as *Firearms and Violence* is that claims about the robustness or fragility of various findings be evaluated with respect to different loss functions, with particular attention to minimax and minimax regret calculations as supplements to the standard Bayesian ones.

SHOULD AGGREGATE CRIME REGRESSIONS BE ABANDONED?

One response to the discussion in this paper would be to search for alternative ways of uncovering aggregate criminological facts. The critiques we have raised are part of the source of interest in so-called natural experiments, in which an exogenous event of some type allows a comparison of aggregate crime outcomes (see Levitt, 1996, for a nice example). In his appendix to the *Firearms and Violence* study, Horowitz (2005) makes a broad general argument against the use of regression models to elucidate the determinants of crime, specifically in terms of evaluating policy effects.

While his focus is on concealed weapons laws, his claims apply with equal force to other crime contexts. According to Horowitz, "In summary, the problems posed by high-dimensional estimation, misspecified models, and lack of correct knowledge of the correct set of explanatory variables seem insurmountable with observational data" (National Research Council, 2005, p. 308). In contrast, he argues that random assignment of policies could in principle reveal their effects; in particular, he discusses how random assignment can allow for the estimation of average treatment effects (a particular piece of legislation, such as shall-issue concealed weapons laws, is an example of a treatment).

We of course concur that there does not exist an algorithm to infallibly identify the "true" model of crime (or for that matter, other phenomena) when the universe of candidate models is broad enough. However, we do not believe this means that crime regressions cannot be informative about policy. Different models have both different ex ante levels of plausibility and ex post levels of goodness of fit for a given body of observational data. The different concealed weapons regressions with and without socioeconomic controls are not equally ex ante plausible, given the state of social science. And we do not know, given our priors, how the relative goodness of fit of the different models analyzed in the National Academies report would translate into different posterior model probabilities.

Our discussion of the assumptions that underlie the interpretation of aggregate crime regressions may all be interpreted as examples for Horowitz's arguments about the limitations of regression analysis of crime. We do not claim to have an answer to the question of how to integrate the different types of model uncertainty we have discussed into a single integrated framework, let alone introduce such factors as the extension of the basic crime model to intertemporal decision making. Our disagreement with Horowitz is that we see a role for empirical models in informing policy discussion, even though the researcher is aware of untestable or unappealing assumptions underlying them. The way in which models are used to inform beliefs necessarily requires judgments; this necessity does not mean that the models are uninformative. A researcher brings a body of social science and statistical knowledge to bear in the assessment of empirical results; this knowledge matters in assessing the dependence of a result on an assumption. Put differently, not all assumptions are equally arbitrary.

The need for assumptions is not unique to regression analysis with observational data; all empirical work is theory-laden (to use Quine's phrase). An experiment of the type proposed by Horowitz with respect to shall-issue weapons permit laws—randomized legalization across states—would, if one is to use the findings to inform policy makers, require assumptions about (1) the degree to which potential criminals can alter the locations in which crimes are committed, (2) the nature of migration by potential criminals across state boundaries both before the experiment and in response to it, (3) the effect on the current crime choices of potential criminals of the knowledge that an experiment that may affect future laws in their state of residence is being conducted, etc. Also, the translation of findings from such an experiment into a recommendation for those states that did not implement the policy requires exchangeability assumptions on the states. Does one assume that the deterrent effect of the law is identical across states? If state-level deterrent effects are heterogeneous, how is this heterogeneity to be modeled—via random effects, varying coefficients, or some other method?[9] Randomized experiments cannot avoid the need for judgments; as described in detail in Heckman (2000, 2005), judgment is intrinsic to social scientific inquiry.

Overall, we do not see good reasons to regard natural experiments as superior to regressions with observational data in terms of their relative utility as means of understanding crime.[10] It is straightforward to construct examples in which one methodology can provide insights that the other does not. Each has a contribution to make in criminological research.

[9]Abbring and Heckman (2007) provide a comprehensive overview of the assumptions required in developing estimates of treatment effects that account for considerations of the type hinted at in our discussion.

[10]See Heckman (2005) and Manski (2007) for discussion of the limitations of experiments; Heckman and Navarro (2004) compare the strengths and weaknesses of different empirical strategies for uncovering the determinants of individual choice.

CONCLUSION

In this chapter, we have described some issues we regard as important in the econometric study of crime: microfoundations, aggregation, counterfactual analysis, and policy evaluation. We have tried to make clear the various assumptions that must be maintained to interpret aggregate crime regressions with respect to individual behavior and have emphasized how standard uses of these regressions to evaluate policy presuppose a number of assumptions. In light of disagreements about these assumptions, which ultimately underlie claims of fragility or robustness of an empirical result, we have outlined some ways of using model-averaging methods and statistical decision theory to make progress. Throughout, we have emphasized the role of judgment in empirical work, for which no algorithm exists.

ACKNOWLEDGMENTS

We thank the National Science Foundation and University of Wisconsin Graduate School for financial support. Arthur Goldberger and Justin Wolfers provided immensely helpful comments on a previous draft.

REFERENCES

Abbring, Jaap H., and James J. Heckman. (2007). Econometric evaluation of social programs, part III: Distributional treatment effects, dynamic treatment effects, dynamic discrete choice, and general equilibrium policy evaluation. In J. Heckman and E. Leamer (Eds.), *Handbook of econometrics, volume 6*. Amsterdam: Elsevier.

Aldrich, John H., and Forrest D. Nelson. (1984). *Linear probability, logit, and probit models.* Beverly Hills, CA: Sage.

Avramov, Doron. (2002). Stock return predictability and model uncertainty. *Journal of Finance, 64*, 423-458.

Ayres, Ian, and John Donohue, III. (2003). Shooting down the "more guns, less crime" hypothesis. *Stanford Law Review, 55*, 1193-1312.

Becker, Gary S. (1968). Crime and punishment: An economic analysis. *Journal of Political Economy, 78*(2), 169-217.

Becker, Gary S. (1993). Nobel lecture: The economic way of looking at behavior. *Journal of Political Economy, 101*(3), 385-409.

Bernard, Andrew B., and Steven N. Durlauf. (1995). Convergence in international output. *Journal of Applied Econometrics, 10*(2), 97-108.

Bernard, Andrew B., and Steven N. Durlauf. (1996). Interpreting tests of the convergence hypothesis. *Journal of Econometrics, 71*(1-2), 161-173.

Berry, Steven, James Levinsohn, and Ariel Pakes. (1995). Automobile prices in market equilibrium. *Econometrica, 63*(4), 841-890.

Black, Dan A., and Daniel S. Nagin. (1998). Do right-to-carry laws deter violent crimes? *Journal of Legal Studies, 27*(1), 209-219.

Blundell, Richard, and Thomas Stoker. (2005). Heterogeneity and aggregation. *Journal of Economic Literature, 43*(2), 347-391.

Brock, William A., and Steven Durlauf. (2001). Growth economics and reality. *World Bank Economic Review, 15*, 229-272.

Brock, William A., Steven Durlauf, and Kenneth West. (2003). Policy analysis in uncertain economic environments (with discussion). *Brookings Papers on Economic Activity, 1*, 235-322.

Brock, William A., Steven Durlauf, and Kenneth West. (2007). Model uncertainty and policy evaluation: Some theory and empirics. *Journal of Econometrics, 136*(2), 629-664.

Brock, William A., Steven Durlauf, James Nason, and Giacomo Rondina. (2007). Simple versus optimal rules as guides to policy. *Journal of Monetary Economics, 54*(5), 1372-1396.

Cantor, David, and Kenneth C. Land. (1985). Unemployment and crime rates in the post-World War II United States: A theoretical and empirical investigation. *American Sociological Review, 50*, 317-332.

Cohen-Cole, Ethan, Steven Durlauf, Jeffrey Fagan, and Daniel Nagin. (2008). *Model uncertainty and the deterrent effect of capital punishment. American Law and Economics Review,* forthcoming.

Dezhbakhsh, Hashem, Paul Rubin, and Joanna M. Shepherd. (2003). Does capital punishment have a deterrent effect? New evidence from post-moratorium panel data. *American Law and Economics Review, 5*(2), 344-376.

Donohue, John, and Steven Levitt. (2001). The impact of legalized abortion on crime. *Quarterly Journal of Economics, 116*(2), 379-420.

Donohue, John, and Justin Wolfers. (2005). Uses and abuses of empirical evidence in the death penalty debate. *Stanford Law Review, 58*(3), 791-846.

Doppelhofer, Gernot, Ronald I. Miller, and Xavier Sala-i-Martin. (2004). Determinants of long-term growth: A Bayesian averaging of classical estimates (BACE) approach. *American Economic Review, 94*(4), 813-835.

Draper, David. (1995). Assessment and propagation of model uncertainty. *Journal of the Royal Statistical Society, Series B, 57*, 45-70.

Durlauf, Steven, Salvador Navarro, and David Rivers. (2008). *Notes on the econometrics of deterrence.* Unpublished working paper, Department of Economics, University of Wisconsin, Madison.

Ehrlich, Isaac. (1972). The deterrent effect of criminal law enforcement. *Journal of Legal Studies, 1*(2), 259-276.

Ehrlich, Isaac. (1973). Participation in illegal activities: A theoretical and empirical investigation. *Journal of Political Economy, 81*(3), 521-565.

Fernandez, Carmen, Eduardo Ley, and Mark Steel. (2001). Model uncertainty in cross-country growth regressions. *Journal of Applied Econometrics, 16*(5), 563-576.

Garratt, Anthony, Kevin Lee, M. Hashem Pesaran, and Yongcheol Shin. (2003). Forecasting uncertainties in macroeconometric modelling: An application to the UK economy. *Journal of the American Statistical Association, 98*(464), 829-838.

Gaus, Gerald F. (2006). *Social complexity and evolved moral principles.* Unpublished paper, University of Arizona.

Gelman, Andrew, James S. Liebman, Valerie West, and Alexander Kiss. (2004). A broken system: The persistent patterns of reversals of death sentences in the United States. *Journal of Empirical Legal Studies, 1*(2), 209-261.

Goldberger, Arthur S. (1991). *A course in econometrics.* Cambridge, MA: Harvard University Press.

Greenberg, David. (2001). Time series analysis of crime rates. *Journal of Quantitative Criminology, 17*(4), 291-327.

Hansen, Lars Peter, and Thomas J. Sargent. (2007). *Robustness.* Princeton, NJ: Princeton University Press.

Heckman, James L. (2000). Causal parameters and policy analysis in economics: A twentieth century retrospective. *Quarterly Journal of Economics, 115*(1), 45-97.

Heckman, James L. (2005). The scientific model of causality. *Sociological Methodology, 35*, 1-98.

Heckman, James L., and Salvador Navarro. (2004). Using matching, instrumental variables, and control functions to estimate economic choice models. *Review of Economics and Statistics, 86*(1), 30-57.

Heckman, James L., and Salvador Navarro. (2007). Dynamic discrete choices and dynamic treatment effects. *Journal of Econometrics, 136*(2), 341-396.

Horowitz, Joel L. (2005). Statistical issues in the evaluation of right-to-carry laws. In National Research Council, *Firearms and violence: A critical review* (pp. 299-308), Committee to Improve Research Information and Data on Firearms, Charles F. Wellford, John V. Pepper, and Carol V. Petrie (Eds.), Committee on Law and Justice, Division of Behavioral and Social Sciences and Education. Washington, DC: The National Academies Press.

LaFree, Gary. (2005). Evidence for elite convergence in cross-national homicide victimization trends, 1956 to 2000. *The Sociological Quarterly, 46*, 191-211.

Leamer, Edward E. (1978). *Specification searches*. New York: John Wiley & Sons.

Levitt, Steven D. (1996). The effect of prison population size on crime rates: Evidence from prison overcrowding litigation. *Quarterly Journal of Economics, 111*, 319-351.

Levitt, Steven D. (2004). Understanding why crime fell in the 1990s: Four factors that explain the decline and six that do not. *Journal of Economic Perspectives, 18*(1), 163-190.

Lott, John R. (1998). The concealed-handgun debate. *Journal of Legal Studies, 27*(1), 221-291.

Lott, John R., and David B. Mustard. (1997). Crime, deterrence, and right-to-carry concealed handguns. *Journal of Legal Studies, 26*(1), 1-68.

Mankiw, N. Gregory, David Romer, and David N. Weil. (1992). A contribution to the empirics of economic growth. *Quarterly Journal of Economics, 107*(2), 407-437.

Manski, Charles F. (2005). Statistical treatment rules for heterogeneous populations. *Econometrica, 72*, 1221-1246.

Manski, Charles F. (2006). Minimax-regret treatment choice with missing outcome data. *Journal of Econometrics, 139*(1), 105-115.

Manski, Charles F. (2007). *Identification for prediction and decision*. Cambridge, MA: Harvard University Press.

Marschak, Jacob. (1953). Economic measurements for policy and prediction. In William C. Hood and Tjalling C. Koopmans (Eds.), *Studies in econometric method*. New York: John Wiley & Sons.

Matzkin, Rosa L. (1992). Nonparametric and distribution-free estimation of the binary threshold crossing and the binary choice models. *Econometrica, 60*(2), 239-270.

National Research Council. (2005). *Firearms and violence: A critical review*. Committee to Improve Research Information and Data on Firearms, Charles F. Wellford, John V. Pepper, and Carol V. Petrie (Eds.), Committee on Law and Justice, Division of Behavioral and Social Sciences and Education. Washington, DC: The National Academies Press.

Navarro, Salvador. (2007). Control functions. In Lawrence E. Blume and Steven Durlauf (Eds.), *New Palgrave dictionary of economics* (revised ed.). London: Palgrave-Macmillan.

O'Brien, Robert M. (1999). Measuring the convergence/divergence of "serious crime" arrest rates for males and females: 1960-1995. *Journal of Quantitative Criminology, 15*(1), 97-114.

Plassmann, Florenz, and John Whitley. (2003). Confirming "more guns, less crime." *Stanford Law Review, 55*, 1313-1369.

Quine, Willard Van Orman. (1951). Two dogmas of empiricism. *Philosophical Review, 60*, 20-43.

Raftery, Adrian E., David Madigan, and Jennifer A. Hoeting. (1997). Bayesian model averaging for linear regression models. *Journal of the American Statistical Association, 92*(437), 179-191.

Savage, Leonard J. (1951). The theory of statistical decision. *Journal of the American Statistical Association, 46*, 55-67.

Sen, Amartya. (1979). Utilitarianism and welfarism, *Journal of Philosophy, 76*(9), 463-489.

Stoker, Thomas M. (1993). Empirical approaches to the problem of aggregation over individuals. *Journal of Economic Literature, 31*(4), 1827-1874.

Sunstein, Cass R., and Adrian Vermeule. (2005). Is capital punishment morally required? Acts, omissions and life-life tradeoffs. *Stanford Law Review, 58*(3), 703-751.

Wald, Abraham. (1950). *Statistical decision functions.* New York: John Wiley & Sons.